W9-DIM-026

Managing Innovation
  Edwin A. Gee and Chaplin Tyler

The Management System: Systems Are for People
  Leslie H. Matthies

Financial Accounting Estimates through Statistical Sampling by Computer
  Maurice S. Newman

Forecasting Methods for Management, Second Edition
  Steven C. Wheelwright and Spyros Makridakis

Decision Making and Planning for the Corporate Treasurer
  Harold Bierman, Jr.

Corporate Financial Planning Models
  Henry I. Meyer

Strategies in Business
  Shea Smith, III, and John E. Walsh, Jr.

Program-Management Control Systems
  Joseph A. Maciariello

Contemporary Cash Management: Principles, Practices, Perspective
  Paul J. Beehler

Dynamic Cost Reduction
  Irving Dlugatch

Inventory Control for the Financial Executive
  Thomas S. Dudick and Ross Cornell

Inventory Control
for the
Financial Executive

Inventory Control
for the
Financial Executive

THOMAS S. DUDICK
ROSS CORNELL

Robert Manning Strozier Library

NOV 20 1978

Tallahassee, Florida

A Ronald Press Publication

JOHN WILEY & SONS, New York · Chichester · Brisbane · Toronto

Robert Manning Strozier Library

NOV 29 1979

Tallahassee, Florida

Copyright © 1979 by John Wiley & Sons, Inc.

All rights reserved. Published simultaneously in Canada.

Reproduction or translation of any part of this work
beyond that permitted by Sections 107 or 108 of the
1976 United States Copyright Act without the permission
of the copyright owner is unlawful. Requests for
permission or further information should be addressed to
the Permissions Department, John Wiley & Sons, Inc.

Library of Congress Cataloging in Publication Data:

Dudick, Thomas S
  Inventory control for the financial executive.

  (Systems and controls for financial management series)
  "A Ronald Press publication."
  Includes index.
  1. Inventory control. 2. Inventories—Accounting.

I. Cornell, Ross, joint author. II. Title.
HD55.D8   658.7'87   79-10699
ISBN 0-471-01503-2

Printed in the United States of America

10 9 8 7 6 5 4 3 2 1

SERIES PREFACE

No one needs to tell the reader that the world is changing. He sees it all too clearly. The immutable, the constant, the unchanging of a decade or two ago no longer represent the latest thinking—on *any* subject, whether morals, medicine, politics, economics, or religion. Change has always been with us, but the pace has been accelerating, especially in the postwar years.

Business, particularly with the advent of the electronic computer some 20 years ago, has also undergone change. New disciplines have sprung up. New professions are born. New skills are in demand. And the need is ever greater to blend the new skills with those of the older professions to meet the demands of modern business.

The accounting and financial functions certainly are no exception. The constancy of change is as pervasive in these fields as it is in any other. Industry is moving toward an integration of many of the information gathering, processing, and analyzing functions under the impetus of the so-called systems approach. Such corporate territory has been, traditionally, the responsibility of the accountant and the financial man. It still is, to a large extent—but times are changing.

Does this, then, spell the early demise of the accountant as we know him today? Does it augur a lessening of influence for the financial specialists in today's corporate hierarchy? We think not. We maintain, however, that it is incumbent upon today's accountant and today's financial man to learn *today's* thinking and to *use today's* skills. It is for this reason the Systems and Controls for the Financial Management Series is being developed.

Recognizing the broad spectrum of interests and activities that the series title encompasses, we plan a number of volumes, each representing the latest thinking, written by a recognized authority, on a particular facet of the financial man's responsibilities. The subjects contemplated for discussion within the series range from production accounting systems to planning, to corporate records, to control of cash. Each book is an in-depth study of one subject within this group. Each is intended to be a practical, working tool for the businessman in general and the financial man and accountant in particular.

ROBERT L. SHULTIS
FRANK M. MASTROMANO

PREFACE

The period following World War II was marked by an explosive growth, in which company after company was merged into larger entities—to a point where a few giants now dominate most industries. Manufacturers outdid each other to gain customer favor. The result was an explosive increase in the number and variety of products that were offered for sale—with a corresponding increase in the number of items in inventory.

Although inventory control requirements have changed radically, a large number of companies still cling to myths of inventory accountability that date back to earlier periods when it was practical to control inventory through the use of manually posted kardex records. In those earlier years, when products were simpler and fewer in number, the flow of inventory into and out of the factory and warehouses was more direct and clearcut.

The competitive nature of the marketplace has resulted in a high degree of automation that requires tooling, expensive and complex equipment, and a variety of different materials. Lead times become more and more important. Inventories of component parts and subassemblies must be accumulated in lots that fulfill the economics of manufacture. This means that lead times, safety stocks, and economic order quantities must be determined with greater care.

This book recognizes the more complex nature of modern day production by emphasizing the important role inventories play as buffer zones between the supplier and the company, as well as between the company and the customer. With the present increased complexity of manufacture, the book discusses lead times that can no longer be applied on an across-the-board formula to all products. It discusses the costs of carrying inventories, the need for increased skills in scheduling production, and better techniques in manufacturing and material handling.

Not only does the book deal with control of physical units; it also includes chapters devoted to problems in valuing inventory (Chapters 3 and 10). It reviews the problems many companies have experienced in reconciling the values of inventory carried on the books with the values from physical inventory. In many cases, such discrepancy is not due to disappearance of the physical units, but rather to the inconsistency of values applied to input as compared with values assigned to shipments. The book also points out that there are other distorting factors, such as counting rework twice—once when the item has been fabricated, and again when a defect has been corrected. This frequently happens when controls are weak.

Many companies still value inventory on the "single bucket" approach. Purchases of material, direct-labor payroll costs, and overhead are added as incurred. Relief of inventory at time of shipment, extended by a standard value (or a percentage factor applied to the sales value of shipment), is used as the basis for reducing the inventory.

Proper costing of production and inventory is discussed from the vantage point of an integrated computerized system in which the physical units controlled by the production and inventory group provide the basis for costing that is used to obtain the inventory valuations.

THOMAS S. DUDICK
ROSS H. CORNELL

New York, New York
April 1979

CONTENTS

formula approach . . . Weaknesses in the cost formula approach. What does work . . . Six steps in developing an effective policy: *Discussing and applying the policy steps . . . Flexibility of policy . . . Implementing the six step inventory policy.*

What does inventory include . . . What is included in inventory carrying cost: *Inventory related costs are not always carrying costs of inventory . . . Rent equivalent costs . . . Taxes and insurance . . . Operational costs—Equipment depreciation and maintenance . . . Electricity . . . Stockhandling . . . Breakage and obsolescence; Financing costs . . . Putting it all together—Rent equivalent costs . . . Taxes and insurance . . . Operational costs (Equipment depreciation and maintenance . . . Electricity . . . Stockhandling . . . Breakage and obsolescence) . . . Cost of money; Tallying up the cost.* Penalty costs: *Production penalty costs . . . Sales penalty costs . . . Capital penalty costs.* Inventory models . . . Recognizing cost behavior: *Warehouse capacity . . . Purchased services.*

The law of averages . . . Playing the odds . . . The manager looks at probability . . . Computer simulations . . . Inventory planning models.

Misapplied technology: *The human factor in inventory control . . . Overreliance on the computer . . . No systematic approach.* Operations review: *Steps to follow—Collecting facts . . . Analyzing performance data . . . Identifying symptoms . . . Testing suspected problems.* Measuring the impact of inventory problems.

Inventory management—control of physical units versus financial controls . . . How to approach systems planning

. . . Inventory points: *Basic procedures for treating inventory points.* The order-point/order-quantity model . . . Min–max model . . . Replenishment model . . . Combining orders . . . Allocating orders.

Deterministic laws versus laws of probability . . . Business applications . . . Probability forecasts . . . No escape from forecasts . . . Business properties of forecasts: *Importance of being specific . . . Timing considerations . . . Frequency of forecasting . . . Margin of error—Method 1 . . . Method 2.* Forecasting methods . . . Forecasting techniques.

Measuring performance . . . Monitoring procedures . . . Empirical inventory control: *Conditions for empirical controls.*

Overview of computerization . . . Indented bill of materials . . . Structuring the costs used for inventory valuation . . . Source of manufacturing data . . . Developing the product cost . . . Transaction listings . . . Journalizing the transactions for the cost system: *Purchase price variance . . . Input into production . . . Raw material issues . . . Fabricated parts transferred into stock . . . Transfers from finished goods to WIP stockroom . . . Transfers from WIP stockroom . . . Customer returns . . . Components in finished goods stock returned to production . . . Completed production transferred to finished goods . . . Floor work-in-process . . . Shipments during the month . . . Variance analysis.*

Inventory Control
for the
Financial Executive

CHAPTER 1

INVENTORY—THE ECONOMIC BUFFER ZONE

Inventories are a major asset and represent a sizable investment in businesses that sell or manufacture products. In extraction, manufacturing, wholesaling, retailing, import/exporting, and other fields, inventories constitute one of the largest controllable assets of the business. The business executive must account for and control inventory by careful and continuous attention.

It is the changing and renewable nature of inventory that demands the constancy of attention. In contrast with permanent assets, such as plant and equipment, an item in inventory serves its function and then is removed—all in a few months. Thus the inventory status must be reassessed every few months or more often.

The two major economic purposes of inventories are:

• Buffer zones in the system of production and distribution.
• Investment or speculation.

Our concern in this book is with the buffer zone function served by inventories. A good illustration is the well-known bottle of "Cola." We expect our local retailer to have a sufficient supply to permit us to "down one" immediately and to stock up our refrigerators. The retailer, in turn, expects the bottler to maintain a supply to immediately restock the shelves. The bottler looks to suppliers to maintain adequate stocks of the necessary raw materials.

In its use as the economic buffer zone, inventory functions on an item-by-item basis. If the customer wants to buy a bottle of 32-ounce Cola and it is not in stock, it may not suffice to have plenty of Cola in the 10-, 16-, or 64-ounce bottles. The salesman knows this but the financial executive reviews inventory in dollars on the balance sheet and may overlook it. The situation referred to indicates a "mix problem." It does no good to have the right amount of inventory overall if the mix is wrong. As a department store manager once put it "Half of what I have I don't need, and half of what I need I don't have."

IMPACT OF COMPETITION ON INVENTORY

Inventories of goods ready to use (finished products), constitute a major portion of many business inventories. They are required by businesses with industrial customers as well as those providing consumer goods. Many industries set delivery standards of a few days. Failure to meet these standards will result in sales lost to competitors. Because of the increased size of buffer inventories that are needed, inventories become a "battleground" between the supplier and the user—both want the other to maintain the larger share of the buffer.

The aluminum fabricator who rolls sheets from ingot can have production disrupted if the supplier does not have ingots available. The purchaser of sheets who stamps out aluminum parts depends on the supplier of aluminum sheet to have it available. Whether such suppliers are outside companies or divisions within the same company, the problem is just as real. Whether the buyer or the seller maintains the buffer depends on competitive pressures. The balance of competitive pressure can tip depending on whether material is in short supply or plentiful.

When material is in short supply, the suppliers dictate the terms; when plentiful, the user calls the shots. Interestingly enough, when materials are in great demand, prices are higher and the user must increase inventories to provide the buffer stocks—all at a higher investment. When materials are plentiful, they are lower in price and the supplier is more willing to maintain higher buffer zones. This is one of the contradictions that affects inventories—a situation that can shift within a few months and which is frequently overlooked by many financial managers seeking to control the investment.

Many companies can build finished goods inventories to a stage just short of the final product that is sold. This constitutes the basic product to which options are added when the shipment schedule becomes available. This approach reduces the magnitude of the finished goods inventories while still satisfying customer demand. In many cases, the options are packaging or decals. Exercising these options before orders are in can tie up inventories in stock because of the wrong package or incorrect decal. This flexibility can also be extended to work-in-process, particularly when the company fabricates its own parts. By maintaining inventories at various stages of manufacture and assembly, which is called work-in-process inventory, the company can lower its overall investment in inventory assets and still meet competitive pressures.

Work-in-process inventory also serves as a buffer between production stages. When operations within work-in-process are numerous, buffer areas are usually needed in some of the operations. Manufacture of hypodermic needles is a good example: Thin tubing is cut and sharpened and then the barrel is cut and formed. Next, the needle, barrel, and other parts are assembled. The following processes include sterilization, quality inspection, and packing. In all, more than 30 operations in five production areas are involved. Manufacture in each area is supervised separately. Consequently, the timing and quantities of parts produced do not always coincide, which necessitates inventories to smooth out the differences. These buffer inventories serve the same purpose within work-in-process production centers as the finished goods inventory serves between manufacturer and customers.

If finished goods inventory serves as the front end economic buffer, materials inventory serves as the back end. Because vendor deliveries are unpredictable, the company must either maintain stocks or see its production occasionally interrupted because of lack of needed materials. The same tug-of-war over inventories occurs between company and vendors as occurs between company and customers. In times of plentiful materials the company can pressure vendors to meet precise delivery schedules—thus forcing more of the inventory investment away from the company and onto the vendors. When materials are scarce the tug-of-war goes the other way. The financial executive must keep in mind the financial impact of this situation and its interrelationship with pricing. Shifting inventory to the vendor is financially equivalent to a price discount or reduction. However, the operating and budgeting consequences can be different. Further, the exact financial trade-off between inventories and pricing can be difficult to ascertain.

INVENTORY CONTROL VARIES WITH THE NATURE OF INVENTORY

Control of types of buffer inventories differs, as discussed in later chapters. Raw materials, for example, are required because vendor deliveries are erratic; input is not completely predictable and therefore cannot be controlled directly by the company. Work-in-process inventories permit direct control by company management of both the inventory input and output, thus procedures differ from those used for raw materials. Finished goods control is influenced partly by management and partly by customer demand which can be highly unpredictable.

Accounting records maintained for inventory have historically influenced inventory control methods. When "up-to-the-minute" perpetual records are maintained on an item-by-item basis, control techniques are more effective than those available with less timely records prepared on an aggregated basis. The cost of preparing and maintaining the more detailed information may not be justified by the marginal improvement in control. However, cost per bit of information is rapidly declining as computer technology improves, so that yesterday's decision as to the cost/benefit of inventory information may not be valid today.

IMPACT OF COMPANY OPERATIONAL POLICIES

Company facilities and processes influence the level of inventory. If in production all operations are laid out in a straight line flow, then relatively little work-in-process inventory is needed. If processes of production are physically separate or if control is divided, inventory requirements increase.

The physical structure of the distribution system also contributes to inventory requirements. When level of service and customer demand are constant, the amount of inventory increases in proportion to the square root of the number of distribution points. For four warehouses, for example, to serve the same customers as one warehouse did previously, inventory levels double (square root of $4 = 2$).

The inventory level increases because inventory is controlled at the stockkeeping unit (SKU) level. A stockkeeping unit is a product at an inventory location. When the locations increase from one to four, the SKUs must be duplicated at each location. The demand for the products is now spread over four SKUs so that the demand for each SKU is roughly one fourth. However, the inventory required for this lower demand at each of the four warehouses does not go down one fourth. Safety stock requirements put a "drag" on the inventory level reduction—hence the use of an estimate based on square root. This point as it relates to service levels is discussed in Chapter 3.

MANAGEMENT VIEWS OF INVENTORY

Attitude concerning inventory appears to be job related. Thus, attitudes can be categorized as sales, purchasing, production, and finance attitudes.

The two basic attitudes are desire for higher inventories or desire for lower inventories.

Sales attitude is expressed as: "We can't risk stockouts." "If we don't have the requested item, we'll lose the business and the customer's other business." "We have to offer a complete line or competitors will get the business."

Purchasing and production personnel insist on enough inventory to keep production flexible, permitting them to shift production to other products when there is a downturn in certain items. Production managers have been known to want to continue running production beyond the scheduled quantities when equipment is running efficiently with low scrap.

Sales managers and product managers want higher inventories and "lobby" effectively for them. In some companies, implementing the materials management function is considered a partial answer to the high inventory advocates by applying downward pressures on inventories. While undeniably increasing the professionalism of inventory control, materials management personnel may be reluctant to do this, if it creates conflicts with well established sales executives.

Sales and production managers share a product or SKU orientation toward identifying inventory. Their reports and needs are frequently stated in units. The salesman thinks about inventory as 350 cases of A16-160 red and 1350 cases of A-16-160 green. Accounting managers deal with budgets and monthly management reports, and think of inventory in terms of dollars. Their unit is not likely to be A16-160 red, but rather inventory dollars in the fabrication cost center and at the Buffalo plant. These views must be considered when discussing inventory with managers from various functional areas of the business.

COST EFFECTIVE INVENTORIES

Inventory as the economic buffer zone makes its role in business more understandable. However, every benefit has its cost. The cost/benefit trade-off becomes deceptively complicated, partly because inventory is continuously changing. Inventory is controlled not by one big decision but rather a series of small ones—each decision addressing one item at one location for an appropriate time period. Executives are naturally reluctant to allocate time to such small decisions; hence, inventory is managed on a day-to-day basis at lower supervisory levels.

The complexity of the cost/benefit determination for inventories is increased by the quantitative nature of inventory control. Such control lends

EXHIBIT 1-1   INVENTORY COST/BENEFIT ISSUE: ATTITUDES OF VARIOUS FUNCTIONAL MANAGERS

SALES WANTS:	HIGH INVENTORY
CUSTOMER SERVICE WANTS:	HIGH INVENTORY
MARKETING WANTS:	HIGH INVENTORY
DISTRIBUTION WANTS:	HIGH INVENTORY
PRODUCTION WANTS:	HIGH INVENTORY
MATERIALS HANDLING WANTS:	HIGH INVENTORY
PURCHASING WANTS:	HIGH INVENTORY

WHO WANTS LOW INVENTORY?
THE FINANCIAL EXECUTIVE WANTS LOW AND
PROPERLY MANAGED INVENTORIES!

itself to quantitative techniques and, as a result, a large body of technology has developed in inventory control. That technology can be difficult and/or expensive to understand and apply properly.

Even though quantitative methods have been introduced, inventory is largely managed by judgment and hunch, especially in regard to materials and finished goods because important factors are beyond the direct control of the company and the data needed to make informed cost/benefit decisions is not available. Few companies know with any certainty the impact on sales of various changes in finished goods inventory policy. This is an area dictated by experience and judgment. But how objective is the judgment? Exhibit 1-1 illustrates the attitudes of managers in various functional areas of a company.

Exhibit 1-2 presents the results of an analysis of inventories. This "worst case" demonstrates results of poor inventory management. For each SKU, the average monthly usage was calculated over a 6-month

EXHIBIT 1-2   COST/BENEFIT ISSUE ILLUSTRATED

WORK-IN-PROCESS INVENTORY		
Months Usage in Stock	Inventory at Cost	Percentage of Cost
Out of stock	0	0.0%
0 to 3 months	$ 46,400.58	4.8
3 to 6 months	96,208.93	9.9
More than 6 months	825,394.57	85.3
Total	$968,004.08	100.0%

IS THIS ASSET PROPERLY MANAGED?

period and then divided into the inventory on hand to determine the on-hand figure in terms of months' usage in stock. The inventory value was then classified according to months' inventory as shown in Exhibit 1-2.

Consider that lead time to replenish the inventory was about 1 month, reorder lot sizes were not a consideration, and there were no problems such as rail strikes or union negotiations at the time. Was the dollar investment justified by the benefits of the inventory as a buffer? Could the production stages have been buffered by investing less in inventory? Was that asset properly managed? Obviously it was not.

THE ROLE OF THE FINANCIAL EXECUTIVE

The financial executive safeguards company assets and insures that they are properly managed. This certainly applies to inventory. Exhibit 1-1 illustrates the functional areas within a company that are directly concerned with inventories. That each department desires higher inventory levels indicates a lack of objectivity regarding cost/benefit analysis. If the financial officer does not pressure inventory downward no one else will.

Because inventory is managed by a series of small decisions, financial executives desiring to reduce inventories must get more deeply involved. They must recognize that the day-to-day decisions have been pushed to the lower levels of management. Challenging individual decisions of an inventory supervisor is not effective control. Should the lot size of the run have been 500 rather than 2000? The production scheduler undoubtedly has a good reason for the 2000 lot size runs. Since this person is on the spot with the most information, it is difficult to challenge his decision. Generally, the financial executive must review the inventory situation overall and then establish policy guidelines for the supervisors, thus controlling by monitoring compliance with policy. The accounting-finance function is well suited to this task.

The accounting-finance function becomes involved in inventory control for another reason. The data processing section frequently reports to the financial executive. Its services are used for costing production and cost of sales, as well as costing transfers among the major segments of inventory. Accounting procedures require costing of the same inventory transactions needed by the materials management group in following physical units through the plant. It is logical that the policy guidelines for inventory control fit both accounting and the materials management needs.

Many managers in business, unfortunately, look upon the computer to magically solve inventory problems. This is wishful thinking. The role of manager as the decision maker has not been changed by the computer.

Only at a routine level can the computer be programmed to make decisions. If this changes in the future it will be evolutionary rather than revolutionary. Major factors in inventory management are not measurable —at least not economically. As an example, how many companies can answer, "How much in sales is lost if you run out of stock?" Probably few. Designing an industrial experiment to get the answer could be extremely complicated and impractical because it would necessitate questioning customers. An experienced executive has an idea what the answer is, being, in a sense, a complex computer who has been assimilating and analyzing information for years.

The procedures covered in this book make extensive use of the "human computer." We discuss setting inventory policy, identifying problems, and conducting operations in conformity with stated policy. The policy comes from the "human computer" which won't burn up endless hours groping for the answer. The executive may do some groping but he generally knows when to stop analyzing and to come up with a decision. The financial executive must know when to use the human computer and when to switch over to the digital computer.

INVENTORY COSTING

Cost accounting is an important part of inventory management for a manufacturing company. Half the cost/benefit equation is based on costs. To determine the value of inventories, dollar values are applied to the physical units that are controlled and accounted for on inventory status reports (perpetuals). The inventory balances on these status reports should be regularly verified through cycle counts that take into account the magnitude of dollar values when selecting items to be counted with high frequency. Obviously, the items with lower values would be counted less frequently.

Unfortunately, too many companies determine inventory valuations without reference to the individual physical units being accounted for on the monthly inventory status reports. Many company procedures consist of a single pool of inventory on the books to which material purchases are added and labor and overhead costs inputted. At the other end, shipments out of inventory are frequently costed at arbitrary values which do not necessarily equate with the input values. The result is often a year-end physical-to-book adjustment that corrects the erroneous profits (or losses) recorded during the year.

This book describes how inventories can be managed. Chapter 6 should be helpful in structuring an approach to identifying problems. Chapters

2 and 10 concentrate on the cost accounting aspects of inventory management—tying physical accountability by the computer with costing through use of standards. We have not constructed a theory of inventory management that answers every problem. The procedures we describe have been tried and have worked. We invite you to share our experience.

CHAPTER 2

YEAR-END "PHYSICAL TO BOOK" DISCREPANCIES —ACCOUNTABILITY FOR LOSSES AND WASTE

Better control of operations through more informative reporting to management is the subject of many books and papers. Much of this deals with format (i.e., reporting by responsibility, profitability by product line, and marginal contribution). It is surprising how many writers and speakers overlook proper inventory accountability and valuation as a necessary ingredient of accurate reporting. Accountability for waste and spoilage (called scrap by some) is often brushed over lightly as if it were merely a problem of proper reporting. While proper reporting of production losses is important to good inventory accountability, other factors affect inventory accuracy.

The first part of the chapter deals with inventory accountability as it relates to year-end physical versus book problems. The second part covers waste and spoilage.

YEAR-END PHYSICAL INVENTORY TO BOOK DISCREPANCIES

Hundreds of manufacturing companies, at year-end, find that an 11 months' profit has seriously deteriorated because of a large difference between "physical" and "book." Only inventory shortages that result in lawsuits make the headlines:

$5 MILLION INVENTORY SHORTAGE
AT ABC CORPORATION; SEVERAL
LAWSUITS IN THE OFFING.

These represent only the tip of the iceberg. The average executive is not aware of the many occurrences because no tabulation is available. In fact, because the occurrence is an embarrassment to the financial executive, it is suppressed rather than publicized. Most times the shortages are not real losses—the discrepancy being the result of a poor cost system that under-relieves inventories during the year, requiring adjustment at year-end. This raises several questions:

1. Why is correct inventory valuation so important?
2. How do discrepancies occur?
3. What is the solution?

Why Proper Inventory Valuation Is so Important

Good inventory accountability assures correct reporting of profits during interim periods as well as at year-end.

1. Nothing is more disconcerting to the general manager responsible for the profit goals of his operation than to think for 11 months of the year that he is meeting the business plan, only to find in the twelfth month that a large inventory difference between physical and book wipes out much of the profit. Often when this happens, a promising career can be demolished overnight. This can happen not only to the financial executive, but to the general manager of the operation as well.

   Often, they become defensive, arguing that the discrepancy between physical and book is only 1% of throughput (flow of production). They imply: "How much more accuracy can you expect with the massive movement of material and parts in a year?"

   While it seems logical to equate the magnitude of the discrepancy with the volume of throughput, the more frequently used measure in the real world of business is the impact on profits. The difference is demonstrated below:

	Company A	Company B
Annual throughput	$10,000,000	$10,000,000
(Factory cost of production)		
Inventory discrepancy	$ 100,000	$ 100,000
Percent to throughput	1%	1%
Pretax profit	$ 1,000,000	$ 200,000
Percent discrepancy to profit	10%	50%

   Obviously, a more unfavorable reaction can be expected from Company B's management and stockholders than from Company A even though the amount of inventory discrepancy and throughput are exactly the same.

2. Proper inventory accountability is needed because quarterly submissions are required by the Securities and Exchange Commission. A company whose inventory is overstated on its books may show overstated profits in the first three quarters and a relatively poor performance for the fourth quarter after adjusting to the physical. This does not represent acceptable reporting.

3. Stock analysts who make recommendations to clients on the basis of reported earnings can be greatly misled by incorrect profits resulting from overstated earnings. This can be detrimental to a company seeking to raise capital.

Why Discrepancies Occur

Inventory discrepancies occur in a number of ways. The following case studies illustrate the more typical occurrences.

Company A

This company has one inventory pool on the books. There is no breakdown among raw material, work-in-process, and finished goods.

Input into inventory is based on the actual cost of material purchased and the actual direct labor as recorded on the payroll. Overhead is applied on the basis of a predetermined overhead rate on direct labor.

Output. Relief to inventory is determined on the basis of "standard" costs applied to shipments. These are developed to approximate actual costs. Because the rate of cost escalation accelerated during the year, the standards used for costing sales have fallen far short of actual costs. As a result, the book inventory is substantially higher than the value of the physical inventory, so that profits reported in earlier months are now reduced substantially.

Company B

No formal standards program.

Input. In an attempt to approximate a standard cost system, actual labor costs are factored by estimated efficiency factors. Material input is therefore considered to be based on standard prices.

Output. To arrive at the cost of sales, an historically experienced percentage is applied to each month's sales. As in Company A, the basis of output is not consistent with input. The percentage applied to sales is 51%. Because the mix of products has changed during the year to include more of the high material content items, the actual cost of sales turns out to be 57%. Because of this underrelief of 6%, there is an inventory discrepancy of about $1 million.

Companies A and B need to establish uniform standards for both input and output.

COMPANY C

Because of a defect in a newly launched product, customers have been authorized to return the product for replacement of the defective part. As the returns begin to accumulate, paperwork falls behind. The controller therefore resorts to a physical inventory each month to account for the blacklog of returned products. This results in an overstatement of inventory since most of the items are still the property of the customers. Returns from customers cannot be picked up as inventory until a credit has been issued to the customer.

COMPANY D

Rework is characteristic of many products. In doing rework, it is important to carefully monitor the production count to assure that double-counting is avoided—once when the original work is done and again when the defect is corrected.

Company D makes a product that has been subject to about 10% rework. Its controls to assure accurate counting are somewhat weak. As a result, double-counting has caused an inventory buildup on the books that was unknown until the book and physical inventories were compared at year-end.

COMPANY E

Has a formalized standard cost system. The same standards used for costing individual operations add up to the total standard product costs used for arriving at cost of sales. However, because losses in production are not fully accounted for, at year-end the inventory shortage between physical and book is $465,000.

Reporting production losses through direct paper work is easier said than done. Frequently, such losses occur because material thickness and widths (particularly in metal stamping) exceed specifications. In plastics molding, mold wear can result in use of more material than called for. Since the end product in this company has an average factory cost of only 25 cents per unit, this is certainly not enough to warrant expensive monitoring to assure that all losses are correctly and fully accounted for.

The solution is to report the good finished components and subassemblies only when accepted into stock, thus automatically excluding waste and spoilage. This approach, which is applicable to many companies, is discussed later.

The experience of Companies A, B, C, D, and E illustrate circumstances that cause a large inventory discrepancy. The number and variety of such occurrences are almost limitless. Positive steps, which consider variations in cost flow, minimize the potential causes of discrepancies.

Variations in Cost Flow

Inventory accounting procedures are based on the type of cost flow, which, in turn, is based on the actual production flow of the product being manufactured.

A custom product is an entity unto itself, production flow being patterned around making specific products for specific customers. The flow of material, labor, and overhead is directed toward satisfying the requirements for that specific product. When completed, it is shipped to the customer out of work-in-process rather than out of a finished goods warehouse. In a number of instances, companies make custom products from standard interchangeable components. Thus, the production flow for components can be similar to the flow in making standard products for stock while the assembly of the finished unit can be similar to that of custom products.

A standard product is usually built to stock and sold out of finished goods. The production flow can be pictured as a steady stream of material, labor, and overhead flowing into work-in-process through the various operations. From work-in-process, the flow is through the finished goods inventory from which shipments are made.

Job Costing

The job costing system generally utilizes two basic inventory accounts:

1. Raw material.
2. Work-in-process (jobs in process).

While purchases are normally directed into the raw material inventory account and then issued to jobs as needed, this is not always the case; material purchased specifically for a job can bypass the raw material inventory account. Direct labor is charged directly against the job on which the work is performed.

Inventory accountability under job costing is relatively simple. As each job is completed, all accumulated costs charged to that job are cleared out of inventory, leaving no unaccounted-for residual quantities. If relief is made at the standard cost of the finished job (or estimated cost), the resulting residual quantity represents a variance. This would be cleared out of work-in-process as a separate step.

The job costing method has disadvantages, however, because such a system requires substantially more work than a process cost system. As an example, a company with annual sales of less than $10 million could have 500 jobs in process. Job shops tend to "borrow" from one job to meet priority requirements of another. When such borrowing is not documented, the accuracy of the inventory value carried on the books becomes questionable. While process costing is simpler and therefore less costly, it cannot be substituted for job costing when customized production and costing are required.

The type of product or service dictates the type of cost system required. When the product or service is unique and its specific cost must be known, then the job cost system is mandatory. In a process type business in which standardized products are built to stock, rather than to a customer's order, a standard cost process flow system is more suitable.

Standard Costing in a Process Flow

A process (repetitive) business requires three basic inventory accounts:

1. Raw material.
2. Work-in-process.
3. Finished goods.

Many companies that have greatly improved the credibility of financial statements through better inventory accountability are still vulnerable to year-end discrepancies because incipient problems are not reflected in the paperwork that documents the various transactions affecting the inventory. Examples are: overreporting of production, excessive use of material that is unreported, and rejects that are not completely accounted for.

As is illustrated later, the work-in-process account should be broken down further to identify items stored in a controlled stockroom and those that make up the floor work-in-process. Accounting systems rarely recognize this breakdown in work-in-process, and thereby miss an opportunity for better accountability of inventory.

Most of the foregoing problems that result in underrelief of inventory in a process flow system occur in work-in-process. Efforts to correct the reporting frequently become highly frustrating exercises because the cost of the cure often far exceeds the benefits, particularly when low unit values are involved.

Accountability for Inventory

True accountability of inventory requires two steps:

• Accountability for the physical units.
• Assigning dollar values to the physical units accounted for.

The accounting department rarely has the tools necessary for good physical accountability. This is done by the production and inventory control group whose major responsibility is to:

- Issue requisitions for purchase of material.
- Issue shop orders for production of components and subassemblies as well as the finished product.
- Maintain perpetual records of items in inventory.

With the introduction of the computer in maintaining perpetual records of all stockroom inventories and, in many cases, status reports of floor inventories, it behooves the accountant to make better use of the same paperwork that is used for moving material in and out of the various stores accounts.

The big "hangup" of many accounting departments lies in the work-in-process inventory. The accountant looks upon this as a single pool of costs. The production and inventory control group identifies work-in-process in at least two segments: finished parts in work-in-process inventory that contains two or more controlled areas:

- Components (manufactured and purchased parts).
- Subassemblies.
- Unpacked goods (finished goods that have not yet been packed).

The components and subassembly stockrooms are usually enclosed areas while the unpacked goods are in an open area located at the end of the production line. Although the latter area is not enclosed, it is closely controlled, as are the other two.

Receipts into all three areas are based on counts of items that have been inspected and accepted by the inspector. The smaller items are weighed and scale counted through use of conversion factors. The larger items are accounted for individually.

The tickets representing receipts into stock and issues out of stock are numbered sequentially. Each day's receipts and issues are batched and forwarded to the data processing department for processing. The pre-printed numbers are listed sequentially for both the receipts and issues to determine if any tickets are missing. If there is a gap, the issuer of the ticket is asked for an accounting. Usually missing numbers are tickets that were voided and thrown out. Insistence on full accountability reminds new personnel that every transaction must be documented.

The quantities received into and those issued out of each controlled area are used as the basis for adjusting the "on-hand" figures on the perpetual inventory status report for each stockroom. (The same procedure is followed for raw material and finished goods.) The same paperwork used to adjust perpetual inventories should be the basis for input into inventory on the books.

Before discussing accountability for floor work-in-process, let us cover cycle counting, the assurance that the units in stock are correct.

Importance of Cycle Counts

No perpetual inventory can be run "ad infinitum" without regular verification. The preferred method is cycle counting, so named because of the systematic selection of items to be counted. Two basic considerations for effective cycle counting are:

- Proper cutoffs.
- Frequency of counting.

Proper Cutoffs

Any paperwork that documents the transactions affecting the perpetual inventory usually lags by a day or more because the documents must be reviewed, accounted for in numerical sequence, batched, and then processed before the perpetual records correctly reflect the status of the items covered by the paperwork.

All such delayed transactions must be accounted for when the physical units counted are compared with the balances shown on the inventory status report. This reconciliation is as important as the physical count.

Determining the Frequency of Counting

Selecting and categorizing items to be counted assures accuracy of stockroom inventories. First, each item in inventory is listed sequentially, by dollar value.

Categorizing the Inventory

Next, the inventory is divided into four categories identified as A, B, C, and D. This must be done on a judgmental basis, keeping in mind the following guidelines:

> The A and B items, taken together, should account for about 80% of the value. The B items ideally should be roughly half of the A items in dollar value.

As between C and D items, the categorization should leave 50 to 60% of the total items and about 10% of the total dollar value in the D classification. The following figures illustrate the desired breakdown into four categories:

Items	Number of Items	Percentage of Total Items	Percentage of Total Value
A	1,350	7.4%	48%
B	2,300	12.6	26
C	3,200	17.5	16
D	11,400	62.5	10
Total	18,250	100.0%	100%

Cycle Counting Schedule

Once the categories have been determined, a frequency for counting must be established. A suggested schedule is shown below:

Items	
A	Every 2 months
B	Every 3 months
C	Every 6 months
D	Every 12 months

Since the A and B items account for 74% of the total inventory value and require counting only 20% of the total number of items, cycle counts for these two categories are scheduled frequently. The D items, which represent more than 60% of the total number of items in inventory but only 10% of the total value, can safely be scheduled for counting once a year.

Over and above verification through cycle counting, there is an automatic verification opportunity for each item in which an issue depletes the supply. In some instances, negative quantities appear on the inventory status report (perpetual). This can result when a part number is misidentified. Negative balances should never be automatically adjusted to zero because this is tantamount to a writeup of inventory. Every effort should be made to determine the reason for the error.

Overview of Cycle Counting Requirements

Cycle counting is a full-time job that must be taken seriously. It cannot be treated as "fill-in" work when time allows. Because this program can require as many as 150 items to be counted each work day, the computer must provide the daily listing of items to be counted. This listing should also provide space for the inventory control clerk to show the actual number in stock as well as the cutoff reconciliation quantities.

Accounting for Floor Work-In-Process

Once the stockroom work-in-process inventories are accounted for, only the floor inventories remain to be discussed. These are the to-be-processed raw materials lying around the work places and items that have been partially processed as well as those to be accepted into stockrooms.

If the floor work-in-process is in "pipeline stock" it can be accounted for by carrying a fixed dollar value on the books. If there are "expansion points" at which the amount of floor inventories fluctuates, it may be necessary to take physical inventories at such points and to adjust the fixed value carried on the books.

Some production and inventory control departments account for floor work-in-process through shop orders which utilize "travelers" or shop orders to identify the production at each point of the process as well as the number of units lost through defective workmanship or materials. Where such information exists, the balances on the shop orders can be costed to arrive at the value of the floor work-in-process.

Some accountants monitor floor inventories by accounting for movement from cost center to cost center. While this method seems to be theoretically proper, it can result in a fictitious buildup on the books with the resulting discrepancy at year-end when the book value is compared with the physical value. The weakness in this method is that production figures on an operation-by-operation basis, even if correct, would result in input into inventory of costs that would be too high because of losses in later operations.

If such losses were removed from the inventory, the net result would be approximately correct. However, in the real world, reporting of production losses is one of the weak links in inventory accountability. It is a rare company that can boast of reliability in reporting of such losses, leaving as the most practical alternative the acceptance into inventory of only the costs of those items that are physically received into the various stockrooms. Although we favor this method, we recognize that accountability for losses and waste facilitates corrective action.

ACCOUNTABILITY FOR LOSSES AND WASTE

Too often the accounting system, which admittedly has the important job of reporting the financial condition of the business to the owners, results in a paperwork routine that fully occupies too many financial groups to the extent that the more pertinent day-to-day controls are never properly implemented. While the financial executive is responsible for making up payrolls, billing customers, paying suppliers, monitoring inventories, controlling capital acquisitions, preparing budgets, and summarizing expenditures, he must, in spite of these demands, find a way to implement timely cost controls, one of which includes production losses and waste. He must enlist the aid of other members in the organization: production control in preparing information needed for measuring material utilization and the quality group for reporting and control of production losses. In most companies, substantial amounts of good basic information needs only to be correlated and recast into meaningful and actionable reports.

The phraseology "accounting for losses and waste," taken alone, is somewhat misleading because it implies that losses and waste are known as soon as incurred. Losses refers to units (usually fabricated components) that are not of acceptable quality and cannot be reworked. Waste refers to material that is used in excess of the quantities specified in the production standard allowances. In metal stamping, excess usage of material could be caused by using metal strip that is on the high side of the dimensional specifications called for in the production standards. In molding, waste can result from worn molds.

Losses and waste cannot be properly accounted for in many instances because production is not screened immediately after fabrication. This is frequently done just before acceptance into a controlled stock area and following a wheelabrading, tumbling, or cleaning operation. Some parts— foundry castings, for instance—can have hidden defects under the surface that are not evident until the boring or grinding operation takes place.

The financial executive is looked upon by fellow managers as the catalyst in the assembly, interpretation, and distribution of this information. This section discusses the types of analysis and reports that are necessary for controlling losses and waste more effectively.

Control of Material Losses

Material is probably the most difficult element of manufacturing cost to account for. Actual usage is not known in many instances until an inventory is taken. Taking inventories can be expensive and time-consuming. This undoubtedly is one of the reasons material is not accounted for more frequently. It is not sufficient to report material (and labor) efficiencies once a month or after a job is completed. Management must have this information on a more timely and more frequent basis.

Although material accountability presents some real problems, the case for control is not hopeless. Although many items of material need to be accounted for, a few items usually make up much of the total. Even if an inventory is required in order to properly report material usage on a more frequent basis, the inventory need only cover the few items. This is the selective control technique.

Selective Control Technique for Material Control

One company controls material much better through use of this technique. An analysis shows that 87 different material items are used in normal production and that 14 of these account for 52% of the value. Although fuller than 52% coverage is desirable (27 items are required for 85% coverage), in the interest of economy and speed only 14 items are controlled at the outset.

Arrangements have been made with the factory to take an inventory of the 14 key items each Friday shortly before close of work. The stockroom also furnishes the financial group with figures showing the number of items issued and returned to stock. These are furnished daily along with the number of units that are produced and accepted by the stockroom. Receipt of these figures daily permits cursory checks to detect unusually low or unusually high activity; as a result, the financial group has become more production oriented because questions have to be answered by production personnel.

Daily receipt of production and issue figures makes it easier to accumulate the figures during the week so the final day's production and issues need only to be added to the prior 4 days' totals. As soon as the inventory information is available, each item is summarized and the material utilization percentage determined, as illustrated in Exhibit 2-1.

The beginning inventory is always the same as the preceding week's ending inventory, unless an error is found. Issues to the floor are added to the beginning inventory to determine the total amount of material available. This figure is reduced by returns to stock, which sometimes are high because they represent rejects due to poor workmanship by a department. The adjusted amount is then reduced by the ending inventory to arrive at the amount of material usage. This, divided into the output or production, results in a material utilization percentage.

Part 198986 shown in Exhibit 2-1 is illustrative of this type of control. The beginning inventory amounts to 8820 units; 69,000 units are issued to cover the next 2 weeks' production requirements. The 11,000 returns to stock represent defective parts. The entire amount of material available, less returns, is used to produce 24,066 finished parts—a material utilization of only 36%.

Investigation into this low percentage reveals that the quality of the

EXHIBIT 2-1   WEEKLY MATERIAL UTILIZATION REPORT (figures in units)
w/e _____

Part #	Beginning Inventory	Issues to Floor	Returns	Ending Inventory	Material Usage	Production	Utilization Percentage
135812	98,156			2,926	95,230	82,812	87%
138819	98,000	18,045		26,000	90,045	82,812	92
144404	5,400	96,750		10,750	91,400	82,812	90
211362	3,500	63,500			67,000	51,891	77
223414	860	252,695	3,010	8,624	241,921	252,190	104
201134	8,000	378,510	6,000	3,080	377,430	252,170	67
199966	15,530	133,000		7,224	141,306	101,527	72
211633	14,217	33,400		26,307	21,310	19,683	92
198986	8,820	69,000	11,000		66,820	24,066	36
253007	1,550	35,650	21,130	3,000	13,070	5,689	44
244031	3,640	10,500	2,860	3,920	7,360	5,689	77
22306	2,000	8,150		1,000	9,150	5,689	62
23364	15,754	88,540	6,653	12,507	85,134	65,482	77
19966	5,370	104,275	6,900	19,800	82,945	65,482	79

parts issued from stock is generally poor. Only 11,000 have been returned to stock (although more should have been returned) because of a rush order for a customer requiring immediate delivery. As a result of poorly fitting parts, more than 66,000 have been used to make 24,000 finished units.

Since this experience the financial group watches for large returns to stock as a clue to low utilization. To prevent similar problems in the future, rush production of parts such as 198986 are minimized by maintaining a min-max inventory in stock sufficient to take care of 2 or 3 weeks' production requirements. Now when issues are made to the floor, there is greater assurance that the parts are not defective because adequate lead times are provided all departments to eliminate waste due to haste. Utilization figures are inspected and trends are carefully watched to determine how to improve utilization.

This report also provides a weekly analysis of inventory of the 14 dominant items. If an inventory remains too high and is untouched for 4 weeks in a row, questions are asked, and frequently it is possible to obtain orders to reduce the inventory to tolerable limits. This eliminates later obsolescence and consequent writeoffs.

Maintaining this type of report in units rather than in dollars eliminates much work in giving a dollar value to the figures. Since the 14 items represent over half the value of all materials used, there is no need to incur additional cost to reconfirm this fact each week.

PRODUCTION FLOW

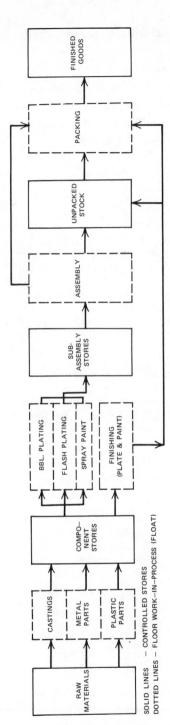

SOLID LINES — CONTROLLED STORES
DOTTED LINES — FLOOR WORK—IN—PROCESS (FLOAT)

EXHIBIT 2-1 PRODUCTION FLOW

Monitoring Spoilage

It is not always necessary to account for inventory changes to obtain effective control. When the flow of the product and its components can be monitored so "unaccounted-for disappearance" is not an important factor, an analysis of spoilage provides adequate control. This type of control is usually more economical than the weekly material utilization report. It is also more timely because spoilage information can be provided hourly if need be.

One of the companies whose material cost control procedures has been studied prepares a daily spoilage report which shows the number of each unit rejected (minor items omitted). If the defect can be reworked, the spoilage quantity is adjusted and the rework cost noted. This report is issued each morning for the preceding day, with a short statement explaining major causes of an unusually high spoilage rate.

The information on the daily report is summarized weekly by type of unit and defect causing the rejection. Dollar values are then assigned and a listing is made in order of dollar magnitude of spoilage, with the highest cost items appearing at the top of the list. A specimen copy of this report is shown in Exhibit 2-2.

The part number rejected is shown as well as the final product in which the part is used. The week's scheduled production is shown in order to determine the magnitude of rejects. While a "Percent Rejects to Week's Scheduled Production" might be useful for this purpose, it was decided that every additional column adds to the complexity of the report and to

EXHIBIT 2-2 WEEKLY SPOILAGE REPORT (dollar value of rejects)

w/e _____

Part #	Used on Product No.	Week's Scheduled Production	No. of Rejects	Type of Defect	Total Cost
603	78396	300	19	116	$ 625.38
301	69842	150	9	43	531.52
673	39461	75	8	52	503.61
498	21312	890	150	14	342.16
306	14398	250	14	16	221.03
403	31982	600	32	6	114.32
106	21699	300	25	55	98.14
198	4443	250	8	62	41.10
					$2,477.26

Annualized total: This week's	$123,863.00
Prior week's	$114,132.75

the preparation time. The next to the last column shows the reject code while the last column shows the dollar cost of the rejects. The total week's rejects of $2,477.26 is annualized to emphasize the magnitude of spoilage. The prior week's annualized total is also shown for comparison.

The report is closed out at the close of business on Tuesday and issued Wednesday morning. In a weekly meeting held on Wednesday shortly after the report is distributed, the quality assurance group and production foremen discuss the causes of spoilage and suggest remedies. Primary emphasis is placed on the first three items, which account for 70% of the rejects. If time permits, the fourth item, which accounts for another 14%, is discussed. When appropriate, other parties such as the purchasing agent or material control supervisor is called in. The purchasing agent might be called in on a discussion of quality of parts or other materials being purchased while the material control supervisor might be called in on a discussion dealing with defects due to rough handling of parts or improper storage. Actual participation by these parties has a more salu-tary effect than a telephoned complaint delivered in haste and received in haste. The mid-week meeting permits action the same week as the decisions and recommendations are made. The results are carefully re-viewed in the following week's meeting to determine if the problems have been corrected.

Another company which assembles components that, once assembled, cannot be taken apart for repair, summarizes weekly spoilage in units on a cumulative basis. The figures correspond with the sequence of opera-tions, and are illustrated in Exhibit 2-3. In the first assembly operation 100 units were started but one was rejected, showing 99.0% good. Operation 2 shows 99 starts with one rejected. Operation 3, with 98 starts because two had already been rejected, resulted in three rejects, or 96.9% good units. Operations 4 and 5 follow the same pattern.

The cumulative "percentage Good" shows the cumulative effect of losses all along the line. While this figure is readily apparent by looking at the "Good Units" column and relating this to 100 starts at operation 1, it is not always possible in actual practice to determine this figure in this manner because all units started in each operation are not always com-pletely processed and forwarded to the next operation in the same week. Exhibit 2-4 is a more typical example.

EXHIBIT 2-3   WEEKLY SPOILAGE REPORT (units scrapped)
w/e _____

Assembly Operations	No. of Starts	Good Units	Percentage Good to Starts	Cum. Percentage Good	Rejects
1	100	99	99.0%	99.0%	1
2	99	98	99.0	98.0	1
3	98	95	96.9	95.0	3
4	95	75	78.9	74.9	20
5	75	65	86.7	65.0	10

EXHIBIT 2-4   WEEKLY SPOILAGE REPORT

Assembly Operations	No. of Starts	Good Units	Percentage Good to Starts	Cum. Percentage Good	Rejects
1	145	145	100.0%	100.0%	—
2	140	134	95.7	95.7	6
3	42	41	97.6	93.4	1
4	41	36	87.8	82.0	5

The cumulative percentage good is calculated as follows:

100.0% in operation 1 multiplied by 95.7% in operation 2 = 95.7%
95.7% in operation 2 multiplied by 97.6% in operation 3 = 93.4%
93.4% in operation 3 multiplied by 87.8% in operation 4 = 82.0%

The cumulative percentage of rejects highlights the total impact of accumulated spoilage. It appraises the overall effect of the rejects rather than looking at only a segment at a time. Referring again to Exhibit 2-3, it should be little consolation to management to see that operations 1, 2, and 3 are running better than 90% when only 65% of all units started are good.

This type of control highlights such losses without requiring time-consuming cost calculations. While application of costs to the units would better equate for relative values, the additional information obtained may not justify the delay in issuance of the report.

OTHER INVENTORY DISCREPANCIES

Although unreported losses and waste must be considered when physical and book inventories differ, this is not necessarily the predominant factor. Inconsistency in valuation of input versus output is probably a larger factor. This would include instances in which partial and completed production are costed at values that are not consistent with the costs assigned to finished products shipped to customers. The earlier examples of companies A, B, C, D, and E cite specific experiences in such valuation inconsistencies.

Like many occurrences in the dynamics of modern business, accountability for losses and waste is so intertwined with other factors affecting inventory that it is frequently difficult and economically not practical to sort out the factors and evaluate them individually.

CHAPTER 3

FORMULATING INVENTORY POLICY

Inventory policy is the set of executive level directives that establishes guidelines for inventory management. Day-to-day management of inventories, on the other hand, consists of many small decisions made by many inventory controllers.* These decisions are subject to a variety of pressures made under continually changing conditions. The level of detail is too small to justify executive review of the individual decisions. Thus control is exercised by setting performance standards and monitoring actual performance against the standards. The alternative—no policy—is equivalent to no executive control over inventories. What is not always fully appreciated is that a vague, intangible, or highly subjective inventory policy is also equivalent to no executive control over inventories.

CUSTOMERS ARE PART OF INVENTORY POLICY

At a meeting of executives at one company the sales vice president said: "There's no loyalty in this business; whenever our competitor gives a 10% price cut we lose the customer. I wish I knew how to overcome this kind of temperament."

Studies by marketing research groups relating the company's sales to its own price discounts support the vice president's view that sales of their products are very sensitive to pricing. While the importance of pricing is obvious to most persons, the advantages of good service may not be so clearly recognized. One district sales manager, puzzled by the loss of an important customer, said: "We've always met competitive prices and even undercut our competitors when necessary." A review of correspondence from various customers reveals numerous complaints about broken delivery promises. Recent examples are:

---

* These are usually employees reporting to the production control department or equivalent.

- Delivery scheduled to arrive on November 7 arrived November 22.
- Delivery scheduled to arrive on January 8 was rescheduled for January 12. Half the shipment arrived on January 14 and the customer was notified that the balance could not be delivered until January 21.

Consequently the customer had to alter production schedules as well as delay deliveries to his customers. These examples represent the negative costs of poor service.

In addition to the obvious positive side of good service, a benefit that can be even greater than price discount is the reduced amount of inventory that the customer has to carry. With inventory carrying costs approximating 25% of the value of the inventory, good service permits the customer to reduce inventories to a minimum and thus avoid excess carrying charges.*

SUPPLIERS ARE PART OF INVENTORY POLICY

The ability of suppliers to meet shipping schedules influences the buyer's material and work-in-process inventories. Inventory policy should take into account company efficiency as well as supplier performance. A supplier's difficulty in meeting shipping schedules is not always caused by low level of inventory. More often than not, he has too many of the wrong items in inventory and not enough of those that are needed by the buyer. Frequent call by the company's salesmen relaying customer complaints interrupt schedules and are costly. Accelerating customer complaints can snowball rescheduling causing failure to meet schedules. The increased cost results from numerous production interruptions and changeovers. Part of the problem may be due to confusion because the buyer does not provide the supplier with accurate forecasts of requirements.

CASE HISTORY OF A PAPER PRODUCTS COMPANY

This company, let's call it the ABC Paper Products Company, produces about 300 items. These include napkins, towels, industrial cleaning tissues, and personal and facial tissues. The manufacturing operations are located in the Northwest and in the South with the warehouses centered in major metropolitan areas. Public warehouses under short-term lease arrangements are used for the most part. Generally, the products can be shipped from any mill to any warehouse. There are a few exceptions, however. As an example, the products made of coarser wood from the

---

* See Chapter 4, "Inventory Carrying Charges."

Northwest are not readily saleable in the central and eastern states because of roughness.

Sales Characteristics

Sales are made primarily to industrial customers and such institutions as schools, hospitals, and government agencies. Large quantities are also sold to food chains for resale in their retail outlets. Paper jobbers are not used. Food chains and large industrial customers order on a national basis with shipments throughout the country. The orders, which are triggered by favorable prices, are usually large and frequently call for delivery on a release basis (that is, the company has annual contracts with the customer, and shipments are made at specified intervals and quantities).

The pattern of sales reflects little in the way of seasonal fluctuations. Periodic purchases because of favorable pricing result in greater fluctuations than does seasonal buying. Thus, the leveling of production to maintain a constant work force could be controlled by staging promotions at strategic times.

Usually consumer products are promoted, not industrial items. The consumer products are promoted regionally rather than nationally.

Inventory Control

Work-in-process inventories, which consist of cut logs, pulp, and roll paper, are relatively small. Most of the inventory dollars represent finished goods stored at the various warehouse locations. Such inventory amounts overall to a 3-month supply.

There is some concern about the management of inventories, as depicted in Exhibit 3-1. The item shown, which is typical of the other items in inventory, reflects the end-of-week balance at the New York warehouse.

During January the warehouse received large stocks from the manufacturing plants. These arrived during February and exceeded that month's sales, with the result that the inventory balance increased. In late March and April the balance was at a satisfactory level for filling orders on an ongoing basis. Restocking orders were placed, but because of overstock in February small quantities were ordered. Since these orders were small in relation to the shipments, the inventory balance was reduced. In May, the item was out of stock. Throughout the summer, the warehouse was periodically out of stock for certain items. Orders continued to be placed according to the pattern set in March and April when inventory was being worked down; stocks were therefore insufficient for the conditions in May, June, and July.

Under existing procedures this situation prevails until "lobbying" by the regional sales manager results in executive awareness of the out-of-stock situation. Then, another surge of production orders increases the inventory. This sequence of "feast or famine" has been repeated over and over for almost every item in inventory.

To correct the situation, management has formed a committee to develop scientific techniques for managing inventory. Discussions held with

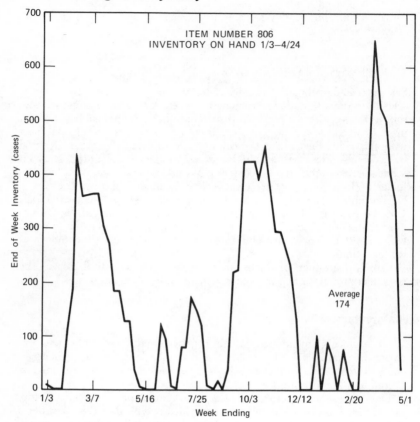

EXHIBIT 3-1 WAREHOUSE INVENTORY REPORT

representatives of production, sales, and finance have not come up with any important conclusions except agreement that service is important. This is the extent of inventory policy. Since no performance standard has ever been set nor method of service measurement agreed upon, all participants are left with their own ideas of what constitutes sound inventory control.

To compound the problem, inventory decisions are dominated more and more by the sales department with production and finance continually on the defensive. While it is bad management for a sales group to take over control of inventory, it is equally reprehensible for other groups to do such a poor job that such action is considered necessary.

WHY SET POLICY

The situation of the paper products company is not unusual. Because the marketing organization is pressured to bring in sales, it wants products available for immediate shipment irrespective of the resulting high levels of inventory. The production executive finds that he cannot produce the product efficiently when there are frequent changes to satisfy an immediate sales need. The financial executive, on the other hand, wants to conserve capital by holding inventories at an optimum level.

If inventory policy is not clearly defined, these conflicting interests cause frustration and discord. Frequently, one of these interests prevails because of a dominating personality. Dominance by any faction is never in the best interests of a company.

A vague inventory policy can be as bad as no policy. In both cases middle management and operating supervisors are left to their own devices with no clear understanding of what is required. Policies must provide meaningful guidelines such as: "98% of all units of catalog items ordered will be shipped from stock within 3 days."

The percentage established, such as the 98%, could apply to the company as a whole; it could vary by warehouse, by nature of the product, or by customer grouping. Stating the policy in specific terms provides all segments of the company with guidelines that should minimize the conflicting interests and foster more cooperation among the departments. Equally important is the articulation of a specific service policy that can become part of the company's selling aid to reassure the customer that delivery promises will be honored.

INVENTORY POLICY AND THE COMPUTER

It is not unusual for a company to have 15,000 to 20,000 or more items in inventory. These are not only finished products but manufactured components, purchased parts, and raw materials. To keep a record of the quantities in the various stockrooms, the movements in and out of each stockroom and work-in-process area, as well as the many analytical and control factors is a tremendous job. The computer takes over a burdensome and costly manual task.

When use of the computer in inventory accountability became practical, many writers described how computers should take over inventory management as follows: Translate all conflicting inventory objectives into cost denominators. Program the computer to interpret customer service in terms of cost of stockouts, backorders, split shipments, delayed shipments, and other related factors. Then express production service in terms of setup cost, size of run, and the like. After this has been translated into inventory unit cost, develop a formula that ties all these costs together to arrive at an overall cost of inventory. This formula applies the cost factors (stockout rate, order size, cost of capital) and calculates the minimum inventory cost which results from taking these factors into account. The result is considered to be inventory policy. Then, according to the policy, production is run in two shifts, say 258 days a year; the distribution group obtains a new warehouse in Miami, for example, and the company rejects those orders that do not fit in with the policy prescribed by the computer.

Although universities continue to teach these procedures, few companies follow them because they recognize that inventory policy requires judgmental considerations. The lack of formal analysis or decision rules means that the computer cannot be programmed to formulate inventory policy.

Today, many companies consider their inventory management automated even though the automation may apply to little more than record keeping and reporting. Inventory stock status reports are maintained and management is provided with current exception data to monitor inventory performance. At the policy level, the computer has little to do with inventory management.

For many companies, the limitations of automated inventory management with respect to policy surfaced during the 1974–1975 recession. The energy crisis, high inflation, and then the recession changed business conditions so rapidly that many time-honored inventory policies became obsolete overnight. Many executives whose inventory records were automated discovered that their company had no mechanism, automated or otherwise, for setting policy—and therefore no control over inventory.

DEFICIENCIES OF THE COST FORMULA APPROACH

The failure of the "all cost" approach to inventory policy has left a gap in automated inventory management as practiced in most companies. The starting point in filling this gap through a comprehensive inventory management program is to examine the reasons for the failure and then to determine practical methods to overcome the difficulties.

Failure of the "textbook" approach to setting inventory policy can be attributed to one or more of the following:

• The textbook procedures for determining policy are not adaptive to dynamic business conditions.
• Certain assumptions are not realistic.
• Cost information is not available.

Typically, management revises and improves inventory policy by assigning the task to a staff team in the systems group. This group collects and analyzes data, interviews the appropriate operating personnel, and finally presents recommendations for executive review and approval.

Executives studying the recommendations become dissatisfied because the recommendations contain some or all of the faults mentioned above. But because executives are usually not specialists in inventory management, they cannot explain their dissatisfaction. Therefore, they either recommend further study or reluctantly accept the proposal with the hope that the problem areas will be worked out in use. Usually the objections are forgotten, leaving things much the way they were before.

The paper products company described earlier in this chapter provides an example of what doesn't work in setting inventory policy.

> The problems of too much inventory of some items and too little of others, too much inventory at one time and too little at another time, have existed for some time. The sales and production departments have "squared off," each blaming the other for the problems plaguing the company. The systems department has been instructed to study the problem and to suggest an inventory policy and how to implement it. After extensive studies and interviews at the plants and warehouses, the group has issued a report explaining the causes of the inventory problems and recommending improvements.

An Example of the Cost Formula Approach

The following are some key points in the report:

1. There is too much inventory and too little customer service (a reiteration of a well known fact).

2. Causes: bad scheduling, incorrect lot sizes, poor forecasts, too frequent product changes, and generally poor factory performance in getting out the product.

3. Recommendations: Calculate the cost of a stockout, cost of carrying inventories, and overall percentage of stockouts. Determine the overall inventory level that would minimize all costs. Then slant company policy to maintain the overall stockout rate and the overall inventory investment at the levels determined by the analysis.

4. Determine the overall policy level. Then allocate inventory to individual items based on average sales. Stock each item with a 2-month supply. Policy: The production department maintains that level for all items at all times.

5. Assign a task force to improve forecasting procedures. Base production scheduling on the average projected demand.

6. Improve the scheduling of deliveries from plants to warehouses so that warehouse orders arrive on schedule.

Management has reviewed the report and recommendations without enthusiasm but has approved a study that should improve forecasting procedures. The attempt to determine overall inventory cost minimization, as recommended, has been seriously delayed because the controller's department cannot provide information on costs of carrying inventory—a task that has been started a number of times but not completed during the time period in which it was needed. It has also been difficult to elicit the kind of creative thinking that would provide information on the cost of stockouts in order to determine inventory levels.

Weaknesses of this Cost Formula Solution

The recommendations to allocate an acceptable overall level of inventory to individual items based on average sales contains a basic weakness. The assumption that a fixed number of months' requirement is a suitable method for determining inventory needs of the various items overlooks the fact that:

- Many items are manfactured at more than one location. Items shipped from the East coast and from the Northwest require different lengths of time in transportation. Obviously, the amount of allowed inventory must take into account the longer pipelines that must be kept filled.
- For some items the demand patterns are fairly stable while for others they are somewhat erratic. The level of inventory for stable items would therefore differ from that for the erratic.
- Certain items are produced constantly; others intermittently, with lot size considerations. Here, again, the amount of inventory will differ for these two conditions.
- Promotions affect demand; inventory stocking rules should account for this.
- Items sold to large chains must take such demand factors into account: Items not sold to chains require a different level of stocking.

Any recommendation suggesting a 2-month average inventory for all items must be erroneous. Because the marketplace changes rapidly, the system for inventorying has to be flexible and dynamic rather than rigid across-the-board. Flexibility should allow the company to provide for advance orders, consignment stock, product substitution, product life cycles, discounts, customer returns, slow-moving items, obsolete stock, preferential customers, changes in tax rates, changing warehouse costs, manufacturing obsolescence, automation, and production capacity.

Also to be considered: 1. What would policy be with respect to the introduction of new items into inventory? 2. How can the system provide for a possible rail strike, a strike at one of the manufacturing facilities, or some other exigency that affects demand? The executive knows instinctively that recommendations for control of inventory have to be flexible, allowing for unexpected and expected changes.

The study at the paper products company did not consider inventory policy sufficiently. A cost formula was developed, based purely on analysis of company data. Where data was missing, the systems personnel made assumptions without the benefit of experience. The formula developed was based on erroneous assumptions and was so inflexible that by the law of averages, half of the items would have insufficient inventory to meet customer service requirements while the other half would be in excess of needs. Thus excess inventory was automatically built into the system at the start, and additional "crash" scheduling would be needed to satisfy customer needs for the items that would be in short supply.

WHAT DOES WORK?

The following are six steps for developing sound inventory policies. Not all of these are suitable for every company but those that are serve as a good reference point.

1. Identify the relevant areas to be included in the policy.
2. Determine the basis of measuring performance in the relevant areas.
3. Establish standards for acceptable performance. If possible, specify upper and lower limits for compliance.
4. Identify the executive point of control to assure that policies are being properly carried out.
5. Define the changes in business conditions that will trigger a reevaluation of inventory policy.
6. Design the mechanism to act as a test of the effect of policy changes on operations.

Discussing and Applying Policy Steps

The first step in developing a sound inventory policy is to identify the areas to be incorporated into the policy. The areas affecting customer service such as stockout rates and order processing time are generally high on the priority list for wholesalers and certain manufacturers. Downtime is high on the list for companies in the processing industry. A checklist of areas that should be considered in the development of policy is included in Exhibit 3-2. This list has been compiled from a number of inventory projects for companies in widely varied businesses.

**EXHIBIT 3-2 CHECKLIST: AREAS THAT SHOULD BE COVERED
BY INVENTORY POLICY**

Inventory turnover	Setup time
Inventory value	Expediting
Stockout rates	Overtime
Order processing time	Intercompany transfers
Delivery time	Intracompany transfers
Backorders	Obsolete inventory
Order frequency	Slow moving inventory
Split orders	Cancellations
Lead times	Inventory location
Returns	Product changes
Substitutions	Production run size
Hedge inventory	Quality rejection criteria
Consignment stock	Certified vendors
Process downtime	Incoming inspection
Routing	Cycle counting
Bills of material	Engineering changes
Requirements forecasting	Assignment of responsibility
Machine downtime	

Each area in the checklist should be reviewed, first to identify applicability and then in light of current inventory performance, classified with respect to policy. Certain areas warrant a policy statement—some will be categorized as actionable, while others will have low priority, depending on the company.

The following case study demonstrates a high priority area:

A new president of a gear manufacturing company has given top priority to assessing inventory problems. He has concluded that work-in-process is far too large and that much work is required to improve inventory management. Guidelines are needed. In discussions with plant personnel, problems have been raised. Because foremen in various departments schedule their own production, in-process inventory components have become unbalanced and the overall inventory is almost twice as great as necessary. Sales forecasts are bad, vendor deliveries are poor, and expediting procedures are disorganized.

However, careful review shows that the lack of policies relating to production scheduling has resulted in independent scheduling by a number of supervisors on an ad hoc basis. None has guidelines nor understands the overall situation in the plant. Wanting to help other departmental supervisors and to spare themselves the criticism that goes with stockouts, they have created excess inventories. The solution is to give high priority to establishing inventory policy in the areas affecting production schedules—overtime, machine downtime, production run sizes, and so forth.

In some instances where a review or revision of an existing policy is indicated, immediate change may not be practical. For example, if changes in customer service are contemplated, proposed alternatives could be checked out with selected customers. Before determining what changes to make in inventory policy, the company has to complete investigatory work.

In a program for developing inventory policy, all executives and other key personnel affected by such policy should be parties in discussions that affect their areas of responsibility. Many individual areas, representing segments of inventory policy, are governed by overall inventory policy guidelines. The chief financial executive may, for example, establish that inventory must not exceed a total company value of $18 million and it must turn over at least five times a year.

Frequently, policy is confused by differences of opinion between production and sales. In such instances a staff team should investigate the issues and recommend a policy that satisfies both. If differences cannot be reconciled through this approach, a higher level executive should settle the issues. Fortunately, such disputes are in the minority. In most instances accord is reached without exhaustive analysis and arbitration.

Policy must be formulated in quantifiable terms whenever possible. Since this aspect of measurability might be useful to the financial group, this group should also be involved. The limits within which measurement of acceptable performance is determined should be spelled out in the policy furnished to this group.

Policy must be stated in specific terms that are easy to apply. A statement such as "5% stockout rate" may appear definitive enough. However, it can be interpreted in many ways. Is the rate measured in dollars? In boxes? Line items? Number of orders? Or some other denominator? Often, orders containing many line items are received. Because one or two of the items are sometimes backordered, service performance may be penalized even though overall performance may be excellent.

> In one of the companies whose procedures were studied, the inventory policy required that 95% of customer orders be shipped within 5 days. The new report showing shipping performance indicated performance as being 65%. Upon investigation, it was found that the orders that contributed to this low performance were those received in advance. Orders shipped on schedule were being recorded as late in terms of the date the order was received. Performance looked bad but was actually good. The problem was quickly corrected by changing the date from which performance was measured.

The foregoing illustrations emphasize the need for specificity in developing policy. In the more complex cases, it would be well to present illustrative examples under various situations that might occur, particularly in exceptional cases.

Most companies evaluate inventory turnover on an overall basis, calculating turns on the total value carried on the balance sheet. For purposes of control the policy should provide for more definitive measurements. To illustrate, two companies may both have five inventory turns per year. If one has little in-process inventory and the other has a substantial portion of its total inventory in manufactured parts, five turns per year may not reflect comparable performance attainments. Since the "flowthrough" of work-in-process is normally more rapid than that of finished products, the latter company with its predominance of work-in-process is not actually performing as well as the former company, assuming that the products are similar.

This example illustrates the desirability of basing measurements on meaningful segments for purposes of control. In line with accountability by responsibility, control should be segmented further so that the performance of supervisors responsible for smaller segments of the inventory can also be measured. Since the whole is a sum of the parts, good performance in the segments of inventory assures good overall performance.

Flexibility of Policy

The policy that works well in a seller's market may become an albatross when a buyer's market prevails. As an example, customer returns during a seller's market, when demand is greater than supply, may allow return of only defective goods or goods shipped in error. During a buyer's market these allowances are frequently loosened. It is also possible that other allowances, such as acceptance of smaller size orders, may be made without the penalty of setup charges. For this reason, persons who establish policy must provide the mechanics for changing policy when circumstances so dictate. They must also define which policies are subject to change. Failure to provide for such changes in advance could burden the company with a rigidity that will not permit even the simplest of changes.

Implementing the Six-Step Inventory Policy

For companies starting with no inventory policy at all, implementing the six-step inventory policy requires much detailed work, particularly if the company is in a variety of businesses. Fortunately, the inventory policy program can be implemented piecemeal.

The inventory committee of the ABC Paper Product Company is in this situation and is finally "getting on with it." The resources required for a comprehensive review of policy have not been made available in full measure. The program, therefore, has to be implemented piecemeal. When the obsolete inventory segment was being evaluated, the committee considered whether the obsolescence was potentially related to several other areas such as slow-moving stock, product changes, and production run sizes.

Discussions with the operating personnel indicate that obsolete inventory in the company is related primarily to product changes. Therefore, the committee has decided to address the problem of defining inventory policy for obsolete inventory and for product changes as they relate to obsolete inventory. By comparison with the other areas on the checklist, Exhibit 3-2, obsolete inventory is judged to be of prime importance.

The second step involves determining the basis of measuring performance. Those responsible for the program raised the question, What constitutes obsolescence? Does an item become obsolete when it is dropped from the catalog? What happens when it was dropped from the national catalog but is still selling in some areas of the country? What happens when production resumes after an item has been declared obsolete? Frequently, the obsolete product and its replacement differ merely in decorative features. Should the old product be reworked to make it salable or should it be scrapped? Answers to these questions are worked out as part of determining the definitions of obsolescence. The unit of measurement adopted for the new defintion of "obsolete" is dollar value. (Rather than weight or units.) Implementation of this step—getting a clear definition and assignment of a dollar value to obsolescence—leads to the next steps, which are setting standards assigning responsibility for such losses. This responsibility has been placed with the sales department. Because new product introduction is the responsibility of product managers, and obsolete inventory is created primarily as a result of introducing replacement products, assigning the responsibility of the obsolete inventory to the appropriate product managers combines the responsibility with those executives exercising effective authority over the size of the obsolete inventories.

Because responsibility is assigned to product managers, they are consulted to determine appropriate standards to use in gauging obsolete inventory performance. Several important facts of the business are brought out by these interviews. The first fact is that product improvements (replacements) are usually in response to market pressures such as competitors' new product introductions. Under these conditions the timing of replacement introduction is dictated by the market place and not by the size of inventory in stock. The second fact is that the secondary market for replaced (obsolete) product declines as time passes. The obsolete product can be sold for a number of months after its replacement, but as time passes the possibilities of a sale are less and less.

After considering these facts, the ABC company decides to set obsolete inventory standards in terms of "time" rather than "amount." A good performance is one in which the obsolete inventory is sold through secondary markets within 6 months, and a poor performance is one in which the disposition of obsolete inventory is not so rapid. These standards are in contrast to the usual practice of defining a good performance in terms of a small dollar level of obsolete inventory. In terms of management motivation the distinction is significant. By selecting the correct standard, product managers are not inhibited from making the product changes dictated by the marketplace. At the same time they are motivated to "clean out" the obsolete inventory in a cost effective way.

Achieving good executive control over inventory is probably one of the most difficult tasks encountered in asset management. One reason for the difficulty is the tendency to try to control on an overall basis without first developing step-by-step guidelines. Just as one must learn the alphabet in order to learn the language, so one must develop policy as the foundation for more logical inventory control.

CHAPTER 4

INVENTORY
CARRYING CHARGES

In a manufacturing plant, inventory can represent as much as 50% of the total investment (receivables excluded). The floor space required for receiving, storing, and staging inventories can amount to more than 45% of total floor area at the factory location. The amount of investment and rent equivalent costs alone provide the clue that carrying inventory is costly.

WHAT DOES INVENTORY INCLUDE

The word "inventory" has different meanings to different persons. To many, inventory means finished products ready to ship to customers as well as some raw materials. Work-in-process is seen as a relatively small "pipeline" supply of products in process of manufacture.

Actually, in many manufacturing companies, work-in-process is much more than pipeline stock; it can be half of the total investment in inventory because much of it is made up of components which require a fair amount of lead time. Frequently, components can be used for a variety of finished products. Thus, a large stock must be available for the variety of combinations that are required in assembling finished products.

To reduce investment in inventories, companies often build up stocks of components and subassemblies in work-in-process rather than finished goods. Assembling the finished product does not require much lead time; it therefore makes more sense to many managements to have the common components and subassemblies available to provide any combination of finished products that may be required.

WHAT IS INCLUDED IN INVENTORY CARRYING COST

Terminology, as well as the nature of costs related to carrying inventories, can vary from company to company. The discussion in this chapter is a composite of several companies, and differences in terminology have been taken care of by grouping certain costs under a broader category. Variations in the magnitude of individual costs have been smoothed so the figures presented in this chapter more closely approximate an average than a midpoint of extremes. The items making up carrying costs are broken down into the following categories:

Rent Equivalent Costs
> Building maintenance services
> Building depreciation and/or rent
> Fuel oil
> Real estate taxes

Taxes and Insurance
> Personal property taxes
> Liability and fire insurance

Operational Costs
> Equipment depreciation and maintenance
> Electricity
> Stockhandling
> Breakage and obsolescence

Financing
> Cost of money

Inventory Related Costs Are Not Always Carrying Costs of Inventory

Often certain manufacturing operations are best performed in a warehouse in which the finished product is readily available. Examples of some of these operations are:

- Tests made on certain pharmaceutical products after a short holding period.
- Branding and packaging when a product can be sold under more than a single label.
- Final testing and calibration of electronic equipment.

In such circumstances, the various costs are adjusted to reduce them by the amount of such expenditure attributable to the manufacturing operation. Such adjustments have been made to the costs presented in this chapter.

Rent Equivalent Costs

These are the costs associated with housing the inventory. They include the building and building equipment depreciation and/or rentals; building maintenance services such as cleaning and maintenance of the building structures; fuel oil, real estate taxes; and public liability insurance.

Rent equivalent costs are applied as cost per square foot. This is generally a single plant-wide figure that averages the cost per square foot for factory, office, and warehouse areas.

Managers who want to perform well against budgets object to averaging the cost per square foot:

> Why charge my warehouse and shipping facilities the same rental as the factory and offices? We don't need 70 degree temperatures in the warehouse—we're closer to 60 degrees. Besides, the cost of constructing our warehouse is less per foot than that of the manufacturing areas.

The counter argument frequently raised is:

> True, the warehouse doesn't need the higher temperatures, but when the doors are open in the various parts of the warehouse, temperatures in the entire factory are lowered. Also, while warehouse construction is cheaper per square foot, these areas are usually built higher than the factory and office areas.

There is little to be gained in attempting to refine costs per square foot to take into account such arguments. Actually, the counter arguments are credible, particularly because much of the stockroom storage area for work-in-process is located in the factory area. It would be far better to develop the carrying cost of inventory in a simplified manner so that carrying costs are known and controlled rather than spinning wheels with refinements that are little more accurate than a simply developed average cost per square foot.

Taxes and Insurance

Although real estate taxes are part of occupancy costs, personal property taxes are not. The latter are assessments made by municipalities on equipment and on inventories, the basis being value rather than space occupied. While some taxing authorities assess as of a certain date each year, some base the tax on the average inventory during the year. The method used in this study was average inventory.

Fire insurance costs follow a pattern similar to personal property taxes in that the amount of premium paid is based on the value insured. Public liability, on the other hand, has nothing to do with valuation placed on assets. It covers claims for injury sustained on company property. Accordingly, this cost should be part of the occupancy charge.

Operational Costs

These relate to such costs as depreciation and maintenance, electricity, stockhandling, and inventory shrinkage/obsolescence.

> **Equipment Depreciation and Maintenance:** This covers the amortization of equipment used for handling inventory in storage areas. When products in warehouses are tested, packaged, or otherwise processed prior to shipment, depreciation of the processing equipment would be considered as production cost rather than inventory carrying charges.

> **Electricity:** Electricity is used in stockrooms and warehouses for lighting, charging batteries used in electric powered lift trucks, and for automatic equipment used for storage.

> **Stockhandling:** This includes personnel costs of loading, unloading, stocking shelves, lift truck operation, record keeping, payroll related expenses, freight costs, and supplies. It also includes charges for services performed by the accounting department and the central data processing department.

> **Breakage and Obsolescence:** This category of costs includes the cost of stock that must be written off the books because of breakage in handling. It also includes a provision for obsolescence. This figure is developed from experience during the past 5 years adjusted for known conditions that might affect historically derived information.

Financing Costs

The cost of money is frequently based on the anticipated prime rate for the coming year. This average prime rate is applied not only to the average inventory value during the year but also to the carrying cost of that inventory.

Putting it all together

The various expenses making up the carrying costs of inventory are summarized in Exhibit 4-1. These represent a composite of costs for companies carrying an average inventory of $5,637,600. The three lines showing the vertical breakdown are:

Line 1: By category of expense, the amount of each expense associated with the cost of carrying all inventories.

Line 2: The portion of total costs on line 1 chargeable to production operations performed in the inventory storage areas.

Line 3: The net cost applicable to carrying inventories.

The horizontal breakdown is developed as follows:

Rent Equivalent Costs: These costs are apportioned to production and to inventory storage areas on the basis of the square footage occupied. The amount apportioned to inventory storage areas is then split on the same basis between areas used for storage and those areas in which manufacturing operations are performed to the finished products in inventory.

We include real estate taxes under rent equivalent costs because they are more closely related to that category than to "Taxes/Insurance."

Taxes/Insurance: Personal property taxes are apportioned among the assets subject to the tax on the basis of the relative values of each. The amount of money shown for this category is the amount applicable to the value of the inventory.

Public liability insurance claims show, historically, that they are occasioned more by personal injuries than by damage to property. Some are claims of injuries sustained by nonemployees outside the premises of the actual building. Accordingly, this item is considered as a rent equivalent cost and is assigned to the various functions on the basis of square footage occupied.

Fire Insurance premiums are based on property value. The apportionment of this item is therefore based on a breakdown among buildings, manufacturing equipment, and inventory.

Operational Costs: These are functional costs related to managing inventory or performing a production operation on products in inventory. Such costs include depreciation on equipment, electricity, stockhandling, and inventory losses such as breakage and obsolescence. The portion applicable to production and to inventory storage is obtained through analysis and judgment rather than through allocations. The analysis consists of the following:

Equipment Depreciation and Maintenance: The actual amount of depreciation for the production operations is determined by accumulating the book depreciation for such equipment as electronic testers and packaging equipment. Maintenance is based on historical experience.

For the inventory storage function, depreciation and maintenance include lift trucks and the other automatic handling equipment in use. No attempt is made to allocate any lift truck costs to the production operations even though the trucks deliver products to and from the center in which the work is being done; the cost is considered nominal.

Electricity: This cost is distributed on the basis of a survey made by the chief electrician. The study takes into account the amount of electricity required to operate each piece of equipment (connected load). This connected load is then multiplied by the total hours of use before extending the hours by cost. Electricity costs are broken down for the individual operational areas located in the inventory areas.

Stockhandling: This covers all labor and nonlabor costs related to movement, storage, and warehouse record keeping. It includes wages paid to receiving and shipping personnel, to lift truck operators, company truckdrivers, clerical help, and warehouse supervisors. Included also in this category are the fringe benefits related to payroll, office expenses, and warehouse supplies.

Breakage and Obsolescence: Allowances for shrinkage (breakage) are based on historical data. Allowances used for obsolescence take into account the anticipated life cycle of the product when practical; otherwise past experience is used.

Cost of Money: One of the principal factors contributing to the cost of carrying inventories is the interest on money. In the 1950s interest

EXHIBIT 4-1 COSTS OF CARRYING INVENTORY

	Rent Equivalent Costs			
	Bldg. Mtnce. Services	Dep. and/or Rent	Fuel Oil	Real Estate Taxes
1. All inventory storage areas	$67,114	$136,200	$12,788	$67,068
2. Less: Costs applicable to production	10,080	12,300	1,917	10,060
3. Net inventory carrying cost	57,034	123,900	10,871	57,008

rates on money were typically under 5%; in recent years rates run closer to 10%.

Interest rates do fluctuate, making it difficult to be precise. This must necessarily be a judgmental decision based on an estimated prime rate for the period during which the carrying cost of inventory is being calculated.

Tallying up the Cost

Exhibit 4-1 summarizes the various costs associated with carrying inventory. Line 3, "Net inventory carrying cost," summarizes each cost element. The carrying cost is $1,225,020 for the year for an inventory valued at $5,637,600. This cost represents 21.7% of the inventory value. If the items in inventory that are subject to further production operations were to be added, this would increase the 21.7% by 5.8% to a total inventory carrying cost of 27.5%

A surprisingly large number of companies in 1974 and 1975 went out on a limb to increase their stocks of inventory in anticipation of increased prices. One of the companies used in this case study purchased a year's supply in anticipation of avoiding a 10% increase in price. The cost of carrying this additional inventory was in excess of the anticipated saving which, incidentally, never materialized because prices dropped 5% rather than increasing 10%. The cost of money, alone, during this period was about the same amount as the anticipated saving.

Carrying inventory costs money. Although interest rates vary and some costs are not affected by small changes in inventory levels, it would behoove company managements to calculate carrying costs using Exhibit 4-1 as a guide. If such calculations are not made yet, then it would be well to use the figures in this study.

The inventory-related costs discussed up to this point are those for the sheer volume of inventory maintained. As we saw in the case study based on typical companies, such inventory-related items can cost as much as 25 cents (or more) per dollar of stock.

Taxes/Insurance		Operational Costs					Total
Personal Propty. Taxes	Liab. & Fire Ins.	Equip. Dep.	Electricity	Stockhandling	Bkge. & Obsolescence	Cost of Money	Inventory Carrying Cost
$87,024	$8,593	$14,100	$19,800	$239,300	$336,700	$563,760	$1,552,447
6,600	1,290	12,060	12,420	85,200	120,500	55,000	327,427
80,424	7,303	2,040	7,380	154,100	216,200	508,760	1,225,020

PENALTY COSTS

Penalty costs are inventory-related costs that are not readily identified or measured. These might also be referred to as the cost of nonfulfillment. The penalty can accrue from three sources:

Production: The extra cost that is incurred because of "crash" production schedules due to a shortage of inventory.

Sales: Profits that have been lost because of not having stock to sell.

Capital: Money cost of excess inventories.

These costs are not always identifiable as such in the books of account, yet they must be considered in any inventory planning program that is contemplated.

Production Penalty Costs

This category of cost would be measured by comparing the cost when an optimum sized production run is put through, with the cost incurred in producing the inventory under shortage conditions. The penalty is made up of such factors as an excessive number of setups, lost machine productivity, overtime premium, and higher scrap losses because of shorter runs. In short, production penalty costs are the extra costs over and above leveled production.

The key to measuring excess costs that result in penalty costs, is to determine a "norm" from which the measurement is made. The norm is elusive. What is considered to be a norm in one study may not be applicable in another case even though the basic conditions appear to be the same.

Consider the case of a manufacturer analyzing the costs attendant with obtaining temporary warehouse space to handle the "surge" production built up in advance of the heavy selling season. The carrying costs would be increased by the amount of rental and handling costs. The penalty costs, on the other hand, would be the extra production costs incurred if he doesn't rent the warehouse. This would be the addition of an extra shift with the extra supervision, payment of shift premium, and probably premium pay for Saturday work. The penalty cost would also include the extra supervision and the loss of productivity due to hiring new employees for a short period of time. Computations of this type are not available in the books of account. They must be made by someone familiar with the operations and knowledgeable in costs of production.

Sales Penalty Costs

Chapter 5 discusses a technique that can be applied in measuring sales penalty costs attributable to stockouts. Many companies seeking to measure such costs request their salesmen to submit information on lost sales. However, they find such data unreliable. It is possible on a statistical basis to clean up the data and thus obtain a reasonable approximation of lost sales. The "clean up" takes into account product substitution, customer demand that was delayed but not lost, and compensating sales. While this is being done, the information is audited and verified.

Capital Penalty Costs

Like the other two penalty costs, this one is somewhat imprecise. Although there is general unanimity that capital charges for inventory are warranted, there are differences of opinion as to how the amount of this charge should be determined. The rates that are suggested range from as much as 25%—the company's expected return on investment—to the rate paid on the company's convertible debentures. Those who argue the higher rate say that if the money were not tied up in inventory it would be invested in company projects that would return 25% (assuming that this is a currently attainable rate of return). The opportunity cost, therefore, is 25%. The group favoring the lower rate contends that since inventory is a long-term investment, the money cost assessed to it should correspond with the money cost assessed against long-term debt.

Although opinions differ in generalizations such as the foregoing, greater agreement exists in specific situations. Take the case of one metal fabricator who used short-term bank loans at an effective rate of 14%. Poor production scheduling had led to excessive inventories. As the inventory was brought down to more reasonable levels, the funds were applied to reduce the bank loans. In this specific case, there was no argument as to what interest rate should be applied to arrive at the penalty cost of the excessive inventory.

Generally, manufacturing inventories take on the aspects of long-term investments, thus being viewed as an investment with opportunity cost potential. Inventories of retailers and wholesalers, on the other hand, bear a closer cost relationship to short-term money rates. The same applies to the inventories of import-export firms.

While there are differences in costing alternatives, there is little argument that minimizing excess inventories assures minimal inventory carrying costs.

INVENTORY MODELS AND CARRYING CHARGES

Texts on inventory control devote much space to explaining inventory models. These are usually a series of formulas relating cost data, operating statistics, and production factors. It is natural to ask, "How does this affect my department?" "Which factors would increase proportionately, which disproportionately, which would have no effect at all?" A recognition of the resulting costs must be tempered by a recognition of questions such as these.

The aforementioned formulas are arranged so that if actual values are given for the cost data and operating data, the formulas can be solved mathematically for the factors. In this way, inventory order points, order quantities, lot sizes, and minimum/maximums are determined. For a number of reasons, these models are frequently misapplied and this can have a serious impact on the accuracy of the indicated inventory levels. Failure to properly assess cost behavior is one of the reasons.

By way of illustrating the mechanics, we discuss one of the basic models. Although this model is too elementary for use in most situations, it has nonetheless been misapplied in a number of companies. The following symbols are used in the model:

TC = total cost per cycle
SC = setup cost
CC = inventory carrying cost per unit per time period
OC = out-of-stock cost
T = time between orders

TI = time inventory is in stock
TO = time inventory is out of stock
OQ = order quantity
MI = maximum inventory level
MBO = maximum backorder level

The assumptions governing the inventory behavior are shown in Exhibit 4-2. Time is represented by the horizontal axis and the inventory level by the vertical axis. When the line falls below the horizontal axis, inventory is in an out-of-stock position and backorders can be expected to accumulate. A fixed quantity is ordered each time, and the lead time between receipt of successive orders is taken to be constant. The cost components are computed as follows:

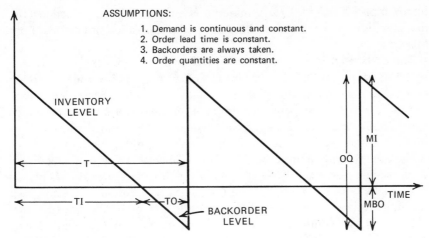

ASSUMPTIONS:
1. Demand is continuous and constant.
2. Order lead time is constant.
3. Backorders are always taken.
4. Order quantities are constant.

EXHIBIT 4-2   INVENTORY MODEL

Cost of carrying inventory $= CC \times \dfrac{MI}{2} \times TI$

Cost of out of stock $= OC \times \dfrac{MBO}{2} \times TO$

Setup cost $= SC$

Since the maximum inventory is MI and inventory decreases at a uniform rate, the average inventory during the time period TI is $\dfrac{MI}{2}$. The cost of carrying inventory is cost per unit per time period, CC, times the average inventory, $\dfrac{MI}{2}$, times the number of time periods, TI. The other cost components are derived in a similar manner.

The total cost per cycle is the combination of the three cost components:

$$TC = CC \times \frac{MI}{2} \times TI + OC \times \frac{MBO}{2} \times TO + SC$$

The average cost per unit of time is:

$$AC = \frac{I}{T}\left[CC \times \frac{MI}{2} \times TI + OC \times \frac{MBO}{2} \times TO + SC\right]$$

Calculus is then used to find the minimum value of AC as a function of the variables in the formula. The values of the variables that give the minimum AC then become part of the inventory rules. In this way order points, order quantities, and the other related factors are determined. If, for example, $MBO = 0$ for minimum AC, the conclusion based on the model will be to set inventory levels so that out-of-stock situations do not arise.

The costs used in the formula, SC, CC, and OC, are constants. To say that SC (setup cost) is a constant is to say that this inventory carrying cost is the same no matter what the level of inventory. This obviously is not the case. If a company, for example, doubles the number of setups because of product line changes, this change must be embodied in the formula. The formula must be sensitive to realistic production requirements.

Continuing with setup costs, another deficiency is the tendency to ignore machine center differences and to use overall averages. A person with plain business sense recognizes the vast differences among such machines as presses, lathes, millers, molding, and automatic assembly machines. But some employees contend, "It all averages out anyway so why try to get specific?" They probably want to average it out to avoid having to determine the amount of setup by machine center.

Averaging out results in overinventorying some items and underinventorying others. Most companies that have adequate labor reporting procedures can obtain the proper breakdown by machine. Usually, it is necessary to go beyond the accounting records when making such analyses. The same applies to the other data needed to develop the formulas. Effective use of a formula is much like effective use of the computer. Output is only as good as input.

Further problems inherent in using inventory models are indicated by the assumptions given in Exhibit 4-2. Demand is assumed to be both continuous and constant. If this is not the case, the model may be inappropriate and the output of the model meaningless. The same conclusion applies to the other assumptions used in the model. Perhaps the most difficult assumption to satisfy is that out-of-stock costs are known. Frequently companies have no objective basis for determining these costs. Since the results of the model are sensitive to the magnitude of the out of stock costs, poor cost estimates can lead to poor inventory management. A sounder approach would be to rely on a service policy set by executives who have extensive experience in the effects of out-of-stock conditions.

RECOGNIZING COST BEHAVIOR

To monitor its inventory carrying costs, a company must be alert to the cost behavior of its own facilities as well as the pricing policies of those from whom it purchases services. Illustrative of the first point is the impact of warehouse capacity.

Warehouse capacity

Common business practice when building a new warehouse is to antici-pate future growth. Therefore, unit inventory carrying costs are higher when the warehouse is not fully utilized. As the inventory increases, unit costs diminish and facilities become strained. The company may rent out-side facilities if it considers the situation temporary, or it may enlarge the present warehouse if it anticipates additional growth. In either event, it is likely that warehouse costs will take a jump. Such changes must be considered if the company is to make sound decisions in managing inven-tory.

Some companies, faced with rising warehouse costs because of newer and higher cost facilities, have found it possible with the larger volume of business to justify labor-saving methods in material handling within the warehouse. Some have gone to completely automated warehouses.

The "stair-step" type of increase referred to above applies to other costs as well. The addition of a clerical employee can have this effect; adding another shift in which the workers are paid a shift premium and to which a supervisory group must be added also causes costs to move up a step. Even money costs can take a jump when existing lines of credit are ex-hausted and new sources must be found.

Purchased services

Sometimes companies utilize public warehouses rather than invest capital in constructing warehouses. The advantage is obvious: when the space is no longer needed, the cost ceases.

One Eastern company decided to lease space in public warehouses as well as the trucking services. The company manufactures appliances in the East and sells them in the Midwest as well as the East. Finished products are stored in public warehouses in Cincinnati, Chicago, St. Louis, and Boston. The warehouses' trucking service moves the products from the warehouses to appliance stores. In many instances, the ware-housing and trucking company has found that products moving between the warehouse locations permit two-way loads. This minimizes "dead-hauling" and therefore makes the trucking operation more profitable to the lessor.

In assessing the inventory carrying cost, the appliance manufacturing company has found that the warehousing costs are quite low in com-parison with past costs with its own and with other warehouses. However, the purchased trucking costs are substantially higher than those of com-petitors. It is apparent that the lessor uses "package pricing" in which the warehousing costs are made attractive. It is also apparent that this "low-balling" of space costs is made up by higher trucking charges. Knowing this, the company has reduced its use of the warehouse trucking services and leases its own fleet to make many of the deliveries to the warehouses.

It is apparent from these illustrations that there is more to inventory carrying costs than merely determining what the costs are. Management must also know how to reduce the costs. In the cost analysis relating to inventories, management must be alert to the fact that the costs are not continuously related to operations, but exhibit stair step and other anomalous behavior. In each specific case, the peculiar nature of inventory related costs must be understood in order to reduce costs.

CHAPTER 5

ASSET MANAGEMENT

Almost every company that deals in goods, as opposed to services, is concerned with inventories. For the most part, such inventories constitute one of the largest—if not the largest—controllable class of assets. For example, the asset side of the balance sheet for Chrysler Corporation, presented in Exhibit 5-1, shows that the inventories comprise the largest category on the balance sheet, representing one-third of the corporation assets. In addition, Chrysler lists almost $1 billion in investments and advances to unconsolidated subsidiaries and associates, investments that in part are represented by pipeline inventories of goods not yet in the hands of the final consumer.

Note that the second largest asset category is Property, Plant, and Equipment (net of accumulated depreciation). Note the distinction in the degree of controllability between inventory assets and property, plant, and equipment. The inventory account represents about 2 months' sales and is in a continual state of replacement. Thus, in a 2-month period, most of the inventory turns over, a situation offering a continuous opportunity to make management decisions that improve or worsen the condition of the company. The property, plant, and equipment assets offer no such opportunity. Tooling decisions tend to be made on a model year basis, providing control only when models are changed.

A financial executive must be deeply involved in the inventory planning of his company. His contribution may be essentially analytical. As we discussed in Chapter 1, the primary use of inventories is to provide buffer zones between stages of production and between the company and the consumer.

Because of the uncertainty of future events, the company is faced with a continuing problem of deciding what its positions should be. The resulting inventory positions could be numerous: keep purchase prices down, keep vendors loyal, keep production running efficiently, increase sales, keep customers happy, and, finally, maximize return on investment.

EXHIBIT 5-1 CHRYSLER CORPORATION AND CONSOLIDATED SUBSIDIARIES CONSOLIDATED BALANCES DECEMBER 21, 1976 (in millions of dollars)

CURRENT ASSETS	
Cash	$ 168.4
Time deposits	218.1
Marketable securities—at lower of cost or market	185.5
Accounts receivable (less allowance for doubtful accounts of $25.1 million)	797.6
Inventories—at the lower of cost (substantially first-in, first-out) or market	2,354.0
Prepaid insurance, taxes and other expenses	102.4
Income taxes allocable to the following year	52.3
TOTAL CURRENT ASSETS	**$3,878.3**
INVESTMENTS AND OTHER ASSETS	
Investments in and advances to associated companies outside the United States	53.5
Investments in and advances to unconsolidated subsidiaries	932.8
Other noncurrent assets	84.5
TOTAL INVESTMENTS AND OTHER ASSETS	**$1,070.8**
PROPERTY, PLANT, AND EQUIPMENT	
Land, buildings, machinery, and equipment	3,867.0
Less accumulated depreciation	2,339.8
	1,527.2
Unamortized special tools	560.0
NET PROPERTY, PLANT, AND EQUIPMENT	**2,087.2**
Cost of Investments in Consolidated Subsidiaries	38.1
TOTAL ASSETS	**$7,074.1**

Chapter 3 discusses an organized approach to sorting out the differences in conflicting objectives. Working within this framework, management can properly assess the conflicting benefits and costs of its inventory policies and arrive at one that suits the company. The remainder of the chapter describes some of these analyses.

THE LAW OF AVERAGES

Since the complexity of inventory management is directly related to business uncertainty and since the role of inventories is to cushion that uncertainty, mathematical probability and statistics play an important role in the analysis related to inventories. The technical depths of these sciences is enormous. We could devote this entire book to some of the variations and only scratch the surface. Application of probability and statistics to inventory management has proved effective. Today they are among the most widely used special techniques in business. The theory as well as the practice requires much special study that is beyond the scope of this book. However, some fundamental principles represent the nature of the world we live in.

One principle—the concept of chance—deals with what to expect in an uncertain world. This concept involves three conditions:

1. We are not certain what will happen.
2. We can list the possible events that might occur.
3. We have some idea which events are more likely to occur than others.

Usage of inventories is a good illustration of a chance phenomenon. Exhibit 5-2 shows weekly stockroom withdrawals of a component used in the

EXHIBIT 5-2 WEEKLY DEMAND FOR BUSINESS MACHINE COMPONENT: PART NUMBER 32566

Week/Demand			
1/0	26/0	51/0	77/0
2/0	27/0	52/540	78/0
3/0	28/20	53/0	79/0
4/540	29/0	54/0	80/10
5/0	30/0	55/0	81/0
6/0	31/0	56/0	82/0
7/0	32/540	57/2	83/0
8/0	33/0	58/510	84/0
9/0	34/0	59/0	85/0
10/0	35/0	60/50	86/0
11/0	36/0	61/0	87/0
12/500	37/0	62/0	88/10
13/20	38/0	63/0	89/20
14/0	39/0	64/0	90/510
15/30	40/510	65/0	91/0
16/0	41/0	66/0	92/0
17/0	42/0	67/0	93/0
18/0	43/0	68/0	94/0
19/0	44/0	69/0	95/0
20/0	45/0	70/15	96/0
21/0	46/0	71/20	97/0
22/0	47/0	72/515	98/0
23/0	48/0	73/10	99/0
24/0	49/0	74/0	100/510
25/0	50/0	75/0	101/0
		76/0	102/0

subassembly of a business machine. A lot size of 500 is withdrawn about every 10 weeks, at which time a work order is issued for the subassembly. Since the lot size requisitions are not issued precisely every 10 weeks, we do not know for certain the actual length of time between the lot size requisitions (point 1 above). In Exhibit 5-2 the first time interval is from week 4 to week 12 : 8 weeks. The next interval is 20 weeks, then 8 weeks, 12, 6, 14, 18, and, finally, 10 weeks. We can list the possible events, 1 week, 2 weeks, and so forth, and have some idea as to which intervals are more likely to occur than others (points 2 and 3, above). As an example, a time interval close to 10 weeks is more likely than a short time interval, such as 1, 2, 3, or 4 weeks.

The question of what is likely to happen is frequently a measurement matter. This is true of the weekly sales of business machines shown in Exhibit 5-3. The number of units sold in a week could take on many different values. When dealing with quantities that can take on a wide range of values and infrequently take on exactly the same value, the solution is to break up the range of values into intervals and develop counts. Exhibits 5-4 and 5-5 illustrate this with the sales data from Exhibit 5-3. In Exhibit 5-4, the data is arrayed in ascending order based on the number of units sold. Next, the range of sales is divided into intervals of 50 units, starting with 250. A count is made from Exhibit 5-4 of the number of weeks with sales for the week falling into each interval. For example, in 2 weeks—weeks 4 and 1—the sales were in the range of 250 to 300. Weeks 2 and 7 show sales to be in the interval from 300 to 350. The results are portrayed graphically in Exhibit 5-5. Each bar represents an interval; the height indicates the number of weeks for that interval.

The development of histograms gives meaning to the likelihood of something happening. By aggregating the data for the individual weeks, the pattern of sales becomes clearer. The interval for aggregation is chosen by judgment. The larger the interval, the more aggregated the data. The

EXHIBIT 5-3   WEEKLY SALES OF BUSINESS MACHINES

Week/Units Sold			
1/280	11/531	21/373	31/480
2/335	12/517	22/574	32/420
3/690	13/485	23/485	33/425
4/260	14/540	24/368	34/505
5/388	15/482	25/360	35/625
6/434	16/603	26/620	36/530
7/343	17/504	27/475	37/562
8/421	18/532	28/379	38/460
9/420	19/420	29/560	39/412
10/540	20/532	30/641	40/357

EXHIBIT 5-4 WEEKLY SALES OF BUSINESS MACHINES ARRAYED BY SIZE OF ORDER

Week/Units Sold			
4/260	39/412	15/482	10/540
1/280	9/420	13/485	14/540
2/335	19/420	23/485	29/560
7/343	32/420	17/504	37/562
40/357	8/421	34/505	22/574
25/360	33/425	12/517	16/603
24/368	6/434	36/530	26/620
21/373	38/460	11/531	35/625
28/379	27/475	18/532	30/641
5/388	31/480	20/532	3/690

basic rule is to keep up this process until the data depicts a meaningful pattern.

The data in Exhibits 5-2 and 5-3 represent rather different situations. The variations in the data in Exhibit 5-2 are caused by delays or speedups in the assembly department scheduling. A few interrelated factors affect this scheduling. Further, since the scheduling can be directly controlled by the company, it is frequently possible to know precisely when the component stock (purchased and manufactured parts as well as subassemblies) will be required.

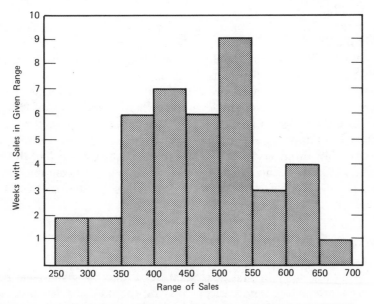

EXHIBIT 5-5 HISTOGRAM OF WEEKLY SALES OF BUSINESS MACHINES

By contrast, the data in Exhibit 5-3 represents sales to many customers. Customers purchase independently and the sale is beyond the direct control of the company. The sales situation is inherently more complex, involving as it does, many more people and factors. Thus, one would expect the sales to be far more difficult to project and the sales inventory more difficult, if not impossible, to control. However, under the law of averages when many independent or unrelated factors come into play, they tend to cancel out each other (average out the variations), resulting in a smooth histogram and becoming fairly predictable.

PLAYING THE ODDS

When a company sells to many customers, demand on sales inventories follows the law of averages. Thus, we can develop a forecast to predict demand. As discussed in Chapter 8, we can never be certain what will happen in the future, the occurrence being a matter of chance. We can, however, with proper analysis, determine what can be expected and manage inventories accordingly.

Exhibit 5-5 shows that the sales pattern of the office machine reflects a fairly stable market. Sales figures are for the basic machine in units. This machine is stocked as a partly assembled product with various options that are assembled to order. By examining the histogram in Exhibit 5-5, we can determine at what level to set inventory and we know what the effect will be.

For example, if it is company service policy to have the basic machine ready for final assembly on, say, 98% of the orders, we now have some idea how much inventory should be carried. In only one case in 40 (2½%) are weekly sales over 650 units. This occurs in week 3 when 690 units are sold. The next largest figure is 641 units in week 30. Using these two figures, if we set the inventory level somewhere in the range of 650 to 700 units, we should get about the required level of service. Setting the inventory level down to, say, 600 units, we would be gearing ourselves to a considerably lower service level, since in the past 40 weeks 5 of the weeks exceeded 600. We cannot expect weekly sales to always continue as in the past, however, for a stable product, change is gradual so this kind of analysis favors the "long odds."

THE MANAGER LOOKS AT PROBABILITY

Providing inventory in sufficient quantities to meet a given level of customer or production service means playing the odds, as demonstrated in the preceding section. The histogram drawn to show the expected frequency of demand on an inventory should make it possible to see the degree of risk associated with a given inventory level. Another measurement problem we must consider is purchases as they affect inventory levels.

Take for instance a low density polyethylene resin as material input to a plant making a variety of products. The demand for the resin is subject to the variability in demand for each of the products using the material. Receipts into inventory are also subject to variability in delivery times and order processing. The plant uses min-max inventory order rules, placing an order whenever inventory falls below the min level. This brings the inventory level to the max. To determine the desired min level, the purchasing agent must find out how much polyethylene will be required from the time the inventory falls below the min to the time when the shipment arrives. This is a combination of the order processing and delivery times. The amount of polyethylene required is thus subject to both the variability in demand and the variability in the lead time for the product. The histogram should incorporate both types of variability in demand and the variability in the lead time for the product.

A difficulty has been experienced in the records of the company whose accounting department maintains figures on weekly usage of polyethylene. A histogram constructed from this data would indicate demand variability but not lead time variability. A histogram showing lead time variability could be constructed from the purchasing records but this would not show demand variability. The purchasing department has tried to work with an average lead time and also with a maximum lead time. The results are not usable in the first instance but are acceptable in the second. Both methods are incorrect: the second method has led to overstocking but makes the purchasing and production departments happy.

When financial management questioned the amount of money tied up in materials, a special analysis was made measuring demand over lead time. When a purchase order was placed, polyethylene usage was measured daily from the date the order was started until the day on which shipment was received. A histogram was constructed showing the variability in these figures—providing management with the means to assess the risk inherent in using a given level of inventory. In one case, because of a rail strike, use of maximum lead times pushed inventory levels up to almost double any reasonable level of risk.

Using the correct formulas, a mathematician could combine the previously existing accounting data on weekly usage with the purchasing data on lead times and come up with a histogram including both factors. This complex calculation is beyond the ability of most employees. As a measurement problem, though, any financial executive can calculate the answer. The task must be correctly defined, however; for example, usage must be measured from the time an order is initiated until the shipment arrives, and then the computer must be programmed to accumulate the figures correctly.

COMPUTER SIMULATIONS

Special measurement is required to determine the correct level for the low-density polyethylene. The accounting figures do not automatically generate data in the desired form but the computer can be simply programmed to calculate this. Certain basic data may not be available. Even historical data may not be available so it may take some months to collect enough actual information to perform the needed measurements. In such instances, computer simulations may provide the solution.

The objective of computer simulation is to create hypothetical data that is representative of the real data that is missing. Exhibit 5-6 shows an application of computer simulation to a situation similar to the polyethylene illustration.

This company assembles air conditioners using motors purchased from an outside vendor. The assembly standard for its 6000 BTU deluxe model is 20 per day. The company uses min-max inventory rules and, as in the polyethylene case, wants to set the min depending on the production during the ordering lead time. The motor vendor provides the company with the other sizes of motors as well as certain other items. Purchase requisitions are submitted for multiple items. Generally, a week is required for delivery; however, as always, delivery times are variable. Partial orders are shipped immediately by the vendor with out-of-stock items following on a rush basis. The company separately puts together information of the lead time variability and production variability data but the absence of the required historical records precludes combining the two.

The upper left portion of Exhibit 5-6 shows the units produced each day. On the average, 9 units are produced on 2 days out of every 100, 10 units on 11 days out of every 100, and so forth. The data on lead times is summarized to the right of the production data. Since the concern is having enough inventory in most cases, early shipments (less than 5 working days), are collected together with shipments that were made in 5 working days. As a further adjustment, the purchasing department has determined to try alternate sources if shipment cannot be promised within 3 weeks. Thus, the trail end of the lead time distribution is replaced as shown in the revised distribution shown at the top right of Exhibit 5-6. The revision shows the lead time in number of working days over 5.

The lower portion of Exhibit 5-6 illustrates how computer simulation is used to generate a histogram of production for lead time on the manufacture of air conditioners. The computer is programmed to generate the number of working days over the basic 5 days. This generation, which is done on a random basis, is presented in the upper portion of Exhibit 5-6. The percentage column indicates the frequency with which different lead time extensions over the basic 5 are required. For example, 51% of the numbers generated would require no additional lead time, 23% would require 1 additional day, 6% would require 2 days, and so forth.

EXHIBIT 5-6 COMPUTER SIMULATION OF INVENTORY REQUIREMENTS

| DAILY PRODUCTION | | LEAD TIME FREQUENCY | | | |
| FREQUENCY | | ORIGINAL | | REVISED | |
UNITS per DAY	PERCENTAGE of DAYS	WORKING DAYS	PERCENTAGE of DAYS	WORKING DAYS over 5	PERCENTAGE of DAYS
9	2%	5 or less	51%	+0	51%
10	11	6	23	+1	23
11	2	7	6	+2	6
12	1	8	4	+3	4
16	2	9	7	+4	7
17	7	10	5	+5	5
18	11	12	1	+7	1
19	17	13	½	+8	½
20	42	15	1	+10	1
21	2			+14	1½
22	3	24	½		
		27	½		
		28	½		
	100%		100%		100%

RANDOM LEAD TIME	RANDOM PRODUCTION UNITS	TOTAL PRODUCTION OVER LEAD TIME
.	.	.
.	.	.
+0	20,20,20,21,17	98
+1	20,18,19,20,20,20	117
+4	9,20,9,18,18,11,12,20,10	127
+1	17,18,9,9,19,22	92
+0	19,19,9,17,20	84
+3	18,19,19,20,20,17,20,19	152
+1	10,20,20,10,18,20	106
+0	19,20,17,20,17	93
+0	19,20,21,21,20	101
+0	18,18,22,18,20	96
+0	20,20,20,20,20	100
+1	19,19,10,20,20,20	108
.	.	.
.	.	.
.	.	.

Next, the computer generates a sequence of random numbers representing 1 day's production. This sequence of random numbers is generated in proportion to the distribution shown under "Daily Production Frequency" in Exhibit 5-6. If the additional lead time is 0, this means that 5 working days have elapsed between initiation of the purchase order and receipt of the motors. The numbers under the heading "Random Production Units" represent the production during this period. The sequence 20, 20, 20, 21, 17 represents production for a 5-day period; a total of 98. The next sequence, which adds up to a total of 117 units represents production for a 6-day lead time period.

The final step in the analysis is to develop a histogram based on the simulated production figures shown in the column "Total Production over Lead Time." Using this histogram as a basis, it was determined that an inventory level of 230 motors is an acceptable level of risk. This was a determination not immediately clear from the original data. The amount is substantially less than the maximum safe inventory obtained by taking the maximum production, 22, times the maximum (revised) lead time of 19 days ($22 \times 19 = 418$ motors).

The figure of 230 units would provide more protection against out-of-stock situations than using the average lead time (6 days) and average daily production of 19½ units. This figure, 117 units, would result in a 50/50 chance of running out.

INVENTORY PLANNING MODELS

The methods described in the preceding sections relate to choosing appropriate inventory levels for stockkeeping units (SKUs). This refers to specific items at specific locations. Making this type of analysis for each of the possible thousands of SKUs can require an effort that may be disproportionate to the potential gain if the method used is not efficient. One approach is to relate the desired inventory level to easily calculated characteristics of the SKU such as average demand and average lead time. Formulas expressing the relationships can then be programmed and included as part of an inventory planning model.

Exhibit 5-7 illustrates the development of one such formula. A random sample of 33 SKUs is selected as representative of items making up the finished products in inventory. The SKUs have been grouped according to the frequency of production run scheduling. The 33 item sample represents SKUs scheduled every 2 weeks. The division includes several plants but the inventories are homogeneous with respect to product quality requirements, scheduling efficiency, material availability, and the like. Sales characteristics are not found to exhibit marked differences at the various plants. For each of the 33 SKUs an analysis is performed to determine the level of inventory required to satisfy division inventory policy.

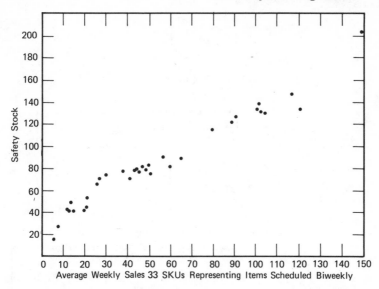

Average Weekly Sales 33 SKUs Representing Items Scheduled Biweekly

EXHIBIT 5-7   RELATED TO AVERAGE SALES

Inventory is then broken down into average 2-week usage periods, referred to as safety stock required to meet service policy needs.

When safety stock is graphed against average weekly sales for the sample items, the safety stock shows the pattern illustrated in Exhibit 5-7. For purposes of the inventory planning model, a formula has been developed for safety stock based on average weekly sales. This is incorporated in the model and used to calculate the required inventory levels for the remaining 4000 SKUs that are scheduled on a biweekly basis. Similarly developed formulas are used for the SKUs scheduled weekly, triweekly, and so forth.

Since this company is expanding its use of public warehouses, the model enables management to calculate the investment in inventory that will be required at each new warehouse facility. The regional sales director provides information on the expected average sales for SKUs out of the warehouses and the safety stock formulas are adjusted to account for the delivery time to the new warehouses. The model is then run to calculate average inventory investment in the warehouse. By combining this with the anticipated warehousing costs, management has determined the overall cost.

Exhibit 5-8 illustrates diagrammatically a fairly sophisticated model composed of three submodels: the inventory level model, production planning model, and financial inventory model. The first model operates simi-

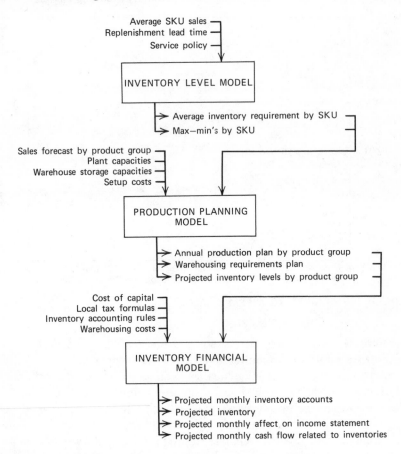

EXHIBIT 5-8   DIAGRAM OF AN INVENTORY PLANNING MODEL

larly to the model described above. The resulting information is inputted, together with the sales forecast and certain production data, into the production planning model. Inventory management and production scheduling rules have been built into this model. In effect, this model, acting as a product group level, simulates the operations in relation to projected sales. The output of this model is a production plan by product group and a schedule of projected inventories.

The final model of the three—the inventory financial model—calculates the balance-sheet/operating-statement effect of the projected inventory plan. This model can be used for tax planning with respect to such matters as the location of inventories and the extent of the application of the LIFO (last-in, first-out) costing principle. The most important feature, however, is the use of current cost of capital to impute a money cost to the investment in inventories. In today's money market, where rates can rise and fall 50% or more in a single year, the company needs a quarterly review of inventory policy.

Computer financial modeling languages facilitate the use of these models. Such languages have many built-in routines for data and file utilization and for standard computations. Such standard financial computations as present value, internal rate of return, standard depreciation formulas, and percentage growth rates have been formulated so that each can be used by programming a few symbols. The user need not even know the underlying formula in order to use the calculations in the model. Double declining balance depreciation, for example, can be formulated in the modeling language so that the model user can obtain depreciation amounts without understanding exactly how they are calculated.

The value of the model as a planning tool is obvious. Monthly output that is useful in budget and operational planning can be generated. Exhibit 5-8 is such a model. Annual output can be obtained to use in capital budget decisions and in corporate planning. Consolidations can be easily put together with the appropriate financial models. The annual type models are an effective tool in merger and acquisition planning. Relocation planning is another type of planning that is more suited to the annual time frame of modeling.

These models are effective if the company carefully formulates operating rules, accounting procedures, and tax conventions and has due regard for the time value of money. Usually, working at a product grouping level for simplicity, the model in effect simulates operations, opens and closes the accounts, and calculates taxes. Careful adherence to the actual operating rules can result in projections sufficiently accurate to serve as a basis for management planning. Using short cuts is sure to result in a highly suspect model. The facts must be carefully laid out.

Exhibits 5-9 and 5-10 show part of the input and output for the inventory financial model. They deal with the projection of inventory asset values. The model is used as part of the monthly pricing review.

The exhibits are included to illustrate ease of use and the degree to which the user of an inventory planning model is removed from the operating rules and formulas. Exhibit 5-9 shows part of the input form which is completed by the manager and given to a secretary trained in time-sharing data entry. Momentarily, the manager has the answer.

Exhibit 5-9 shows part of the data entry related to projecting inventory for one product group. The projection is done on a "units" basis and then costed out by adjusting (weighted average) standard costs for rate changes. Several similar input pages other than the one shown on Exhibit 5-9 were used with this application. Part of the output of the model is shown in Exhibit 5-10.

EXHIBIT 5-9 DATA INPUT FOR THE INVENTORY FINANCIAL MODEL

Product group number	301	0 0 1 7
Production plan by: 1. Monthly Rate of change 2. Monthly increment 3. Specific schedule	302	3
Production plan data: 1. First month (thousands of units),	303	3 7 5
rate (xx.xx%)	304	3 9 0
2. First month (thousands of units),	305	4 0 5
increment (thousands of units)	306	4 0 0
3. 12 months (thousands of units)	307	4 1 0
	308	4 0 0
	309	3 9 7
	310	3 9 2
	311	3 8 8
	312	3 6 9
	313	3 6 7
	314	3 7 4
Materials inflation rate (xx.xx% per year)	315	0 8 5 0
Direct labor inflation rate (xx.xx% per year)	316	0 4 0 0
Overhead inflation rate (xx.xx% per year)	317	0 3 7 5
Product group price changes 1. Number of changes	318	1 7
2. Item price changes	319	0 0 2 1 6 6 0 1 3 7 2 0 6
(item no. xxxxxx, new price per		
unit xxx.xx, first of month xx)	320	0 0 2 2 6 6 0 1 3 7 2 0 6
	321	0 1 7 0 3 5 0 0 9 1 5 0 6

EXHIBIT 5-10   OUTPUT FROM THE INVENTORY FINANCIAL MODEL: INVENTORY INVESTMENT: PRODUCT GROUP 0017

End of Period	Materials	Work-in-Process	Finished Goods Plant	Finished Goods Whse.	Total
12—19x8	$180,617	$108,617	$152,767	$272,580	$714,515
1—19x9	189,323	109,274	156,433	262,495	717,525
2—19x9	195,571	110,460	162,065	255,145	723,241
3—19x9	191,125	108,472	196,261	248,511	744,369
4—19x9	182,142	104,588	242,578	257,954	787,262
5—19x9	174,073	102,057	254,222	271,368	801,720
6—19x9	161,261	98,312	248,121	273,810	781,504
7—19x9	146,751	91,575	201,226	269,429	708,981
8—19x9	155,263	91,811	219,136	282,362	748,572
9—19x9	164,470	100,983	231,845	284,677	781,975
10—19x9	170,471	102,231	214,688	274,543	761,933
11—19x9	$211,916	$104,685	$202,022	$256,917	$775,540

CHAPTER 6

APPROACHING INVENTORY PROBLEMS

From the business vantage point inventory problems are easy to define: too much inventory, too little inventory, or a combination of both (too many items of some and too few of others). The most common problem is a combination of too much inventory overall and an improper balance of the various items.

With the life cycle of many products averaging less than 5 years, it is easy to see that the excess inventory could be in those items used in products being phased out, while the shortages would be in the items needed for the new products coming on stream. Pressure to hold down inventories frequently results in the inventory of new products, the type of inventory needed most being kept in short supply. This, in turn, affects production, causing short runs and more frequent setups.

For all the attention given to inventories in the past 20 or more years, inventory procedures and controls today are virtually the same as those in effect 20 years ago. The automation of inventory control has provided the cosmetics of daily stock status reports and scientifically calculated order points; however, out in the plant operations are pretty much the same as they were before data processing.

The failure to use the computer to its full potential in inventory control relates in large part to the segregation of the science of inventory control from the business of inventory control. The persons knowledgeable about computer capabilities and inventory science have little understanding of plant operations and the needs of operating personnel. Conversely, the persons experienced in production scheduling, purchasing, and stock room control have little understanding of the science of inventory. It is the responsibility of management to bring the two groups together.

70

MISAPPLIED TECHNOLOGY

Much academic research has been devoted to developing models to answer the inventory problems of modern management. These models are based on the use of complex mathematical formulas which assume controlled clinical conditions that rarely occur in the give-and-take of modern competitive business. The practical businessman who must get production out at a profit quickly discredits these models. Although the research has been theoretical, business could benefit from the influx of new ideas about inventory management. However, to use a newly developed idea blindly represents misapplied technology. Industrial experimentation and testing is necessary in order to determine which model formulas correspond to the realities of day-to-day business. Inventory management technology has been misdirected in recent decades. While esoteric inventory models have been examined extensively, little progress has been made in developing the mechanics for executive control of inventories. The research literature asks questions such as: "Which is better—a min-max model with stockastic lead times or an order-point/order-quantity model with dynamic feedback realignment?" Chances are that both models poorly approximate the realities of company needs. With care, satisfactory results might be obtained from both; without care, the results will be bad. Neither of these models in and of itself addresses the questions foremost in the executive's mind: What should be inventory policy with respect to customer service? What total inventory investment is required to provide this service? How can the inventory product mix be improved? What is the best way to reduce inventories below $10,000,000 by year end?

Management needs can be formulated and automated; however, the objectives of model building differ from the most important management objectives. Rather than refining "optimization" the focus should be on control. Management needs the mechanics for quickly identifying the worst cases—where inventory levels are much too large or much too small. Timing is important. If the inventory for Item #250 is rising rapidly because no one realizes a strike has closed down a major customer, action must be taken immediately. Catching potential problems such as this early could prevent a 200 or 300% overstocking of an item (or items). A customer demand change is only one of the reasons why some companies discover a year's supply of some items when their system calls for eight turns a year. Another even greater cause of overstocking and later obsolescence is failure to recognize that a product line is phasing out. For a manufacturer who has 15,000 to 20,000 different component parts and probably 5000 finished products in the line, the potential for overstocking (and understocking) is great.

When inventory is managed well, such situations can be corrected quickly. Too much expediting can be expensive. It could well make the difference between a profitable and unprofitable operation. If a customer is closed down because of a strike, quick direct action must be taken. But because of the hundreds of inventory problems that come up each year, automatic ways of reacting improve the situation. Here, formulas can be used to advantage but the emphasis should be on the direction and magnitude of the changes resulting from the application of the formula and the timing. The formula must prevent the operations from going to extremes and counteraction to problems must not be so great as to result in a whipsaw or overkill approach.

Management also needs a norm by which to identify an inventory problem. Inventory levels, production rates, and order quantities must each have their own measurement against this norm. A deviation from this norm could mean a problem. We discussed formulating such "standards" in Chapter 3 (Formulating Inventory Policy) as they relate to a stabilized operation. But what happens if the company loses some stability of production or a division ceases to be a true going concern? This has happened many times during industry shakeout periods. An example is the upheaval in the electronics industry in the 1960s when semi-conductors were coming into their own and vacuum tubes were phasing downward. The same thing happened with computer manufacturing. Climbing money rates can cause instability in inventory balances and can require attention to determine the impact on inventory policy. So can the opening up of an export market in a foreign market.

Management must continuously change inventory policy in line with changing business factors similar to those just mentioned. Every change in policy can affect thousands of inventory items. Management must provide for automaticity of procedure (not to be confused with automation through use of a computer) to adjust inventories as policy changes. This flexibility requirement of inventory management is frequently neglected.

Because management and inventory specialists cannot "get together," inventory control in many companies is the same as it was a decade or two ago even though computers have been introduced and perpetual inventories (stock status reports) developed. Inventory controllers, typically from production or distribution with backgrounds as stores clerks, loading supervisors, or parts expeditors, appreciate the responsibility involved in controlling a major asset. Until inventory control technology can provide practical solutions to inventory problems, it is unlikely that much progress will be made in implementing more advanced inventory methods that place more of the emphasis on sound inventory policy procedures.

The Human Factor in Inventory Control

Employees want to look good on control reports maintained by management, whether or not their performance warrants a high score. This points up the need to give visibility to the monitoring aspect of inventory management in a way that defeats attempts to manipulate the results. Even more important, is the need to motivate employees by designing reports so that "manipulation to look good" will lead to precisely the behavior desired.

Anyone with experience in this area can attest to the innovative ability of personnel to "fudge" the figures rather than look bad.

At one company, the production scheduler removes items from the "authorized-to-stock" category when the inventory for those items becomes undesirably low. This is done because "out-of-stocks" are measured against "authorized-to-stock" items. After the inventory is built back to approved levels, the items are reinstated on the list.

In another instance, a shipping superintendent "engineers" the reporting system so that advance shipments to one customer net out against failures to ship to another customer. By maintaining a backlog of customers willing to take advance shipment on certain scarce products, the superintendent creates whatever level of service "score" he desires to reflect in the reporting system.

The warehouse superintendent of another company enters a large customer order prematurely. Since customer cancellations are allowed, he asks the customer to enter the order well in advance of the need. When the goods are assembled and ready to ship, he enters a cancellation so that the customer does have to take delivery. "That way, I'll have your order here and ready to go as soon as you need it" is his line. The items ordered in advance are usually high volume items, and therefore go unnoticed. When the advance order is placed, no inventory is held on special allocation for the customer since that would be contrary to company policy. The inventory is therefore available for general use.

It would seem to make little difference that the "bogus" order is placed and then canceled. However, since inventory for the warehouse is controlled by a computer, there is a potential for manipulation. The sales order is entered toward the end of the month while the cancellation is entered the following month. Thus the supervisor introduces a high degree of variability in the computer's sales history. Since sales, net of cancellations, are used as the basis for calculating inventory, manipulations resulting in higher variability means that the computer raises the inventory level even if total sales remain unchanged.

Such "juggling" of figures shows how many well-founded plans can come to grief. Shenanigans such as these are often prompted by arbitrariness on the part of management in mandating hastily conceived inventory reductions. Such reductions can damage good production flow, as well as restrict good service to customers. In these cases, the supervisors feel that they are acting in the best interest of the company. Management should form a partnership with production based on sound inventory policy rather than encouraging an adversary relationship. If inventory reports are carefully planned, the actions taken to look good on the report are the actions desired by management.

Overreliance on the Computer

It is strange logic that a larger computer is the answer to inventory problems. A business with legal problems engages a competent attorney; when tax situations are complex, experienced tax accountants are brought in; product design problems are assigned to design engineers; yet when inventory problems develop, many companies immediately obtain a larger computer.

Inventory control can be improved only by improving the underlying procedures and the skills of the inventory specialists who run the system. Larger computers by themselves will not make for a better production mix, fewer late shipments, or higher inventory turns. Computers carry out programmed instructions. Unless operating procedures are changed, nothing is changed, no matter what the expenditure on computers.

> For example, the president of a steel fabrication business is proud of his automated scheduling and inventory control system. The system has been implemented at his insistence and is the primary purpose for which the computer is used. Each day, data is inputted and the computer calculates desired inventory levels. It also projects sales and prepares a daily production schedule. The latter is hand delivered to the plant manager who secretly sets the schedule aside and continues to run the operations the old way. Nothing has changed. Unless the system designer motivates and trains the operating people to perform with the new tools, no progress is made.

Over-reliance on computers seems to extend to computer packages, "black boxes" containing predetermined programs. The widely held erroneous belief is that if one buys the black box, stockouts cease, turnover improves, and the production line never falters. Again, unless operating personnel can be trained to use the "black boxes" to improve inventory management, nothing has changed.

No Systematic Approach to Identifying Inventory Problems

Everyone talks about inventory but no one does anything about it. So much of the company's working capital is tied up in inventories and so many employees are concerned directly or indirectly with this major investment, that inventory is a constant topic of concern in business. The concern is expressed as: "Customer service is a problem with us." "Customer service is satisfactory but we can't get preferred services for special customers when we need it." "I don't know why scheduling is so bad, but the new automated forecast may help." "We have obsolete inventory and slow-moving items piled up to the rafters."

With such a cross-section of comments it becomes difficult to distinguish fact from opinion. Attitudes are based on isolated events, casual comments, or personal likes and dislikes. As a result of such discussions, a group consensus may be reached in the company and inventory procedures revised. At this point, the revisions probably have specific but limited objectives. However, the group consensus objectives may not be the right ones. They are likely to be based on unsubstantiated opinions.

The questions to ask are: Are the problems correctly diagnosed? What is their magnitude? Are there cost effective alternatives? How are other functional areas related? Are there other problems? Overall, these questions should be integrated into a systematized approach to identifying inventory problems.

A company distributing auto supplies has recently applied this group consensus approach to inventory problems. It has nine warehouses, each carrying approximately the same line of products. Buying is decentralized, with each warehouse determining its own needs. Customer orders, however, are filled on a company-wide basis. Customers in Chicago are supplied from the Chicago warehouse, but if product is not available there then Chicago draws from any of the other eight warehouses. The company is concerned that inventory turnover is poor when measured against industry averages. After much discussion a consensus is reached that the problem is due to untimely stock status reporting. If the warehouse managers could know immediately what is in stock at each warehouse, rather than working off bulky, week-old computer runs, then turnover would improve greatly.

The company decides to develop an on-line, real-time inventory inquiry system. This involves buying a new computer and communications equipment. It also involves a considerable programming effort. The total expense in cash outlay and internal resources runs into hundreds of thousands of dollars. Fortunately the project is abandoned. The reasons for this are involved but come closer to fortuitous circumstances than an intelligent assessment of the situation.

A year later, a new materials manager has been hired and has the advantage of being free from the prejudice formed in previous group discussions. After reviewing operations and assessing the inventory situation he comes to the conclusion that the poor inventory turnover is due to decentralized buying and to lack of company policy with respect to customer service. Therefore, at little expense, management centralizes control of buying and gives the central buyers guidelines for a level of service. As a result, inventory turnover has improved markedly, as has customer service. With better guidelines for purchasing, the need to inquire into the inventory status in every warehouse to satisfy customer needs has been reduced to a negligible level. Human resources, rather than computer resources, have been upgraded.

The inventory specialist has to objectively assess the strengths and weaknesses of existing systems and show management that the problems are as defined by him and that they can be corrected through the procedures that he recommends.

OPERATIONS REVIEW: A SYSTEMATIC APPROACH

Operations review of inventories identifies problems and areas that can be improved. The special value of a review conducted along the lines discussed in this chapter is threefold.

First, operations review is comprehensive. The intent is to examine all aspects of inventory management. This assures an all-inclusive plan for corrective action. There is always the danger that when one segment of inventory is managed better another will deteriorate. As an example, when one manufacturer launched a campaign to reduce backorders, not only were backorders reduced but in-process inventory rose sharply. Thus, all facets of inventory management should be kept in view when attempting to improve systems.

The second advantage of reviewing inventory is that it provides measurements of the magnitude of the problem. These measurements have proven invaluable in getting management to respond to problems appropriately. An operations review at a New England manufacturer illustrates this point.

The company manufactures gears, speed reducers, and certain other related components—essentially high volume, low cost items sold to a mass market. A small part of sales are special orders of large gear assemblies from utilities and other companies in heavy industry. A typical item is machined in lot sizes equal to several months' expected sales and stocked either as a finished product or parts that are later assembled as a finished product. Since the manufactured and purchased parts are standard and the finished products are fairly standardized with interchangeable parts, the company publishes a catalog. This is released to an aggressive sales force. The marketing group analyzes the company's market penetration and recommends areas for special sales emphasis. This group also prepares a sales forecast to serve as a basis for production and sales planning.

The company is particularly proud that its computer has been programmed to determine economic lot sizes and production schedules based on forecasted sales. The assembly line would respond to a shift in demand due to redirected sales.

A part of operations review is to examine how production lot sizes are determined. Actual lot sizes tested against plan show that machine operators have been following the production plan closely. The scheduling plan has also been tested. It shows that the scheduler has been using the lot sizes calculated by the weekly computer scheduling program. The documentation for the scheduling program has been examined; it shows that the program employs a standard EOQ (economic order quantity) formula. A forecast of demand is required for the EOQ calculation, which, according to the production scheduler, is obtained from the marketing group.

Next, the data processing procedures are tested to determine that the forecast is correctly entered in the program. The testing process reveals that the "forecast" used by the scheduling program is always one-sixth of the previous year's sales. The production schedule is therefore based on data that is a year old and not on the marketing forecast.

By the time this error is discovered, the system has been in use for some time and management thinks it is "great." Their reaction is understandable: "This technician reviewing operations says that we aren't scheduling based on the forecast. Marketing says that they are preparing one and production says that they are using it. This guy must be hung up on some theoretical point that doesn't matter. Anyway, all agree the system is working fine."

The system is not working well at all, however. For items with sales this year that are above last year's level, the rescheduled production is too low. Stockouts are frequent and special expedited runs are continuously required. Serious problems are avoided because only about 10% of the items show a significant sales increase over the previous year. In addition, about 8% have declined in sales, so inventory stocks are well above current requirements. Variations of this magnitude are considered to be about normal.

Management must be convinced that the error is fairly large rather than normal. Measurement is needed. A statistical sample of items is selected from items showing a 40% or greater increase in sales over the previous year. The scheduling history and inventory history for these items is recreated, showing the frequency of stockouts and special production runs.

A second statistical sample of items is selected from among the items showing a 20% or greater decrease over last year. For each of these items inventory turns are computed by using current inventories and average sales over the last 3 months. This is presented to management. No further convincing is necessary; scheduling procedures are corrected.

The third advantage of the operations review is that it is a structured approach with a beginning, a fixed number of tasks, and an end. In the real world, where capable personnel are scarce, this makes a big difference. The production vice president who is reluctant to permit a key manager to participate for an indefinite time on a project with no apparent objective, will be more willing to loan him to the project team reviewing operations. The structured approach also enhances the status of the project team. Adopting that approach spares the team members the time-consuming and nonproductive approach of debating what the steps should be.

Expanding the scope is always a problem for special project teams. Problems are always open-ended. The team could go on and on without guidelines such as "do tasks 1, 2, and 3 but not 4, 5, or 6." A structured approach channels efforts into a limited number of useful tasks that can be quickly completed. The successfully completed tasks prove progress to management and spur the progress of the project team. Branching out beyond the scope of the mission should be strictly ruled out. It only dissipates the effort.

Steps to Follow

The operations review at this company illustrates some important steps. We consider the following five steps as being basic:

1. Collect facts.
2. Analyze performance data.
3. Identify symptoms.
4. Test suspected problems.
5. Measure the impact of proposed solutions.

Steps 4 and 5 are discussed in the gear manufacturer's example; in that review steps 1, 2, and 3 are also performed.

Collecting Facts
The project team reviewing inventory may be tempted to bypass this task on the basis that everyone is thoroughly familiar with operations. Collecting facts, however is important as a special task for several reasons.

Not everyone interested in the project has the same background knowledge of operations. Accounting personnel, for example, may be up-to-date on product structure, but completely unfamiliar with the methods used by product engineering personnel for introducing revisions. The materials control manager may be fully aware of customer service requirements but he may not be aware of the cost flow through the cost accounting system. Collecting the facts provides the opportunity for operating personnel to become knowledgeable of other operating areas.

Collecting the facts can also be a boon to communications between the operating and data processing personnel. Without the interplay of working together the data processing specialist may see only the procedures directly related to the computer. To him the bill of materials is in good shape if it is easily accessible on a disk and there is no backlog of data changes to process onto the file. Whether or not the data processing system is functionally adequate for scheduling may not even cross his mind when he assures the group that the "bill of material is in good shape." To the data processing manager, inventory is a set of figures on a report rather than goods on the floor. This is not so unusual because his frame of reference comes from his own work and he isn't much different from the production man who thinks of goods on the floor or the accounting specialist who sees dollar figures rather than goods.

It is up to the nonoperating specialists to adapt to the terminology of plant operations when the focus is on operating problems and their solution. One method of getting the team together on the same footing in fact collection is to have the team complete a fact collection questionnaire such as the one shown in Exhibit 6-1.

The project team should first try to supply the answers itself and then schedule interviews with personnel. This questionnaire could be used as a starting point. Some of the questions will not be applicable and other specialized questions will be added. Answering the questions is usually easy. The hard part is to determine the degree of completeness required in the answers.

Question 1, for example, asks for a statement of company policy with respect to out-of-stock rates and so forth. If there is no policy the answer is "none." However, if there is a policy, it may be vague and require a number of interviews to find out how employees interpret it. Should the differences of interpretation be reconciled? Or should the matter of which variation is right be submitted to a vote? If the key executive is interested, the matter can be submitted to his vote, but will that settle it? Sound business reasons may underlie variations and, official policy notwithstanding, operating personnel will find some way to do what is right.

> Take the case of the garment manufacturer who has heavy stockouts in a line of work pants. A major customer submits orders specifying color but doesn't really care what color is shipped. The plant takes advantage of this to ship whatever color best balances the manufacturing schedule. Technically, this results in a large stockout rate by the official definition; however, the official definition may not be as practical as the "informal" definition used in the plant.

To determine stockout rates one must take into account the exceptions such as the one in which the garment manufacturer was able to choose

EXHIBIT 6-1 INVENTORY MANAGEMENT QUESTIONNAIRE

1. What is company policy with respect to the following?
   a. Out-of-stock rates, backorder rates, and late shipments
   b. Order service time
   c. Customer returns, order cancellations, order modifications, and substitutions
   d. Machine downtime and production interruption
   e. Overtime
   f. Inventory turns for materials, work-in-process, finished goods, and piece parts stores
   g. Obsolete and slow-moving items
   h. Vendor performance
   i. Product and production engineering changes
   j. Data error rates in inventory records
   k. Other pertinent matters (specify)

      . . . .
      . . . .
      . . . .
      . . . .

2. For control purposes, physical inventory is divided into what segments?

3. Which inventory segments are located in restricted areas with receipts and issues documented for control purposes?

4. Is inventory responsibility clearly defined for each inventory segment?

5. Is there an organization chart showing responsibility for the following functional areas?
   a. Production planning
   b. Scheduling
   c. Material control
   d. Storeskeeping
   e. Production and product engineering
   f. Material handling
   g. Receiving and shipping
   h. Quality control
   i. Purchasing

6. Is a stock status report maintained for the following? If so, how frequently is it updated? What information is contained in the report?
   a. Materials
   b. Finished goods
   c. Stores inventories
   d. Work-in-process items

7. What reports are prepared on the following? How frequently are they updated? What information do they contain?
   a. Obsolete or slow moving inventory
   b. Excess inventory

8. What performance measurements are prepared with respect to:
   a. Turnover rates

EXHIBIT 6-1   (Continued)

    b. Out-of-stock rates
    c. Backorder rates
    d. Shipped-on-schedule rates
    e. Machine or production downtime rates
    f. Machine and operator idle time rates
    g. Overtime rates
    h. Customer complaints
    i. Vendor performance
    j. Other (specify):

      . . . .
      . . . .

9. For each performance measurement prepared, what is the history for the past 2 years?

10. How is customer order status tracked and reported?

11. Is there a reliable system for reporting actual production?

12. What records are prepared showing actual versus scheduled production?

13. What records are prepared of partially completed production or work orders?

14. Is the bill of materials structured for production, engineering, and accounting uses? How many copies are maintained and how are they updated?

15. Forecasts are prepared for what items? How accurate are these forecasts?
    a. Within 5%?
    b. Within 10%?
    c. Outside 10%

16. How often are physical inventories taken? Are cycle counting procedures used?

17. What is the magnitude of the errors between physical inventory counts and perpetual records? What is the frequency of such errors?

18. What are the procedures for determining when and how much to order:
    a. Finished goods items
    b. Work-in-process items (subassemblies)
    c. Raw material items
    d. Stores items (piece parts)

19. Which inventory items have their source:
    a. Outside the company and are used only in the company?
    b. Within the company and are used in the company?
    c. Within the company but are used outside the company?

20. Are inventory control procedures appropriate for each situation in Question 19?

21. What are the procedures for production scheduling?

22. If the bill of materials is used for scheduling, is it suitably structured? Does it have all the necessary information such as lead time, production rates, and allowance for scrap?

23. Are parts scheduled in economic manufacturing quantities?

EXHIBIT 6-1   (Continued)

24. Are parts or assemblies scheduled for production only after checking the availability of materials and tools?

25. Which departments have frequent setups and multiple runs for the same items? How does the dispatching system work?

26. What are the procedures for expediting? How many man-hours are spent in that activity?

27. How does the production priority system work?

28. Does the production schedule load jobs to specific persons and machines? Does the routing indicate the due dates by operation?

29. What are the procedures for rescheduling? What is the frequency of change?

30. What is the paperwork procedure for engineering changes? How frequently are they made?

31. What is the amount of nonstandard freight charges, for example, air freight, LTL (less than truckload)?

32. Are there reliable time standards?

33. Are there accurate records of machine and equipment capacities?

34. Are manpower requirements determined well in advance?

35. Are production routing lists current and accurate?

36. Are there large physical-to-book adjustments in the accounting records?

37. Are departmental labor efficiencies available?

38. Is there a continuous program for evaluating vendor service?

---

colors that were plentiful in his inventory. It is difficult to obtain information on exceptions, however, because these are usually not documented. Any computerized system designed to process only the normal transactions will not yield correct results. Provision must be made to obtain information on exceptions as well.

As an example, one retail company automating its credit operations has plans to process two types of contracts that were negotiated with customers. Before the automation is completed, however, six types of contracts are found. Fortunately, "digging" at the start of the project has turned up the other four types. This saves the company from going on line with a system that would fail whenever one of the four mystery contracts came along.

After the project team completes the questionnaire and reviews the answers, the information must be confirmed. Certain portions are obtained from interviews and from interpretation of records as well as reports. Such information is subject to human error, especially if obtained through interviews.

One pitfall is that if the interviewee thinks that he is expected to know the answer, he will give one. Experienced interviewers structure questions to provide internal checks on the answers. As an example of how this works, the director of purchasing of an oil company was asked: "Is purchasing completely centralized in the corporate office?" He said that all purchase orders are placed through this department. Later during a discussion relating to one of the outlying oil fields, the interviewer asked: "About what percentage of your purchases are placed directly from the purchasing representative in the field?" The response was 15 to 20%.

Leading questions test the correctness of information before it is taken for fact. Verification should be obtained by asking other individuals the same questions. A contradiction could be the result of confusion, misunderstanding, or differences between the formal and informal procedures.

Many of the questions in Exhibit 6-1 can be answered by checking reports and analyzing data. Since this can be time-consuming, the project team should review the questions from the point of view of assigning priorities. The questions could be broken down into those relating to particular functional areas. To avoid getting bogged down in data, the project team can select high priority areas to work on first. If these provide promising opportunities for exploration, the company can suspend the review of other areas and move toward improvement of design in the selected areas.

Analyzing Performance Data
The next step in the inventory review is to analyze performance data. Much of the information should be analyzed automatically as it is being accumulated. While the final conclusions cannot be made as yet, the analytical implications can be helpful. What does the data indicate? What does it tell us about the operations? To get meaningful answers we must summarize, compare, and evaluate the facts.

Exhibits 6-2 and 6-3 illustrate the summarizing of data. Exhibit 6-2 shows an inventory card for a manufactured component. This card, which is updated monthly, shows the production for the month, the issues, and the month-end balance. The months are not complete calendar months but the periods between the dates shown on the card. Following the final transaction in the month, the current inventory balance is computed by adding production for the month to the previous ending balance. Issues are subtracted (figures are in units). When work orders are placed for parts to be produced, the units called for are entered in the "Schedule" column. Because of spoilage during production and quality rejects, good production is usually less than scheduled production.

This card and cards for selected other items were obtained when facts

EXHIBIT 6-2   WORK-IN-PROCESS INVENTORY DATA

Date	Production	Issues	Adj.	Balance End of Month	Schedule
12/26		3,804		22,868	60,000
1/31	58,500	6,711		74,657	
2/27		47,262		27,395	120,000
3/26	106,522	13,518		120,399	
4/30		27,144		93,255	
5/28		26,622		66,633	60,000
6/25	58,500	40,485		84,648	
7/20		12,012		72,636	
8/27		36,966		35,678	60,000
9/24	56,862	14,458		78,074	
10/29		20,532		57,542	
11/26		1,188	5,772	62,126	

Description: Item 1 dial   Ordered from: Stamping
Item No: 106-35-17   Where Located: A17, A18, B6

were collected in an inventory review. Reviewing the data on the card alone does not provide the kind of analysis needed. The information must be summarized. The inventory level of the work-in-process inventory of these items must be determined by computing the average ending inventory in number of months (Exhibit 6-3). For each component shown, the month-end inventory was averaged for a 12-month period. The issues were also averaged over the same 12-month period. The average inventory for each item was divided by the average issues to arrive at the average months of inventory for each item. The dial illustrated in Exhibit 6-2 is shown as the first item in Exhibit 6-3. Exhibit 6-3 provides a much clearer overview of the status of work-in-process inventory levels than does Exhibit 6-2.

Knowing the average inventory, as shown in Exhibit 6-3, is not sufficient for good control. The level of inventory must be compared to a standard. The standard could be determined through company policy or it could be based on an industry norm. It might also be determined through an analysis of production lead times, or it could simply be a judgmental decision. As an example, let's use Item 1 in Exhibit 6-3. The bill of materials calls for 1 dial, 1 shackle or extended shackle, 3 discs, 2 spacers, and 1 spring. Assembly was scheduled with two options—the regular shackle or the extended shackle.

If we use the average inventory figures in Exhibit 6-3 as a basis, then 3.1 months' supply proved sufficient for the dial. Why isn't 3.1 months' supply sufficient for the disc or why was 6.2 months' supply stocked for

**EXHIBIT 6-3 WORK-IN-PROCESS INVENTORY: INVENTORY LEVELS OF
SELECTED COMPONENTS**

Item	Component Description	Average Month-End Inventory	Average Monthly Issues	Average Inventory in Months
1	dial	64,826	20,892	3.1
	shackle	38,411	17,768	2.2
	disc	390,611	62,676	6.2
	spacer	142,624	41,783	3.4
	spring	205,442	23,010	8.9
	extended shackle	19,803	3,322	6.0
2	disc	43,584	16,694	2.6
	dial disc	61,228	10,737	5.7
	dial plate	62,464	8,347	7.5
	spring	68,438	8,347	8.2
	bolts	26,904	7,893	3.4
	retainer ring	181,155	8,347	21.7
	extended shackle	40,385	405	99.7

the disc and 8.9 months for the spring? If the product mix can be reasonably estimated, the same would apply to the shackle and extended shackle. From internal consistency alone, the data suggests serious problems with the work-in-process inventory control.

Exhibit 6-4 illustrates another comparison. This time the measurement was made against a standard determined by company policy: a turnover of 5½ times per year for electrical components. This is shown as the horizontal line across the graph and is labeled "goal." The turnover rate for the actual data is calculated by multiplying each month's sales by 12 and dividing by the inventory value at the beginning of each month. The fluctuations in the graph are due more to monthly sales variations than to fluctuations in the inventory.

The company illustrated by Exhibit 6-4 uses the same procedures for all its finished goods. The finished items are segregated by product groups, each of which is overseen by an inventory controller. The inventory turnover is calculated for each controller in the same manner as demonstrated in Exhibit 6-4.

Past performance can provide a basis for measurement. Exhibit 6-5, for example, compares current stockout rates with the equivalent rates for the preceding year. The company has instituted a scientific inventory control program in its finished goods warehouses. Since the primary objective is to improve customer service, the stockout rate is selected as an important measure of the success of the new system. The company's goal for

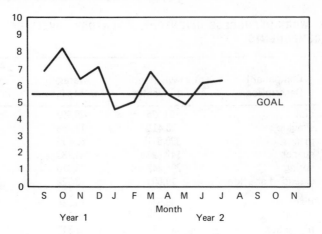

INVENTORY TURN IS DEFINED AS: $\dfrac{\text{CURRENT MONTH'S SALES (AT COST) ANNUALIZED}}{\text{CURRENT MONTH'S BEGINNING INVENTORY}}$

EXHIBIT 6-4   INVENTORY TURNS BY INVENTORY CONTROLLER

stockouts is set at 2%. The bottom line of the graph in Exhibit 6-5 shows the stockout rate for the warehouses on the new program for the period of May through March of the following year. The previous year's stockout rate (upper line in Exhibit 6-5) is also shown. The improvement over the preceding year is obvious.

In selecting data to analyze, consideration is given to the degree of control management can exercise. If work-in-process inventory levels appear to be high as in Exhibit 6-3, management can take steps to lower the levels. In such matters as rail shipment time, management can do little more than jawbone the railroads.

Materiality is an important consideration during the analysis of performance data. In Exhibit 6-3 some of the inventory levels are shown to be 100% or more above reasonable levels. Since this is true for about half the items, a quick calculation tests materiality. With about $5 million in work-in-process inventories, there would be a potential inventory reduction ($5,000,000) × (half the items) × (half the inventory of these items) = $1,250,000. At a carrying cost of 25%, the company could save $312,500 yearly if it reduced the excess items to normal levels. There is no question as to the materiality of this figure even if the fixed costs were excluded from the calculation. In Exhibit 6-4, the performance of the inventory controller appears to have worsened. However, the evidence is inconclusive because the last 2 months were above the goal established as a standard. It would be difficult to argue that material improvement is possible in this case.

In Exhibit 6-5, the new inventory system has reduced the stockout rate

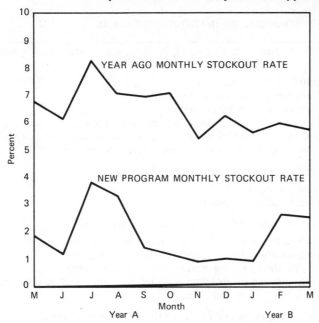

EXHIBIT 6-5   STOCKOUT RATE

more than 60%. Based on accounting information, this is worth about $100,000 per year to the company. However, more information is required. Has the reduction in stockout been purchased at an increase in inventory or operating costs? A check showing that inventory has declined. A revamping of ordering procedures and freight routes has reduced freight costs by an additional $100,000 plus per year. The cost savings of the new system are obviously material.

Identifying Symptoms

In collecting and analyzing data related to inventory performance, some problems become obvious immediately. Frequently, simple computations demonstrate this. Exhibit 6-3 illustrates a work-in-process control problem localized in the production scheduling procedures. This is an example of a symptom—and it is symptoms that we must find in order to identify the real cause of the problems. Another problem symptom is excessive backorders. Management must determine what number of backorders is excessive by first analyzing backorder data and the relationship to number of orders processed. Identifying symptoms early is highly desirable because observations and analyses can be made during the project team's review work. The team will know where to place its emphasis.

Exhibit 6-6 presents a list of symptoms of inventory problems. This can

EXHIBIT 6-6 SYMPTOMS OF INVENTORY PROBLEMS

1. Policy with respect to the following is vague and is not stated in measurable terms:
   a. Customer service level.
   b. Inventory turnover or inventory levels.
   c. Obsolete and slow-moving inventory.
   d. Machine downtime, overtime, line or process interruption.
   e. Order cancellations, substitutions, returns, drop shipments, price discounts, and other mechanics relating to order entry and delivery.

2. Responsibility for maintaining proper inventory levels is:
   a. Not clearly assigned.
   b. Assigned to sales personnel.

3. Reports are not prepared on a regular and current basis:
   a. For stock status, showing inventory levels for all stockkeeping items.
   b. Showing out-of-stock rates and/or backorder levels.
   c. Identifying obsolete, slow-moving, and excess inventory.
   d. Showing production interruptions, rescheduling, and special expediting caused by work-in-process shortages.

4. Inventory reports and data files show a high level of data errors.

5. Inventory levels are not set on forecasts of demand.

6. Production scheduling is not based on forecasts of demand. This assumes, of course, that forecasts are intelligently made.

7. Inventory levels are based on general rules such as 2 months' supply of "everything" rather than rules tailored to various SKUs (stockkeeping units).

8. No ABC classification used.

9. Excessive and worsening:
   a. Stockout rates.
   b. Backorder levels.
   c. Frequency of late shipments.
   d. Obsolete inventory.
   e. Number of purchase orders past due.
   f. Amount of expediting.
   g. Amount of production or machine downtime.

10. Excess inventory condition is material or worsening.

11. Inventory levels of major items are volatile, showing cyclical ups and downs.

12. The production schedule is frequently revised.

13. Lead times are long for:
    a. Production.
    b. Vendor.

14. The bill of materials (BOM) is not effectively structured for production scheduling.

EXHIBIT 6-6 (Continued)

15. Parts demand is not projected by BOM explosion.

16. Items are difficult to locate physically.

17. Certain product lines have defective parts and defective finished products in inventory.

18. Major segments of work-in-process or stores inventories are outside controlled areas.

19. No system for disposing of obsolete inventory on a regular basis.

20. Production schedulers and/or inventory control supervisors rely on informal rather than formal control procedures.

21. Product costs are out of date.

22. Large end-of-quarter inventory adjustments are required.

23. Large adjustments are required when physical verification counts are made.

24. Freight shipments are made at rates in excess of standard rates, i.e., use of air freight and less than carload because of last minute ordering.

25. Backshipments and interwarehouse shipments are permitted.

26. Economic lot quantities are not calculated for production requiring costly setup.

27. Secondary manufacturing departments have much lower labor efficiency than the primary departments.

28. Engineering changes disregard inventory levels.

29. The production schedule is released before the availability of tools and materials is ascertained.

30. The bill of materials file is out of date.

31. Production routings are inaccurate and out of date.

32. Production scheduling does not maintain an accurate work order status file showing progress of each order against plan and recording completed production.

33. The purchasing department does not have automatic followup procedures for overdue orders.

34. Scientific methods are not used to set inventory levels for finished goods.

35. Actual and planned production differ significantly.

36. Setup costs and machine rates are out of date.

37. Material specifications are indefinite and inadequate.

be used as a starting point. Some of the symptoms applicable to one industry may not be applicable to others. Symptoms relating to production scheduling, for example, do not interest wholesale or retail firms whereas they may be interested in deficiencies in demand forecasting.

The list should be modified to suit the particular company. Note that many symptoms listed in Exhibit 6-6 are related to the questions in Exhibit 6-1. The questionnaire was developed by first preparing the list of symptoms and then constructing the questions to gather information relating to the symptoms.

Testing suspected problems

As discussed, Exhibit 6-3 presents the work-in-process inventory levels at a company that is so large that they are a serious problem. The symptom of excess inventory levels is supported by inadequate procedures used for production scheduling. Tighter production controls, scheduling based on forecasted demand, and economic lot sizes are the likely answers to the problem. There could be problems with the likely answers, however (for example, with the accuracy of forecasts), so any solution must be tested further.

The most common type of test consists of collecting and summarizing additional data to check out certain points. Exhibits 6-7 and 6-8 illustrate one such test. The company is a wholesaler with a string of warehouses throughout the Northeast. The review of procedures indicates a possible problem with slow-moving and excess inventory. Purchasing is not centralized—each warehouse determines its own needs based on informal communications with the other warehouse managers. Sales are volatile with the bulk concentrated in a few key customers. Under such circumstances, it is easy for stock to accumulate in items which may have once been in heavy demand but now are slow moving.

A limited examination of inventory has revealed the symptoms but management wants more definitive information. Consequently, a sizable number of items are selected on a statistical basis and the inventory level compared with sales for these items. Exhibit 6-7 demonstrates this. The column at the extreme right lists the months of inventory for various items in the Boston warehouse. This calculation is made as follows:

- The previous 12 months' sales is divided by 12 to obtain an average monthly sales.
- The month-end inventory value is then divided by the average sales per month to obtain the months of inventory on hand.

For example, average monthly sales for BC 301812 was obtained by dividing 10 units by 12 to obtain the quotient .83 unit. Next, the month-

EXHIBIT 6-7 OBSOLETE INVENTORY TEST BOSTON WAREHOUSE—APRIL 19xx

Item No.	Inventory in Units	Unit Cost	Extended Cost	Sales Past 12 Months in Units	Inventory in Months
·	·	·	·	·	·
·	·	·	·	·	·
·	·	·	·	·	·
BC 301812	8	.440	3.52	10	9.6
BC 301821	1	7.460	7.46	14	0.9
BC 301911	60	.380	22.80	0	
BC 320220	19	1.692	32.14	33	
DD 220030	900	.069	62.07	0	
DD 220050	5,550	.031	172.05	1,850	36.0
DD 224250	0	17.610	0	1	0.0
DD 880017	405	1.357	549.46	0	
DD 880019	3,000	.040	120.90	0	
DD 999243	18	.378	6.80	0	
FK 031824	1,800	.189	339.84	0	
FK 031825	1,600	.044	70.24	0	
FK 032024	485	.100	48.50	15	338.0
FK 211817	50	2.100	105.00	50	12.0
FK 301818	2,500	.100	250.00	0	
FK 302120	99,026	.170	16,787.88	50,573	23.50
FK 402304	5,550	.031	170.94	1,850	36.00
FK 402305	15,300	.068	1,043.46	2,200	83.4
·	·	·	·	·	·
·	·	·	·	·	·
·	·	·	·	·	·

EXHIBIT 6-8 SUMMARY OF OBSOLETE INVENTORY TEST BOSTON WAREHOUSE—APRIL 19xx

Month-End Inventory Average Monthly Sales	Number of SKUs	Inventory Value	Percentage of Value
Out of stock, with sales in the last 12 months	2,597	0	0%
Month's inventory supply: Less than 3	1,774	$ 79,175	2.7
3–6	548	143,358	5.0
6–12	979	172,206	6.0
12–60	1,025	575,648	19.9
More than 60	1,354	747,622	25.8
No sales in the last 12 months	11,097	1,175,548	40.6
Total	19,374	$2,893,557	100.0%

end inventory, 8 units, was divided by .83 to obtain the months of inventory on hand 8 ÷ .83 = 9.6 months.

Exhibit 6-8 categorizes inventory by rate of movement. At the sales rates for the preceding 12 months, it would take more than 5 years to sell off the inventory in the last two categories, which account for more than $1,900,000 of the $2,900,000 total—more than 65%. If the next lowest category is added, this percentage would rise to about 85% of the total inventory. With information such as this, management is convinced that it needs to establish better inventory controls.

Another aspect of testing relates to data accuracy. Sometimes inventory symptoms appear to be marginal in impact. The range of possible accuracy could make the difference as to whether the action taken is correct. Unfortunately in many companies the data relating to inventories has a high rate of error. In such instances, information cannot be interpreted unless the error rate is determined.

Exhibit 6-9 shows results of measuring data error in a small manufacturing firm. The review of operating procedures indicates potential problems with the work-in-process inventory, the indication being that bad data is one of the main factors contributing to poor scheduling. Production counts are questionable because the many small manufactured parts are weigh counted and converted to units through use of conversion factors, a procedure that is suspect because the parts vary in

EXHIBIT 6-9 TEST OF ACCURACY OF REPORTING WORK-IN-PROCESS INVENTORY

Item		Ticket Count	Test Count	Difference
6025	Barrel	196	196	0
4091	Outlet	1,200	1,200	0
620	Ring	3,920	3,945	+25
2410	Extension	2,660	2,614	−46
596	Body	538	531	− 7
2409	Extension	1,540	1,526	−14
1401	Tubes	900	900	0
870	Body	530	532	+ 2
580	Body	512	510	− 2
6600	Rotating Adapter	839	841	+ 2
720	Pistons	480	479	− 1
1620	Cylinder	165	159	− 6
1673	Cylinder	50	54	+ 4
.	.	.	.	.
.	.	.	.	.
.	.	.	.	.

thickness. These variations, though not great enough to affect product quality, may be causing differences in production counts from one lot to another.

The purpose of the test illustrated in Exhibit 6-9 is to measure the magnitude of the errors. The tests of the various parts reveal that the margin of error is relatively small. It has been concluded that the thickness of material varies in both directions; the differences largely offset each other. Errors in production counts, therefore, are not a major factor in causing scheduling problems.

MEASURING THE IMPACT OF PROPOSED SOLUTIONS

Good testing procedures may correctly identify the inventory problems, but may not suggest a good solution to the problems. One way of determining a solution is by experimentation—changing methods and then monitoring the resulting changes. Incorrect lot sizes put into production could cause poor inventory turnover. Managers are reluctant, though, to experiment with wholesale changes because it disrupts existing procedures. Also, there is no assurance that the proposed changes will work. The logical course is to make changes on a test basis to see if they are productive—either make only small changes in lot sizes or change only a few lots. This kind of experimentation could be highly productive.

Exhibit 6-10 illustrates another type of experiment.

In this company, one of the symptoms of inventory problems is poor forecasting. An alternative method of forecasting has been discussed but strong arguments against losing consistency with the past have been raised. Because of this, the "devil you know is better than the devil you don't know" argument prevails.

Exhibit 6-10 is a suggested counterargument: to put the two types of forecasting to a test. Note that the existing forecasting procedures under the heading "Company Forecast" are compared with an alternative method shown as "Revised Forecast." During the test both forecasts were prepared under real conditions so that one method could not benefit from 20-20 hindsight. The original company forecast method was then used so as not to incur risk during the test. The deviations from actual results are measured for both forecasts. The average error in units as well as the percentage error is shown for both forecasts. Note that the suggested revised forecast shows results that are much closer to actual results than the forecast presently in use.

Exhibit 6-11 shows the results of applying a test to the rules for restocking a stores inventory.

EXHIBIT 6-10   TEST OF FORECAST ACCURACY (units in thousands)

Month	Actual	Company Forecast	Error	Revised Forecast	Error
11	253	331	+ 78	270	+17
12	208	308	+100	200	− 8
1	167	211	+ 44	184	+17
2	120	132	+ 12	96	−24
3	101	120	+ 19	90	−11
4	72	102	+ 30	88	+16
5	39	80	+ 41	50	+11
6	80	70	− 10	60	−20
7	125	100	− 25	120	− 5
8	109	110	+ 1	110	+ 1
9	110	100	− 10	110	0
10	146	180	+ 34	160	+14
Average/Error/			33.7		12.0
Percentage/Error/			26%		9%

In this company an order point method is used for replenishing inventory: when stocks drop to a certain order point, a new order is placed. Buyers set order points and order quantities based on their judgment as to what quantities are appropriate. The inventory in units at the end of each week is shown by the line marked "Actual." A new method is tested by simulating performance during years A and B. The new method is a min-max system with min and max calculated by a formula. In simulating this new method, vendor lead times are taken to be those of the actual orders (in chronological sequence). Actual damage, errors, and adjustments to orders are presumed to also occur in the simulation. The lower line in Exhibit 6-11 indicates that the min-max method results in lower inventory levels.

Still another method of testing involves a control group. Two sets of data are used. One is the test data while the second is considered to be the control group (actually a sample of data similar to the first). The old procedures continue to be used on the control group to provide the basis of comparison with results of the test group.

Exhibit 6-12 shows the results of such a test. In this case, inventory items are paired, each test item being paired with a nearly similar control item. The test measures the total inventory cost based on recommended inventory ordering and production scheduling procedures for the test items. The control group line in Exhibit 6-12 shows what the total inventory cost is over the same period, using the existing procedures on the control items. The accumulated inventory cost after 30 weeks indi-

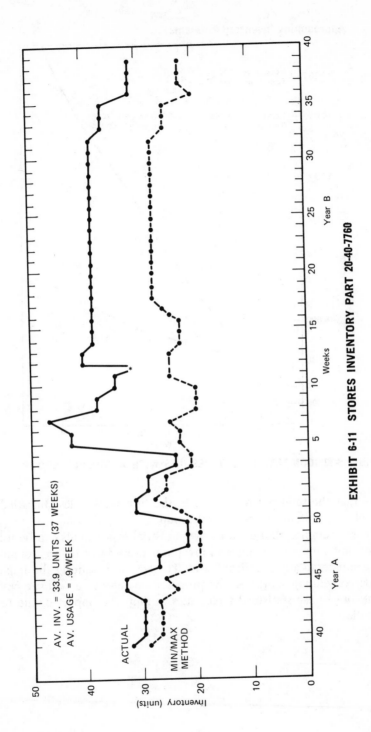

AV. INV. = 33.9 UNITS (37 WEEKS)

AV. USAGE = .9/WEEK

ACTUAL

MIN/MAX
METHOD

Inventory (units)

Year A   Weeks   Year B

EXHIBIT 6-11 STORES INVENTORY PART 20-40-7760

95

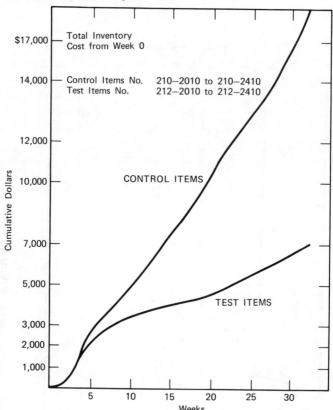

EXHIBIT 6-12 COMPARING TEST RESULTS WITH A CONTROL GROUP

cates that the total inventory cost in the test items is less than half the cost of similar items in the control group.

These examples all illustrate how industrial experiments can be utilized to test out proposed changes in inventory procedures before committing the company in any significant way. The key to measuring the impact of proposed solutions is to test the proposed changes in a realistic environment, but to use statistical techniques to limit the impact of the test on operations.

CHAPTER 7

SYSTEMS PLANNING

Chapter 6 identifies inventory problems and delineates areas needing improvement. Once management has accepted the recommendations resulting from the inventory review, the next task is to determine what should be done to correct the situation and to prevent its recurrence. What changes are required in the accounting, reporting, and operating procedures? How should inventories be managed in the future?

Systems planning is concerned with materials, production, and sales personnel working with inventory. It involves making routine decisions such as determining when and how much inventory to reorder by item, evaluating and updating inventory parameters such as order points, scheduling production runs of specific items, transferring stocks between warehouses, accumulating orders for shipment, inquiring as to the status of customer orders, and the like.

Included in systems planning are the detailed procedures to be followed by those responsible for the inventory related tasks. Systems planning also includes methods of information gathering and analyzing specifically related to inventory control. It might also include decision rules describing what action should be taken in exceptional or nonstandard situations.

This chapter excludes from systems planning such data processing considerations as the selection of hardware, data editing routines, computer file structure, and layout. We are interested, at this point, in the basic system irrespective of whether it operates manually or automatically.

INVENTORY MANAGEMENT—CONTROL OF
PHYSICAL UNITS VERSUS FINANCIAL CONTROLS

Although financial controls are important and must be closely interrelated with control of physical units, we discuss these separately. Chapters 2, 3, 5 and 10 cover the accounting interrelationships.

Financial analysis is a major element in setting inventory policy. The cost trade-off between customer service and inventory investment illustrates a financial consideration that is fundamental to many businesses. This analytical work should be carried out as a separate project as a base for establishing inventory policy. Once inventory policy is confirmed, operating personnel can set aside but not ignore the financial considerations embodied in the plan of action and focus on the operating procedures.

HOW TO APPROACH SYSTEMS PLANNING

Systems planning is more of an art than a science. There are as many different ways to proceed as there are experienced professionals in inventory management. Picking a "best" method for a particular company is probably a futile exercise in unfair comparisons and intangible advantages. Trying to distill out some basic principles from the various possible approaches is a difficult academic exercise which may or may not prove fruitful.

We recommend building a system through use of modules which can be altered to suit particular situations. The problem is broken down into "pieces." The modules of physical inventory might be stores for plant 1, stores for plant 2, materials in the main warehouse, materials in the staging area, materials at plant 1, receiving, and so forth. If one is uncertain about a physical inventory module, it may be too large. It should be broken down further until the module is comprehensible. There is little danger of breaking the modules too fine because they can always be reconstituted into larger modules that "fit" the required design.

Functions should be broken down by the same modular approach. These should be listed (restocking, order checking, expediting, transferring, etc.). If there is some uncertainty, the module is broken down further until the unit is manageable. As an example, the function of feeding the world is a massive sized module but when we break it down into segments such as functions of the local store, the trucking operation, and the warehouse, the modular approach becomes clearer.

Basic procedures deal with determining how much to stock, when and how to reorder—questions that must be answered through inventory management rules. Functions such as measuring obsolete inventory, providing customer priority, monitoring infractions in ordering procedures, or processing quality rejects have an enormous impact on effective inventory management. But lacking the glamour of an order point or order quantity, these are in danger of being neglected in systems planning.

INVENTORY POINTS

In Chapter 1, we covered the reasons for maintaining inventories. Raw material provides the buffer between vendors whose deliveries are erratic and manufacturing, in which efficiency depends on a steady flow of material. The finished components and subassemblies in the work-in-process stockrooms represent a buffer that assures a supply of parts that must be assembled to meet finished goods production schedules. The finished goods stock, in turn, is the buffer between production and the customer who demands good service. One objective of the systems plan is to determine at what points in the operation inventory should be maintained.

For illustrative purposes we use the manufacture of steel tape measures. The steps in the manufacturing operation are diagramed in Exhibit 7-1. Roll steel is purchased for the manufacture of the tape portion. The rolls are slit to the desired widths and lengths (widths of ½" ⅝", etc.; lengths of 10', 25', 50', etc.). The slitting process does not always consume a complete roll so the unused portion remains. As a rule, the roll is slit the entire length but not for the entire width. After being slit and trimmed, the steel strips are fed through a forming machine to curve the strip along its length to permit the tape to be extended some distance along a straight plane. Uncurved tapes are too "floppy" to use.

Next, the strip is fed through a coating and marking machine for imprinting the numerals. The strips are marked on one or both sides. The strips then progress to a subassembly process in which tips are affixed.

Tape housing subassemblies follow a parallel process. Bar and sheet metal is purchased from outside vendors. The metal is cast into the two sides of the tape housing. The low priced housings are stamped out of sheet metal rather than being cast. The housing parts are coated and then combined to form the housing subassembly.

The assembly operation brings together the tape (subassembly), the housing, and certain components purchased from outside vendors (screws, springs, etc.). Assembly is a manual process and involves some commonality of parts. A given tape can be assembled into several different housings to produce different finished products. Likewise, each housing can be fitted with several different tapes—on the average, eight tapes: metric, nonmetric, coated, noncoated, and so forth, while each tape can be assembled in about four different housings.

The assembled tape measures are transferred to the packing operation. Two basic types of packaging are used: simply placing the assembled tape measures in boxes of varying quantities (1 dozen, 2 dozen, etc.) or skin packing them (on a card covered with a clear plastic that is vacuum drawn) and cutting the cards and packing the skin-packed tapes in cartons. The boxes are then stocked in the shipping room ready for shipment.

We have covered the manufacturing process, but at what points in the process should each type of inventory be stocked?

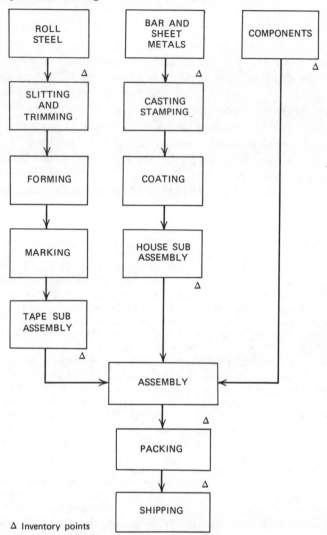

EXHIBIT 7-1 MANUFACTURING PROCESS FOR STEEL TAPE MEASURES

Looking at the extreme case, if no inventory points are maintained receipt of customer orders triggers the whole process illustrated in Exhibit 7-1. The orders are exploded to determine the subassembly and component requirements. The subassemblies, in turn, are exploded to determine the material needed for roll, ingots, and sheet metal. Orders are placed for the appropriate quantities, and then the "waiting game" begins.

When the roll steel arrives, it is slit and the tape subassembly process begins. When the ingot material arrives, the housing subassembly process proceeds. In this case no inventories are maintained and the tape manufacturer has reduced his inventory stocks to zero. Although inventory stock has been reduced to zero, what is the overall cost of maintaining this level of stock? Obviously, this case is unrealistic because no customer would sit and wait for an order that most companies would fill from stock. The job shop approach may work well for production of jet planes and other customized products but certainly not for standard catalogue items. Even if the case were realistic, what would happen to the manufacturing process?

While the components are being stamped out, slit, and formed, the assembly department is idle. Then, when the assembly department received its parts, the component manufacturing area is idle until the next order comes through with the required material. Manufacturing is efficient only when there is a backlog of work for each department to facilitate a steady flow with a minimum of setups. Then, too, imagine the additional cost of material purchases made order by order. In short, the tape manufacturing business (and many others) could be run without inventories—but only at an enormous cost.

Let us now consider the impact of inventories being available at various stages of the manufacturing process, starting with raw material.

The raw material includes small components such as springs and rivets as well as the roll and ingots. In this instance, incoming customer orders are exploded to obtain the subassembly and component requirements. The subassembly requirements are further exploded to determine the material requirements, which are available in stock. In this situation, the purchasing process now proceeds independently of the customer orders. Purchase orders are placed to restock the raw material inventory and, as such, are based on forecasts of material inventory requirements.

Purchasing, thus, is uncoupled from the manufacturing process and this has several advantages. First, customer lead times are improved because the customer has to wait only for the manufacturing process—not for purchasing procedures. Exhibit 7-2 illustrates this diagrammatically on the second line. With raw material readily available, metal fabrication operations start immediately. Another advantage is the increased efficiency in the purchasing operation. Orders can be placed for larger quantities at lower prices because of quantity breaks. Freight costs, likewise, are lower.

Let us next suppose that the tape manufacturer establishes a finished goods inventory (Exhibit 7-2, line 3). As a consequence, customer service is substantially improved because customer orders can be shipped directly out of finished stock. Customer lead time is now reduced to the time required to process the order and to ship it. In this situation, the assembly department is scheduled to maintain finished goods levels according to the restocking requirements. This results in greater efficiency in the assembly department as well as the subassembly stage. More economical lot sizes for subassemblies can now be considered since production is going into inventory.

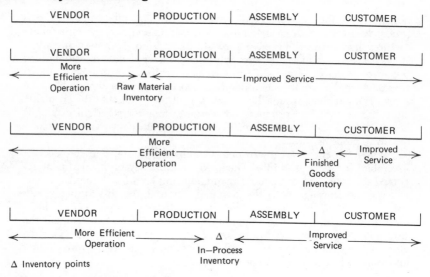

EXHIBIT 7-2 INVENTORY POINTS

Inventory points, properly utilized, permit more efficient operations in the functions immediately preceding the inventory. The inventory also permits improved service in the operations immediately following.

Other inventory points could be established for this example: for assembled but unpacked stock to uncouple the assembly and packing operations; for work-in-process inventories to separate the metals department from the assembly area; for slit and formed but unprinted tapes. Inventory points facilitate:

1. Operational efficiency in areas preceding the inventory.

2. Better service to the areas following the inventory point.

3. Simplified planning.

Competition forces the tape manufacturer to maintain material and finished goods inventory points. How many other points are established is a management decision based on availability of cash, availability of space, and planning skills in the company.

The correct number of inventory points depends on competitive conditions in the industry and the resources available to the company. The requirements for materials and finished goods inventories are usually dictated by the industry. Questions will still remain, however, as to exactly which items must be stocked and what the physical layout and proper distribution network should be.

To determine appropriate work-in-process inventory points is difficult and usually more within management discretion. Planning skills of company personnel can influence decisions greatly. If, for example, the tape measure manufacturer is unable to schedule from raw materials through tape subassemblies, then the process has to be broken down into parts with inventory points uncoupling the several parts. In many industries it has been historical practice to separate the manufacturing process into many short segments for scheduling purposes. Work-in-process stockrooms proliferated with each segment drawing components or subassemblies and returning higher order components or subassemblies to the stockrooms.

Efforts at extending the use of bill of material explosion scheduling have been directed toward increasing the size of the manufacturing segments that can be effectively scheduled, thus reducing the number of inventorying points. With the increased application of data processing in this area, inventory is managed better than with historical methods.

The existence of an inventory point is not always represented by a formalized stock status report. Practice, rather than form, is the deciding factor. If at the completion of a work order at a certain point in the manufacturing process, another work order picks up the subsequent operations, as part of an overall schedule, there is no inventory point even though there will always be a small amount tied up in such inventories. If, on the other hand, the output of one work order remains on the floor in a marshalling area or in a stockroom for a period of time before another work order is issued, then a work-in-process inventory point exists whether or not records are maintained of that inventory.

Basic Procedures for Treating Inventory Points

Having established the points at which inventory should be maintained, we now examine how inventory is managed. If the inventory is truly serving its purpose as an economic buffer, then the basic management question is the same. How should inventory be restocked? Decisions must be made as to when and how much to reorder. Because of the quantitative nature of this decision problem, decision rules can be formulated through the use of a properly developed mathematical formula that will determine when and how much to reorder. Since the rules depend on use of statistical techniques, they will not make the best decision in all instances, however, on the average, they will make very good decisions. In the long run such techniques provide more reliable answers than those given by the most experienced inventory managers who rely solely on judgment.

A number of formulas enter into the restocking decision rules. These are all grouped together in an inventory model. Certain data such as inventory on hand, on order, backorders, and sales projections are input into the model. The model performs computations to determine what items to reorder and in what quantities. If one inventory model can be developed, so can two, three, four, and forty. In fact, constructing inventory models has for years been a rich source of data for publications.

Common assumptions on which models are built are: sales are constant, lead times are constant, there is only one item in inventory, all inventory related costs are accurately known, storage capacity is unlimited, the company can sell more than it can produce, and so forth. By and large, these assumptions are so unrealistic that deducing optimum solutions from the models has little validity.

Models, however, may be useful in spite of their originators. There are considerations that make one model preferable to another. It would therefore be helpful to become familiar with the most widely used models and to understand the practical considerations and advantages of each. To this end we first discuss three basic models:

1. The order-point/order-quantity model.
2. The min-max model.
3. The replenishment model.

Any model being considered should be evaluated with regard to amount of revision required, instability, availability of data required, and ease of use. If the model has to be revised as ordinary business conditions change, its practical value is limited. If ordinary changes in business conditions are magnified by the model causing wider swings in operations, the model would be dangerous to use.

In the absence of any clearly demonstrated performance superiority, consideration should be given to selecting a model that will work on data available or easily made available. Manually performing any computation more difficult than a straight average is generally out of the question, and even at that level of complexity, trouble might be encountered. A model has much to recommend it if it requires the user to do nothing more complex than comparing two numbers to see which is the larger.

THE ORDER-POINT/ORDER-QUANTITY MODEL

The order-point (OP) order-quantity (OQ) model is based on the calculation of two numbers for each stockkeeping unit (SKU). Statistical formulas are available for the calculation of these numbers (OP and OQ) based on historical data and forecast of inventory demand. The decision rule is:

When inventory on hand plus "on order" falls below the OP, then a restocking order is placed for the SKU. The quantity ordered is OQ.

The OP-OQ inventory model is widely used—almost always in connection with automated systems since the calculation of the order points and order quantities becomes complicated and time-consuming when manual procedures are used. Computers are programmed to perform these calculations. For each SKU the quantity on-hand plus that on-order is compared with the order point. If the on-hand plus on-order is below the order point a requisition is initiated. The procedure is simple.

The model has certain assumptions built into the computer applications that limit its usefulness to certain types of inventory. The calculation of OP and OQ is based on a trade-off between inventory carrying costs and setup or ordering costs. The model, therefore, is most useful when these costs are known and when the setup costs are significant. If the required costs are not known with a sufficient degree of accuracy the model will not give reliable results.

The complex equipment required in stamping and forming operations is illustrative of high setup requirements where OP and OQ procedures are applicable. In these instances, the economic production lot size must be calculated because this becomes the OQ for the inventory item.

The OP-OQ model is also used for materials inventory (raw material) where the vendor places order size restrictions on an item-by-item basis as opposed to a total order basis. In these cases, the OQs are set initially to satisfy the vendor's requirements. The OP-OQ model may be applied to finished goods items having similar characteristics—where the quantity assembled or processed is important. Examples are the processing of a large roll of paper, metal, or cloth or the mixing of a batch of chemicals.

OP-OQ models are used in connection with perpetual inventory records. The reorder rule assumes that someone (or some device such as a computer) reviews the inventory level on a daily basis. The rule states that when the inventory level falls below the OP, action is taken. Continuous reviewing is necessary to know when the OP is covered. This is not a hard and fast rule; however, inventories that are not maintained on a perpetual basis are more likely to employ means other than the OP-OQ model.

The ability of this type model to react to changing business conditions depends on the mathematical formulas used to calculate the OPs and OQs as well as how often the parameters are revised. Calculation of OP is based on forecasted demand over lead time and estimated safety stock requirements. The latter will rely heavily on the variation between forecasted demand and actual demand. Elementary OP-OQ models incorporate poor forecasting formulas. In a changing environment, these formulas can "whipsaw," increasing safety stock requirements and thus increasing inventory investment.

Exhibit 7-3 illustrates this instability, showing how a sudden drop in sales caused the model to increase inventory.

About half the sales of this item were made to one customer. The weekly sales including this customer are shown for weeks 1, 2, 3, and 4. At the end of week 4, the customer discontinued his purchases and went to another supplier. Weeks 5, 6, and 7 reflect the sales without this dominant customer. The average weekly sales have dropped from 109,000 cases per week to 48,000, a 44% decrease.

In the OP-OQ model the order point is the sum of two quantities: safety stock (SS) and average inventory demand over the restocking lead time (DLT). As a result of the drop in sales, the model increased safety stock requirements because of the large variations created by the loss of the major customer. The increase in inventory stems from the increase in safety stock requirements. The other component of the order point determination, sales over lead time, was calculated through exponential

EXHIBIT 7-3   POOR RESULTS WITH AN ORDER-POINT/ORDER-QUANTITY MODEL (figures in thousands of cases per week)

		— End of Week Model Calculation —			
Week	Weekly Sales		Safety Stock	Sales Over Lead Time	Order Point
1	107 ↑		90	275	365 ↑
2	113	average = 109	97	290	387 average = 382
3	99	76	315	391	
4	116 ↓	65	329	394	↓
5	52 ↑		134	336	470 ↑
6	46	average = 48	183	304	487 average = 479
7	47 ↓		226	255	481 ↓

$$\frac{48}{109} = 44\% \text{ decrease in sales}$$

$$\frac{479}{382} = 25\% \text{ increase in order point}$$

smoothing. Since exponential smoothing only gradually adjusts to changes in sales, the reduced sales were not immediately reflected in the lead time component of the order point. The net effect of the model was to increase the order point 25% in response to the 44% drop in sales!

Weaknesses such as this can be overcome in the OP-OQ models. Correct mathematical formulation and application of suitable statistical change detection methods can produce workable models. However, specialized skills are required to formulate or apply the models. Unfortunately, commercial models have been oversold on the assurance that all that is necessary is to "plug them in." As a result, hundreds of companies have turned over to the programmers the highly technical task of implementing inventory models. The resulting problems of misapplication are well known.

In spite of this the OP-OQ model has excellent application. The warehousing of bulk commodities provides an example.

A company needs order quantities to provide control of freight costs of movements into the warehouses. Because freight costs are so much less (per pound) when orders are placed for full carloads, overall cost considerations dictate using order quantities based on multiples of a full car.

An analysis of sales history at the warehouse shows some sizable week-to-week fluctuations. Much of this can be explained by special circumstances, however. Delays in getting rail cars lined up and loaded account for most of the week-to-week variations. Other variations due to exceptionally large orders are known several weeks in advance and can be processed as efficiently as regular orders. Overall, demand on the warehouse is fairly regular and predictable.

Because sales have been stable, the lead time component of the order point can be based on average demand levels without concern about a whipsaw effect. This leaves only the safety stock component of the order point to deal with. In Exhibit 7-3 the OP-OQ model erroneously updated the weekly safety stock based on the forecast error that developed when sales suddenly dropped below expectations. This calculation loses sight of the substance of the safety stock. This safety factor is intended to take care of the longer term—to cover variations that occur over a period of time. The erratic effect of one time period should not cause overreaction—this erratic behaviour should be expected. (As an analogy, churches and temples are not built to accommodate the unusual attendance on holy days.) Changes in safety stock should be tied to long-term changes in the level of usage. With this in mind, the safety stock levels for the warehouse are calculated on weekly sales based on historical experience.

Exhibit 7-4 shows graphically the sales variability of a group of products at a warehouse for the purpose of calculating safety stock. Management decided on a 98% service level. This means that 98% of the sales must

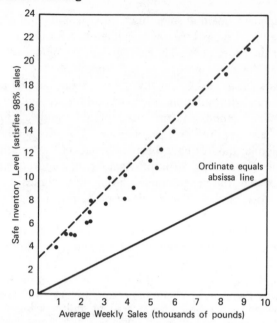

EXHIBIT 7-4 SALES VARIABILITY

be shipped directly out of stock. For each item in the warehouse, weekly sales are examined. These are calculated for the past 26 weeks. Next, a safe inventory level is determined to assure that 98% of the sales can be shipped immediately. In Exhibit 7-4, the safe inventory level is plotted against the average sales for the items shown. The exhibit shows a relationship between the average sales and the safe inventory level. Safety stock is calculated from this relationship and is based on general sales characteristics of the entire warehouse rather than on the recent activity of the particular individual items.

No plan is made for weekly updating of the safety stock levels. Average weekly sales are computed on a regular basis so safety stock can be reset according to the relationship shown in Exhibit 7-4. The actual updating of the safety stock levels (and order point) is left to the tracking system. Such systems are discussed in Chapter 9. At this point, the tracking system provides a measure of excess inventory. As long as both measures are in line with expectations, order points do not have to be updated across the board. On an exception basis, a limited number of changes are made to order points. These correspond to major shifts in demand or shipping patterns.

Exhibit 7-5 shows the stockout rate provided by the tracking system.

EXHIBIT 7-5 STOCKOUT RATE

1	2	3	4	5
Week	Item-Days Out of Stock	Average Demand During Days Out of Stock*	Sales*	Stockout Rate 3 ÷ (3 + 4)
11	38	18,292	1,049,092	1.7%
12	37	20,336	1,252,456	1.6
13	0	0	933,520	.0
14	2	120	944,200	.0
15	8	484	642,284	.1
16	0	0	955,680	.0
17	0	0	621,440	.0
18	0	0	911,880	.0
19	11	2,584	876,144	.3

* Units are pounds.

This shows an early period in the use of the system. The number of item-days out of stock is shown in column 2. For example, if two items are out of stock during the week; the first for 3 days and the second for 4 days, the total item-days out of stock is 3 + 4, or 7 item-days. The same result is reported if one item is out of stock all week. The measure of stockouts used by the warehouse combines the item-days out-of-stock on a weighted average basis. The weighting is made according to the average sales of each item.

For example, if an item has sold an average of 500 pounds per day and is out of stock for 3 days, then the estimated unshipped orders total 3 × 500, or 1500 pounds. These estimates of orders not shipped are totaled to obtain the figures reported in column 3, "Average Demand During Days Out-of-Stock." The actual orders missed because of out-of-stock situations are not available because of a variety of customer reactions. The customer could, for example, withdraw the order or backorder. Backordering has been the more common practice. However, backorders are canceled or shipments delayed if the customer finds an alternative source.

Occasionally, a different grade product is substituted. At times the warehouse ships a better grade at the price of the original order rather than risk losing the sale. Since most of these variations have not been regularly accounted for, substantial record keeping would be necessary to replace the column 3 estimate by the actual figure.

Consideration was given to using dollar value rather than pounds as the unit of measure. This would weight the service level evaluation more heavily in favor of the more expensive items. An analysis showed that the differences in weighting, whether pounds or dollars were used, did not amount to much so no change was made.

The "Sales" column in Exhibit 7-5 shows the total sales of all items for the week. Sales, like the average demand column, are expressed in pounds. The final step in developing the stockout rate is:

1. The sales for the week (column 4) are added to estimated demand during days out-of-stock (column 3: lost sales) to determine the estimated demand.
2. The estimated lost sales (column 3) are then taken as a percentage of estimated demand. The resulting percentage is shown in column 5 as the stockout rate.

The stockout rate, a measure of overall performance, could be low overall yet poor (high) for one or two items that are averaged in the overall rate. This procedure, built with stringent service requirements, assures the virtual elimination of routine stockouts. Any stockouts that do occur can be traced to some exceptional circumstance such as loss of an incoming car in transit.

MIN-MAX MODEL

The rules for using a min-max inventory model are similar to the rules for an OP-OQ model just discussed. With the min-max model, two inventory levels are established for each SKU. The smaller of the two is called the "min" (minimum) and the larger, the "max" (maximum). When working with perpetual inventory records, the restocking rules are:

1. Calculate the current level of inventory on hand plus the "on order" for each item.
2. For each SKU whose inventory balance on hand plus the "on order" is below the min, prepare a restocking requisition.
3. The quantity ordered should be the max less current inventory on hand less current inventory on order.

After the restocking order is placed, the sum of the current inventory on hand plus the new total inventory on order should be equal to the max.

Exhibit 7-6 illustrates how the min-max model works. At the beginning, the card shows a shipment of 10 bags—reducing the balance to 53. On 6/3 two more bags are shipped—further reducing the inventory on hand

EXHIBIT 7-6 PERPETUAL INVENTORY RECORD USING THE MIN-MAX SYSTEM

Date	Reference	Quantity Ordered	After Ship. on Hand	Shipments	ADJ
6/1	SO71663		53	10	
6/3	SO71716		51	2	
6/4	SO71724		33	18	
6/4	R652	27			
6/8	SO71860		8	25	
6/8	R691	25			
6/10	SO71885		3	5	
6/13	recd R652		30		
6/13	SO71968		15	15	
6/13	SO71971		10	5	
6/13	R748	25			

Item No.: B5631–777	Min = 40	Max = 60	Order From Clev.

to 51. The next shipment (6/4) is 18 bags, reducing the balance to 33. Since this is below the min of 40 bags, a requisition is sent to the purchasing department. The amount ordered is the quantity necessary to bring the balance on hand up to the max of 60 (60 minus 33 = 27). Note the min-max information at the bottom of the card.

The next entry (6/8) shows that 25 bags were shipped, reducing the balance to 8. Since the balance of 8 plus the 27 still on order (= 35) is less than the minimum of 40, another requisition is placed. The amount, this time, is equal to 25 (max of 60 less 35).

In the min-max method, the min works in the same way as the OP in an OP-OQ procedure. The difference in the two methods is in the amounts that are ordered. With OP-OQ, the quantity ordered is always OQ. With min-max, the quantity ordered is whatever amount brings the level up to the max. Because the quantity order under min-max varies, this method is not used when vendor conditions or cost considerations dictate an economic order quantity. In retailing and many wholesaling industries where the order (setup) costs are small, the min-max method has good application.

The min-max model is easy to apply. The minimum and maximum inventory levels are understandable to those responsible for inventory record keeping. The min-max method is found in many companies that have never considered the more scientific methods of inventory management. It is a simple system and gains popularity because of this. The calculation of economic order quantities, on the other hand, requires not only good cost information but also the application statistics.

The ability of the min-max model to respond quickly and correctly to changes in demand depends to a great extent on the precise methods used to calculate the min and the max. A carefully thought out model employing a reasonably accurate forecast gives excellent results. Unfortunately, because many companies omit the forecast, excess inventories build up. When demand for an item increases, the reported shortages raise the min and max. There must be a counterbalancing check through use of forecasts or some other analytical method of identifying the minimum and maximum limits that are too high. Unless this is done, inventory levels continually creep up.

In the absence of a good forecast, the min-max method may still be effective provided it is geared to average demand and is not adjusted to trends and cycles. If demand for the inventoried SKUs is highly variable because of "lumpiness" rather than cyclical trends, the best way to handle the problem may be to peg the inventories at average demand—using adequate safety stock and letting the inventory absorb the "lumpiness."

Exhibit 7-7 illustrates shipment data of a manufacturer of industrial equipment. It is a good example of lumpy demand. On a week-by-week basis, sales show great variability, running from zero in some weeks to about 50 in others.

In some cases, lumpy sales can be attributed to the ordering pattern of one predominant customer or to a satellite warehouse. Once the explanations are found, forecasts can be formulated and inventory controls established on the forecasts. In this example, 5 weeks' lead time was required to restock the inventory. The max in this case was established at 120 and the min at 80. The 120 provides for the maximum experienced historical shipment plus an additional allowance. Exhibit 7-8 simulates

EXHIBIT 7-7   AN EXAMPLE OF LUMPY DEMAND

Week/Units Demand			
1/52	11/0	21/52	31/0
2/0	12/52	22/0	32/0
3/0	13/0	23/51	33/0
4/50	14/0	24/0	34/2
5/2	15/0	25/0	35/6
6/3	16/50	26/0	36/45
7/0	17/0	27/2	37/0
8/0	18/0	28/3	38/12
9/0	19/0	29/47	39/50
10/2	20/0	30/5	40/0

EXHIBIT 7-8 A MIN-MAX MODEL APPLIED TO LUMPY DEMAND (MIN = 80; MAX = 120)

Week	Beginning Inventory	Demand	Receipts	Ending Inventory	Orders Placed
1	120	52	0	68	52
2	68	0	0	68	
3	68	0	0	68	
4	68	50	0	18	50
5	18	2	52	68	
6	68	3	0	65	
7	65	0	0	65	
8	65	0	0	65	
9	65	0	50	115	
10	115	2	0	113	
11	113	0	0	113	
12	113	52	0	61	59
13	61	0	0	61	
14	61	0	0	61	
15	61	0	0	61	
16	61	50	0	11	50
17	11	0	59	70	
18	70	0	0	70	
19	70	0	0	70	
20	70	0	0	70	
21	70	52	0	18	52
22	18	0	50	68	
23	68	51	0	17	51
24	17	0	0	17	
25	17	0	0	17	
26	17	0	0	17	
27	17	2	52	67	
28	67	3	51	115	
29	115	47	0	68	52
30	68	5	0	63	
31	63	0	0	63	
32	63	0	0	63	
33	63	0	0	63	
34	63	2	52	113	
35	113	6	0	107	
36	107	45	0	62	58
37	62	0	0	62	
38	62	12	0	50	
39	50	50	0	0	
40	0	0	0	0	

the results. The simulation uses actual demand, the min-max order rules and estimated reorder lead times based on company traffic data.

At week 1, the start of the simulation, the inventory is set at 120 units with none on order. During the week, 52 units are shipped so the inventory is reduced to 68. Since inventory falls below the minimum of 80, an order is placed for 52 units, bringing the inventory back to the maximum of 120. (Ending inventory of 68 plus 52 orders placed.) In weeks 2 and 3 there is no change in inventory. During week 4, 50 units are shipped. The end-of-the-week balance drops to 18 units on hand plus 52 still on order, a total of 70 units. Since this is below the min of 80, an order is placed for 50 units, bringing the sum of on-hand (18) plus on-order (102) up to the max. In week 5, two units are shipped and the order placed in week 1 is received. At the end of the week, 68 units are on hand and 50 units are on order.

This model functions well, with the inventory absorbing the variations in demand. However, note that the overall level of demand remains fairly constant—at about 55 units per month—and that no attempt is made to project trends or cycles in the demand data. Attempts to use simple cyclical projections such as exponential smoothing on this item would likely lead to changing inventory levels which would be out of phase with usage.

In comparison with the order-point/order-quantity model, the min-max is more likely to be used in wholesaling, retailing, and finished goods inventories where there is no compelling reason to order a specific quantity. The OP-OQ model tends to be used more often for work-in-process and materials where specificity of ordering is required.

Exhibit 7-9 shows a weekly stock status report for a warehouse that wholesales electrical parts. The warehouse uses a min-max model for restocking inventory. No minimum order size by item is required and the stock status report is reviewed weekly for placement of orders. The review date is Friday of each week. For each item with available on-hand plus on-order inventory below the min, the computer prints an order flag in the margin of the report.

Inventory is reported separately as available and reserved. When a customer places a firm order and is told that the item is available for shipment at a certain date, the quantity ordered is transferred from "on-hand available" to "on-hand reserved" where it remains until shipped. Future customer orders may not be taken from the on-hand reserved; company policy requires that stock be reserved only against firm orders. The available on-order category represents purchases to restock inventory. The reserved on-order category represents backorders.

The existing order entry procedures facilitate the handling of backorders. If the item is not available in stock when the customer order is received, the order entry clerk enters an inquiry for the anticipated arrival time of the earliest purchase order with no stock reserved against it. The warehouse promises rush delivery to its customer on the day following scheduled arrival. If the customer accepts this delivery date, the appropriate quantity in the purchase order is transferred from on-order available to on-order reserved.

The weekly stock status report in Exhibit 7-9 contains information for adjusting the minimums. This information, shown on the second line of each item record, is average weekly sales over the most recent 26 weeks, the six most recent vendor lead times, and the corresponding inventory lows.

The lead time is the total time in days from the date of the purchase order until the receipt of the stock; it combines order processing time and delivery time.

The inventory low is the on-hand available inventory of the item at the time the new stock is received but does not include the new receipt. The negative balances for the inventory lows indicate that no inventory was on hand and that the indicated number of units had been backordered at that time.

During the weekly inventory review, the stock status report is studied to determine the adequacy of the minimums. Such procedures for adjusting inventory levels are discussed in greater detail in Chapter 9.

A glance at Exhibit 7-9 shows the usefulness of this information. Note the inventory lows for item 14412. Based on an average weekly sales rate of 17 units, the inventory lows range from 3 to 4 weeks of inventory. This appears to be a comfortable level of inventory. Item 14536 has been in a backorder position and is flagged so (*BO*). This information suggests the possibility of raising the minimum for the item. Providing information such as this is part of a feedback mechanism designated to monitor how well things are going and where change is required.

Feedback mechanisms to test and monitor inventory performance are a must for good inventory management. They should be used even with stable inventories. Generally, more reliance can be placed on the feedback mechanisms than on statistical procedures used to estimate mins, OPs, and safety stock. Feedback mechanisms rely on recent past events whereas statistical procedures rely on foresight. Recent hindsight is usually more accurate.

REPLENISHMENT MODEL

In the last example—the min-max model for the wholesaler—the inventory is reviewed weekly rather than monthly and perpetual records are used.

EXHIBIT 7-9   STOCK STATUS REPORT BUFFALO WAREHOUSE

Item Number: 14402	Product Group: Wire	Cost: 1.67 C
Vendor Code: MC Av. Sales	Lead Times: 14 21	Inventory Lows: 242 17
26 Wk: 162	18 16	60 184
	14 14	125 291

		Inventory Available	Inventory Reserved	Inventory Total	
	On Hand	167	150	317	
	On Order	400		400	Max: 1,000
Order	Total	567	150	717	Min: 600

Item Number: 14412	Product Group: Wire	Cost: 1.82 C
Vendor Code: MC Av. Sales	Lead Times: 14 22	Inventory Lows: 67 56
26 Wk: 17	18 21	62 67
	26 17	48 71

		Inventory Available	Inventory Reserved	Inventory Total	
	On Hand	110		110	
	On Order				Max: 150
	Total	110		110	Min: 100

Item Number: 14536	Product Group: Wire	Cost: .85 C
Vendor Code: MC Av. Sales	Lead Time: 18 14	Inventory Lows: 38 16
26 Wk: 37	26 14	−2 25
	22 16	−16 −20

		Inventory Available	Inventory Reserved	Inventory Total	
	On Hand		6	6	
BO	On Order	90	44	134	Max: 180
	Total	90	50	140	Min: 130

The replenishment model is frequently used in cases where it is not feasible to keep perpetual inventory records or where the records cannot be reviewed on a continuous or frequent basis. The replenishment model works in a manner similar to the weekly min-max model, except that there is no min.

The inventory is counted at regular, convenient intervals—weekly, monthly, or any other. Each item is assigned an inventory maximum relating to demand over the time interval between inventory counts. The procedure followed is to subtract the inventory count at each interval from the maximum for the item, and to prepare a stocking requisition for the difference. At each count, then, the inventory is "ordered up" to its max.

The replenishment model has important uses when restocking can be done only at intervals. Spare parts for ships at sea serve as examples. Stores are stocked up before the ship leaves port and, except for emergency air lifts, no other parts are available until the end of the voyage. Replenishment models are also used for inventories such as food in grocery stores where cost effective methods of maintaining stock status reports are not yet widely used. When inventory records are available and daily restocking is possible, the replenishment model is rarely found.

One disadvantage of this model is that it synchronizes all item inventory levels. All items tend to be at their max and at their lows at the same time. With the other inventory models, some items are near their top, others near their low, and others in between; overall, the inventory remains close to average.

The replenishment model responds poorly to a reduction in the demand level of an item. If sales or usage of an item drops off, the replenishment model maintains the item inventory near its max. The min-max and the OP-OQ models, on the other hand, absorb some of the decreased demand by placing orders less frequently.

To correct these deficiencies, some companies using the replenishment model adopt an optional replenishment model. With this version, an order is not automatically placed at every review period. Instead, the inventory count is compared to an inventory min. If the count is below the min, a restocking order is issued. If the count is above the min, no action is taken. This optional replenishment model is actually the min-max model with periodic, rather than continuous, reviews. Exhibit 7-9 could be represented as an optimal replenishment model as well as min-max.

COMBINING ORDERS

Each basic inventory model—OP-OQ, min-max, and replenishment—deals with inventory on an SKU basis. Each item is examined individually in deciding when and how much to order. In practice, the overall inventory at a stocking location must be considered. A model that deals with SKUs on an individual basis is incomplete for good inventory management. The overall considerations depend on the type of stocking point. For materials, considerations to be weighed are incoming freight cost, vendor price breaks, and minimum order sizes. For a manufacturer's finished goods, the assembly scheduling, plant capacity, and labor work load are considerations.

All types of inventory are subject to possible limitations in space or product availability. Generally, inventory can be satisfactorily managed by treating these considerations separately from the rules for controlling a single SKU. The procedures for dealing with the overall considerations then relate to the individual SKU rules—usually through the amount of safety stock provided for each SKU. The overall considerations can generally be divided into those dealing with limitations (allocation) and those dealing without limitations. Allocation problems are discussed in the next section.

The most prevalent consideration relating to the inventory point as a whole is the combining of individual SKU restocking quantities into one order. In retailing and wholesaling businesses a separate purchase order is rarely placed for each item. All items purchased from the same vendor are likely to be listed together on a single order. For manufacturing and processing companies, requests for internal staging requiring truck, rail, or plane are likely to be grouped by destination. Since such grouping of orders complicates planning, a rational assumption is that they would not be grouped unless required by an outside vendor as in cases when minimum order size requirements exist. In other cases grouping could be practiced to obtain price discounts or reduced freight costs.

Whatever the reason for grouping item restocking orders, a sensible approach is to queue up the requisitions. Under the queuing procedure, requisitions are completed for individual SKUs according to the rules in the inventory model. Requisitions are not forwarded to the shipping locations immediately. Instead, they are retained at the inventory point until a sufficient number accumulates. A sufficient number may be defined in terms of dollars, units, weight, volume, or some other appropriate denominator.

Exhibit 7-10 illustrates a reorder sheet for a warehouse distributing industrial paper. Individual SKUs are filled out daily at the warehouse. OP-OQ rules are applied. For each requisition, a line is entered on the reorder sheet. As an example, on June 21, the inventory on hand plus the on order for item A1702 fell below the order point. A requisition was completed for 240 cases and sent to the traffic department. Upon receipt of this requisition the traffic department entered the date, item number, and quantity ordered on the reorder sheet (first line on Exhibit 7-10). The traffic department then entered the product weight and extended the order to get the total weight of the item. Finally, the extended weight is added to the previous weight total on the sheet to arrive at the accumulated weight of the orders being queued.

In the example, an order had been completed on 6/20 so the 6/21 line

EXHIBIT 7-10 REORDER SHEET, LOS ANGELES PLANT

SHIPPING LOCATION: GREENVALE PLANT   TOTAL TO: 40,000 LBS.
PRODUCT LINE: INDUSTRIAL PAPER

Date	Item No.	Quantity to Order	Item Weight	Total Weight	Order Number
6/21	A1702	240	46.8	11,222	
6/22	A5776	110	52.0	16,952	
6/22	A2503	200	38.7	24,692	
6/22	B2101	25	28.0	25,392	
6/22	A1702	240	46.8	36,624	
6/24	B2106	10	28.0	36,904	
6/25	B2107	30	28.0	37,744	
6/27	A5976	60	42.5	40,294	NP8671-5
6/27	A5968	300	52.0	15,600	

for A1702 marks the beginning of the new accumulation of item orders. When the 6/22 line is completed for A5776, the weight on that line, 16,952 pounds, is the combined weight of the 240 cases of A1702 and the 110 cases of A5776. For this sheet the totals are accumulated to 40,000 pounds. This takes place on 6/27 when 60 cases on A5976 brings the total over the 40,000 pound mark. At this point a transfer order is completed and forwarded to the shipping department at the Greenvale plant. This order called for shipment of the eight item orders starting with 6/21 order through the 6/27 order. Item number A1702 appears on 6/21 and on 6/22. These requisitions were combined, so in total seven items were requested.

The objective of this grouping is to obtain full car orders to substantially reduce freight costs. While it is not known in advance exactly what items will be combined in an order, a stopping point, such as the 40,000 pounds, can be determined in advance. There are always some uncertainties, regardless of the precision of the method being followed, and some judgment must be exercised. In the case of the 40,000 pound limit, this can vary depending on the size of the freight car. Since the car that was spotted for loading this shipment is smaller than that required, part of one of the line items has to be left off. Item A1702 is the largest volume item at the warehouse so it has been selected as the swing item. If the full order could not be loaded, the requisition for A1702 would be reduced.

Variations in the procedures described are required to fit the queuing rules to the particular inventory point. If the weight per unit varies but the volume does not, then unit counts may be preferable to weights in determining a full order.

As in all procedures, cross checks and monitoring assure that the rules are being followed. Since item A1702 has been selected as the "swing" item in completing the orders illustrated in Exhibit 7-10, inventory for that item is monitored closely. A separate record is kept of deviations between the original order and the modifications that were made. A review of these differences shows whether the stopping point has been properly set. Chapter 9 expands the discussion of monitoring and feedback procedures.

In working out the procedures for queuing individual SKU orders, it was assumed that one of the basic inventory models was being used to determine the individual SKU orders. If an individual determination was made only according to SKU characteristics (such as its demand forecast), how does the queuing of orders affect the correctness of the SKU level decisions? With the procedure described, the only change is potential delay in processing the individual SKU orders. Instead of being forwarded immediately, the order may reside on a reorder sheet until the predetermined amount accumulates.

The lead time of the SKU is therefore extended. This results in an increase in the order point (OP-OQ models). The minimum increases when the min-max model is used and the max increases when the replenishment model applies. Thus, the effect of combining orders can be taken into account by changing the levels in the inventory model without altering the basic procedures.

Care must be exercised to assure that restocking continues at a uniform rate. If there are numerous items in inventory each with its fair share of demand, the law of averages tends to balance out the changing levels. But if most of the demand is centered in a few large items they could be required at about the same time, thus canceling out the equalization of inventory levels for the various items.

As an illustration, one company has rented a new warehouse and has carefully established min-max levels for each of the items. Each one is stocked at its maximum at the time of the "grand opening." The spread between the min and the max has been set at 2 weeks for each item. When the warehouse starts operating, its favorable location stimulates demand in the area and inventories are quickly pulled down so that just about every item has to be ordered at the same time. After a period of 4 weeks of "mad scrambling," the orders begin to smooth out. This is helped along by temporarily ordering a 3-week supply instead of 2, for half the items. Even after the orders level out, the embarrassment remains. Since each item was originally stocked at its max, the space rented to accommodate that level of inventory is about 40% more than is required. Sales growth did not bring the warehouse up to efficient space utilization until 3 more years had passed.

ALLOCATING ORDERS

We have developed the procedures thus far in this chapter assuming that sufficient resources are available to carry out inventory policy. This is not always a realistic assumption. However, given the desired customer service level and certain other policy considerations, it is possible to calculate the desired inventory level and then to develop working rules to maintain inventory at the proper levels provided:

- Available space.
- Sufficient product.
- Other required resources are available.

If the required resources are not available, the problem of allocation of the scarce resources must be solved. Since this can require complex analysis, a rule to follow is to separate the allocation considerations from the other inventory areas of concern. The first step is to plan inventory assuming unlimited available resources; then tackle the adjustments required because of the shortfall. This assumes, of course, that there are not too many allocation problems to consider.

Problems in allocation arise most frequently when there is a shortage of

- capital
- product
- space

Looking into the problem of space, let us consider a plan to open a new distribution warehouse to service the Dallas–Ft. Worth area. The appropriate inventory levels, based on projected sales for the area and the desired service policy, are given to the facilities engineer. Allowing for the standard aisle and staging areas, 60,000 square feet is required. Next, suppose that the only facility presently available with the required rail connections has only 40,000 square feet and instructions are given to "make do." How can inventory be cut back?

First, the service policy of the warehouse should be reexamined to consider priorities with respect to products and customers. To reduce inventory levels in proportion to the reduction in allowed floor space is not the best solution.

Exhibit 7-11 illustrates a customer priority analysis. The company has a temporary warehouse space shortage. This analysis is carried out for 22 customer groups and 16 product groups. For ease of illustration, only 3 customer groups and 3 product groups are represented in Exhibit 7-11. The objective of the analysis is to start with customer service levels and to determine product service levels.

The analysis utilizes a matrix of average sales. The average sales per month of product group A to customer group I, for example, is 2000 units (see Exhibit 7-11). The average monthly sales of product group A to customer group II is 400 with no sales to customer group III. Different service levels have been tried for the product groups. The objective is to get the product service levels (in Exhibit 7-11) low enough to satisfy the space limitations and to do it in such a way that customer group I would have the best service and customer group III a lower but still acceptable level of service.

As an example, if inventory were set to give service at a 95% level for product group A, 90% for product group B, and 80% for group C, the average service level for group I would be 93% while that for customer groups II and III would be 91% and 83%, respectively. The analysis was carried out on a trial and error basis. More advanced techniques are theoretically applicable to this problem but in view of the subjectivity underlying the customer service requirements it would be difficult to justify their use.

A second approach to space shortage is to base the cutback on item priorities rather than customer priorities. This might be the preferred approach if there are substantial differences in the product margin of the

EXHIBIT 7-11   DETERMINING CUSTOMER SERVICE FROM PRODUCT SERVICE

Average Sales Per Month (in units)				
Product Group Customer Group	A	B	C	Output: customer service level
I	2,000	400	200	$\longrightarrow$ C_1
II	400	800	100	$\longrightarrow$ C_2
III	0	100	200	$\longrightarrow$ C_3
	$\uparrow$	$\uparrow$	$\uparrow$	
Input: product service level	P_1	P_2	P_3	

$$P_1 = 95\% \quad C_1 = \frac{2,000\,P_1 + 400\,P_2 + 200\,P_3}{2,600} = 93\%$$

$$P_2 = 90\% \quad C_2 = \frac{400\,P_1 + 300\,P_2 + 100\,P_3}{1,300} = 91\%$$

$$P_3 = 80\% \quad C_3 = \frac{100\,P_2 + 200\,P_3}{300} = 83\%$$

different items. If certain items are profitable on a direct cost basis but losers on full costing, discontinuance could be considered. Items purchased for resale might be given lower priority over manufactured items. Resale items could be shipped directly to the customer rather than to the warehouse. It seems reasonable to tie service level of the items to the profit margin that the item yields the company.

The approach to inventory allocation resulting from capital shortage is much like the approach taken to correct space shortage. The main difference is that items would be measured in dollar value rather than in the square feet that they occupy. The analysis in Exhibit 7-11 could illustrate this. The difference would be that P's would be reduced until the average inventory in dollars was below the required ceiling. This presumes that the dollar reduction is required for proper evaluation of capital needs.

CHAPTER 8

FORECASTING
INVENTORY REQUIREMENTS

The business world consists of determinists and probabilists. Determinists believe that natural phenomena can be predetermined. They believe that if events don't turn out as expected, either the presumption was wrong in the first place or the actual results appear incorrect because of a measurement error.

The probabilists believe that natural phenomena are governed by the laws of probability.

DETERMINISTIC LAWS VERSUS LAWS OF PROBABILITY

Phenomena governed by the laws of probability are impossible to predict precisely. If gravitation were a probabilistic phenomenon, we could not predict when a falling object would hit the ground, even with all the factors known. The time the object takes to reach the ground would be a random variable and any of a number of slightly different times would be possible. Although prediction of the fall time of an object may be "deterministic," some natural phenomena are clearly probabilistic.

Exhibit 8-1 illustrates a natural phenomenon that follows a probabilistic law. In their famous experiment, Rutherford, Chadwick, and Ellis[*] measured the number of α particles given off by a radioactive substance. A Geiger counter was set up to count the number of particles emitted during 7.5 second intervals. During some time intervals no particles were emitted; during others, one particle; in others, two; and so forth. In all, emission counts were taken for 2608 intervals.

[*] Rutherford, Chadwick, and Ellis: *Radiations from Radioactive Substances,* Cambridge, 1920.

EXHIBIT 8-1   RADIOACTIVE EMISSION: A PROBABILISTIC PHENOMENON

EXPERIMENT: During 7.5 second time intervals, count the number of α particles given off by a radioactive substance.

Count	Number of Time Intervals with Given Count	
0	57	
1	203	Total time intervals: 2,608
2	383	Total particles counted: 10,094
3	525	Average number of particles
4	532	per interval: 3.870
5	408	
6	273	
7	139	
8	45	
9	27	
10 or more	16	

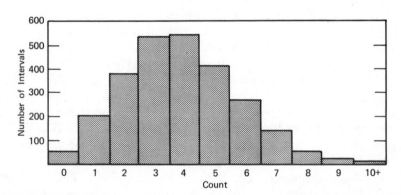

Exhibit 8-1 summarizes the results statistically and graphically. Of the 2608 time intervals, 57 had no emissions at all, 203 had one particle, and so forth. If the radioactive emission were a deterministic phenomenon, then the same number of particles would be emitted during each 7.5 second time period—say, four particles. Then we could forecast this number of every interval.

Although this experiment did not follow a deterministic profile, it did follow a probabilistic pattern. The number of emissions in a given time interval is a random variable following the Poisson probability law. This law does not enable us to predict the exact number of emissions in the next 7.5 second interval but it does enable us to make probability projections. Probability projections are usually qualified, such as, "the chances are 1 in 5 that the number of emissions will be less than 10." We can never be more definite than this.

Business Applications

The radioactive emission example illustrates the probabilistic pattern; we cannot predict precisely the number of particles emitted during each interval. Trillions of atomic particles in the material were in random motion and not in precisely the same state at the beginning of each time period. Therefore, a random element was introduced to the number of emissions. In business such randomness can be expected because many factors affecting business are continually changing.

Although many natural phenomena fall in the category of deterministic (predicting dates and times of eclipses, for example), business data generally fall in the category of probabilistic because of many factors that are random. Exhibit 8-2 illustrates this statistically and graphically for 12-ounce cans of Cola sold at several supermarket outlets. This item was selected because it exhibits stable sales history and is sold in quantities providing ample statistics for study. During the test period represented by Exhibit 8-2 no promotions were conducted either for the Cola or for competing products; there were no price or packagnig changes. The demand pattern did not indicate any pronounced seasonal effect on sales.

Although the underlying factors that would affect demand are stable, there are variations. Undoubtedly these are caused by random purchase decisions. This randomness represents the background arguments raised by the probabilists. If the purchase variations could be identified and the impact readily measured, this would lend support to the determinists' view. If it is difficult to identify and measure the variations, the determinist view is weakened, and the probabilist view prevails. Thus the probabilist view may prevail because of the nature of the phenomenon (e.g., radioactive emissions), or because of limitations in our ability to understand and measure.

Exhibit 8-3 presents statistically and graphically the demand data for another product—10" white paper plates used for outdoor picnics. Although this product had a heavy seasonal demand because the consumer outlets stocked heavily in anticipation of filling summer needs, the histogram in Exhibit 8-3 is not intended to reflect seasonal patterns. Its purpose is to show the ranges of sales within certain parameters. The first range, for example, is 0 to 25 cases. Since 4 months had sales of 25 or fewer cases, the histogram shows 4 as the number of months' inventory for this range of sales. Of the 60 sales figures, 40 fall between 25 to 100 cases—shown by the three highest bars.

EXHIBIT 8-2   DAILY SALES OF COLA (12-OUNCE CANS) SUPERMARKET ROUTES

Day/Cases Sold

1/36	11/23	21/33	31/74
2/41	12/39	22/66	32/18
3/60	13/26	23/46	33/22
4/66	14/19	24/12	34/6
5/78	15/22	25/32	35/49
6/27	16/88	26/75	36/28
7/17	17/47	27/8	37/37
8/29	18/23	28/35	38/44
9/27	19/24	29/60	39/15
10/28	20/36	30/25	40/16

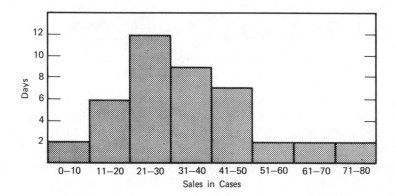

Let's scan the histogram for the first time. Is the variability in the data due to random fluctuations inherent in the sales, or do deterministic elements explain some of the variability? Since, as noted, there is a marked seasonality of the sales, the variability is not completely random, but is related to the month of sale.

This relationship is clear when the data is arranged by month as in Exhibit 8-4. The pattern reflects light sales in January and February which pick up in March. Sales become heavy in April, May, and June. Sales taper off in July and August and are light in September and the months following.

The second table shown in Exhibit 8-4 shows each month's sales as a percentage of total sales for the year. The average percentages for each month are shown at the bottom of each column. We can use these average percentages to adjust the data in Exhibit 8-4 to remove the seasonal effect,

EXHIBIT 8-3 PAPER PLATE MONTHLY SALES (NO SEASONAL DISTINCTION)

81	35	90	58	231	36	25	35	80	165
72	106	85	25	92	191	36	54	121	32
126	179	42	54	40	164	113	51	222	39
242	63	57	71	59	54	94	79	54	38
78	12	31	212	43	40	130	209	41	86
87	41	120	27	28	25	86	45	190	92

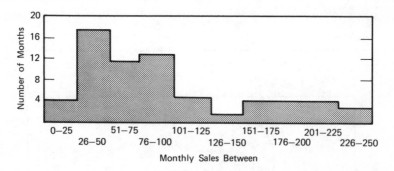

as presented in Exhibit 8-5. The adjusted sales for January of year 1 is 85 cases. This means that sales for the month project into an annual average rate of 85 cases per month when the seasonal factor is considered. In this manner the variability due to the seasonal effect is adjusted out of the data. Exhibit 8-5, then, reflects what the sales would be if the seasonal buying were leveled out. Clearly, this results in less variability in the data.

The histogram at the bottom of Exhibit 8-5 plots the seasonally adjusted data. Compare it to the histogram of the original data given in Exhibit 8-3. The adjusted data presents a much tighter sales pattern. Now, 56 of the 60 monthly sales figures are in the three center ranges, 51–75, 76–100, and 101–125. There is much less variability and consequently the data lends itself to more accurate forecasting. In this case the variability in the original data presented in Exhibit 8-3 is not due entirely to random fluctuations inherent in the business.

The next question relates to Exhibit 8-5. The figures still show a sizable range—42 to 144. Is this variability due to random fluctuations or some deterministic factor? And, if there is a deterministic explanation, is it worth the effort to find and measure the relationship?

In this case, another factor could easily be integrated into an explanation of the sales fluctuations—the business cycle. Sales were unusually low in year 1, a recession year, and picked up steadily after that until year 5.

EXHIBIT 8-4 PAPER PLATE MONTHLY SALES BY MONTH (IN CASES)

Year	Jan.	Feb.	Mar.	Apr.	May	June	July	Aug.	Sept.	Oct.	Nov.	Dec.
1	40	35	87	121	90	130	86	58	38	12	41	54
2	27	28	80	106	165	126	85	86	39	25	32	41
3	43	45	92	231	242	179	113	92	42	25	35	54
4	59	71	120	191	164	190	94	81	54	36	57	79
5	31	36	78	212	222	209	72	63	40	25	54	51

PAPER PLATE SALES
PERCENTAGE OF ANNUAL TOTAL BY MONTH

Year	Jan.	Feb.	Mar.	Apr.	May	June	July	Aug.	Sept.	Oct.	Nov.	Dec.	Total
1	5.1%	4.4%	11.0%	15.3%	11.4%	16.3%	10.9%	7.3%	4.8%	1.5%	5.2%	6.8%	100%
2	3.2	3.3	9.5	12.6	19.7	15.1	10.1	10.2	4.6	3.0	3.8	4.9	100
3	3.6	3.8	7.7	19.4	20.3	15.0	9.5	7.7	3.5	2.1	2.9	4.5	100
4	4.9	5.9	10.0	16.0	13.7	15.9	7.9	6.8	4.5	3.0	4.8	6.6	100
5	2.8%	3.3%	7.1%	19.4%	20.3%	19.1%	6.6%	5.8%	3.7%	2.3%	4.9%	4.7%	100
Average Percentage	3.9%	4.1%	9.1%	16.5%	17.1%	16.3%	9.0%	7.6%	4.2%	2.4%	4.3%	5.5%	100%

**EXHIBIT 8-5   PAPER PLATE MONTHLY SALES ADJUSTED
FOR SEASONAL EFFECT**

Year	Jan.	Feb.	Mar.	Apr.	May	June	July	Aug.	Sept.	Oct.	Nov.	Dec.
1	85	71	80	61	44	57	80	64	75	42	79	82
2	58	57	73	54	80	55	79	94	77	87	62	62
3	92	91	84	117	118	78	105	101	83	87	68	82
4	126	144	110	96	80	83	87	89	107	125	110	120
5	66	73	71	107	108	91	67	69	79	87	105	77

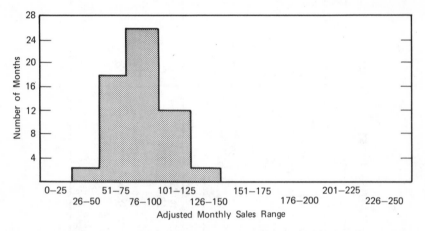

By adjusting for the business cycle, we reduce even further the variability in the sales data. Again, "is the remaining variability random or dependent on other deterministic factors?" If it is random, then no more can be done. The forecast would be prepared by estimating next year's total sales based on the general economy and spreading the annual estimate to the months using the adjusting percentage factors at the bottom of Exhibit 8-4. Any difference between this forecast and actual results would be random and could not be foreseen.

There might be other factors, however. If the geographic area serviced by the warehouse is changed, or alternative markets are developed—say sales to institutions with only minor seasonal fluctuations—then these factors would change the sales pattern. As a rule, a factor important enough to materially affect the sales pattern can be seen, be it competitor action, technological innovation, shift in customer buying habits, legislative constraints, or factors that are directly controllable. The problem is usually one of measurement. What, for example, is the effect of the factor and what degree of counteraction is appropriate?

As noted, the business cycle and seasonal patterns are major factors affecting the sales of the paper plates. The question of whether to proceed further is treated as a practical problem. Even if there are other factors, would inventory performance be improved by integrating these factors into the forecasting procedures?

Let's look at pricing, for example. Competitive prices are known to affect sales of the paper plates but knowledge of competitive discounted prices has not always been available in time. Further, as general policy the company meets competing prices so that any competitive advantage gained by a discount is soon neutralized. The forecast has been analyzed to determine the effect of improved accuracy of inventory accountability. Clearly, the more accurate the forecast, the more closely production and inventories can be tailored to the actual demand. However, the study indicates that the potential for inventory reduction, as a result of an improved forecast, is only 5%, and that improvement appears to be difficult to attain. Thus the remaining variability is treated as random.

Exhibit 8-6 presents data measuring the lead time for delivery to a warehouse. The lead time is in days and is counted from the day the order requisition is completed until the day the product is checked in at the receiving location. The warehouse in this instance is in San Francisco and the shipping plant is in Wisconsin. All shipments are by rail, except for the shipment on order #4 in December. Because the warehouse operates 7 days a week and has excellent unloading facilities, cars are unloaded almost immediately upon arrival. The loading at the plant is well run with sizable inventories maintained there, so that orders are processed promptly. The variability in lead times is due largely to the railroad—either delays in transit or delays in making cars available.

Lead time is important in inventory planning. Warehouse stocks are generally set to cover sales during the lead time period plus a suitable safety stock. Some software packages used for inventory control assume that lead time is a constant. A mere glance at Exhibit 8-6 shows how erroneous this assumption is. If this software package were actually adopted, what lead time would be built into it? Forty days would cover all items shown on Exhibit 8-6 but would require an excessively high inventory. Twenty days would be more reasonable but there would be trouble with 17 of the 46 shipments (excepting the item with the 4-day lead time which was shipped by air freight). If inventory policy is not clearly defined and proper controls set up, the only alternative is to play it by ear. If the variability in lead times is thought to be caused by some deterministic factors, then one could analyze those factors and use them to decide when the lead time would be 14 days, 21 days, 26 days, and so forth.

Rail performance was analyzed for possible seasonal variations in lead

EXHIBIT 8-6 LEAD TIMES FOR SHIPMENTS TO WAREHOUSE

Order Number	Month Ordered											
	Jan.	Feb.	Mar.	Apr.	May	June	July	Aug.	Sept.	Oct.	Nov.	Dec.
1	12	22	16	30	24	39	14	16	14	18	18	17
2	20	19	15	31	21	28	20	12	20	11		20
3	12	14	14	18	16	38		14	20	20		18
4	14	22	15	26	21			22				4
5			32	20	22							20
6				29	21							28

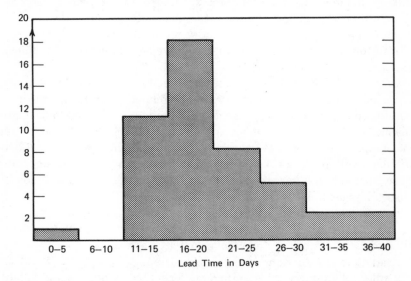

Lead Time in Days

time. The three long lead times shown in June are a clue to the difficulty: the rail cars were in high demand in the farming communities.

The possibility that one railroad was more consistent than another was also investigated because consistency in lead times is more important than shorter lead times with less consistency. Using a railroad that consistently delivers in 21 days to a certain point would permit lower inventories than using a railroad that had variations running between 14 and 28 days. The results of this analysis did not provide a clear enough basis for projecting the rail lead times so this was considered to be essentially random.

The basic interpretation of inventory as a buffer between two points suggests that we need to project two quantities in order to determine what the inventory level should be. These two quantities relate to an input rate and an output rate. The output, or demand, for finished goods in-

EXHIBIT 8-7   YIELDS FROM A BATCH CHEMICAL PROCESS

		Batch Numbers		
1–5	6–10	11–15	16–20	21–25
115	99	81	90	100
128	67	103	135	70
99	133	90	80	102
63	92	81	92	69
144	103	45	77	83

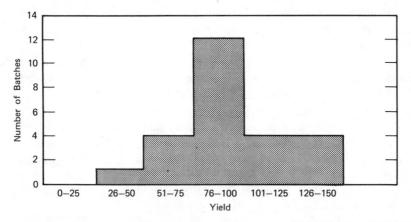

ventories is controlled by factors external to the company maintaining the inventory.

Demand is thus the subject of considerable attention in forecasting. The input into inventory raises similar questions. In the case of the distributor or retailer, the input may be variable because of fluctuations in lead times as discussed previously. In the case of the producer, the input may also be variable even though the process is under his control. This is especially true of process industries such as the chemical industry.

Exhibit 8-7, for example, shows a series of yields from a batch chemical process. The largest batch of 144 is more than three times as large as the smallest batch of 45. The daily yield is added to inventory and becomes material input for another process. Even though requirements are determined several days in advance so that outflow could be known exactly, the variability in the production process necessitates inventorying. Since the process cannot be controlled precisely, the yield could be insufficient for the next production step. To assure continuity of plant operation, it is necessary to maintain an inventory to make up the difference between an unusually low yield and the requirement for the next production step. If the process yield could be maintained at a nearly constant rate, the inventory would not be needed.

The variability of the process yield is depicted in the histogram in Exhibit 8-7. Ranges of yield are marked along the horizontal axis. The number of batches with yields within various ranges are shown vertically. Twelve of the 25 yields are in the range of 76–100.

Forecasting the yield of a process such as this is conceptually different from forecasting the sales of paper plates. The process is controlled by the company while the sales of paper plates, to a large extent, are not. Forecasting, in the case of the chemical process, means finding out the effect of certain factors in the process and then using these factors to regulate the output. The factors referred to are temperature, pressure, process time, and catalysts.

In the determinist's view, variations in yields are due to variations in these factors and that by measuring the relationships one could regulate the yield. The probabilist thinks the yield variations are built into the nature of the process and are therefore unavoidable.

A middle-of-the-road approach assumes that some variability can be explained by the temperature, pressure, and other factors, but some variability is completely random. In this case, the determinist-probabilist question is best left to the chemical engineer. As businessmen, we want to be practical. If an engineeer has an answer it should be used. Otherwise, it is best to treat the variability as random.

PROBABILITY FORECASTS

The data on production, sales, and lead times discussed thus far show much variability which is typical of data used in inventory control. Rarely can we know in advance the precise inventory demand or time of product delivery. As discussed, if variability is inherent in the operation, nothing can be done about it. We have covered the possibility of determining factors that explain this variability. However, the examples in the previous section do not explain all the variability. This also is typical of the data encountered in inventory control. For example it is either inherently impossible to determine or it requires too much effort to determine demand lead times precisely.

Management, in using forecasts, must understand that uncertainty is based on some randomness. Most executives today were educated in deterministic sciences. Without realizing it, they are determinists and believe that with enough effort and thought, it is possible, for example, to forecast exact sales of paper plates for next month. This is unfortunate because (1) the wrong method of forecasting will be used and (2) any difference between the forecast and the actual results will be interpreted as an error.

Let's relate this to the earlier example of radioactive disintegration, clearly a probabilistic phenomenon. What is the projected count in the next 7.5-second period? Physicists tell us that it is impossible to know at the start of the period. It could be 0, 1, 2, 3, 4, 5, 6, or more. If 4 is picked—a good guess—the chances of being right are about one in five; if 7 is picked the probabilities of being correct are about one in twenty. Any answer would most likely be incorrect.

Coming up with a specific number is the wrong way to forecast most business phenomena. The random element is usually present, meaning that a probability forecast is appropriate, which suggests a distribution, not a specific number. The distribution recognizes that a number of different things can happen and it determines the probability or chance of each one occurring.

Exhibit 8-8 shows several distributions. The first is associated with rolling one die. Any number from 1 to 6 can come up, and all are equally probable. Thus the chance of rolling a particular number is 1 in 6, or 16 2/3%. If both dice are rolled, the total could be any number from 2 to 12. In this case, the chances are not the same. Of the 36 possible permutations (6×6), a 2 could only be obtained by rolling a one on each of the dice. The odds are 1 in 36, or 2.8%. A 3, however, could be rolled in two different ways: 1 and 2 or 2 and 1. The odds are then 2 in 36, or 5.6%.

A correct forecast of the outcome of rolling both dice is shown in Exhibit 8-8. A table taken from the standard normal distribution is also shown. The outcome is stated in ranges above and below zero while the probability column shows the chances that the various throws will fall within each range. The table shows a 19.2% chance of an outcome between 0 and 1/2, while only a 2.2% chance that it will be greater than 2.

This is the probability forecast. Occasionally the results are presented as a tabled distribution. More often the forecast is presented as a specified number together with a confidence limit or margin of error. The number is the average or expected value of the distribution. The confidence limit or margin of error is a measure of the variability of the possible outcomes. These two characteristics—the average or best estimate and a measure of the variability—provide most of what we need to know about distribution for inventory purposes. When the distribution is presented in this manner, watch out for misinterpretation by deterministic-minded executives. They are predisposed to see the best estimate, not the confidence limits.

EXHIBIT 8-8 DISTRIBUTIONS

Possible Outcomes	Probability	Outcome Ranges	Probability
1 Die		Standard Normal	
1	16 2/3%	less than —2	2.2%
2	16 2/3	—2 : —1½	4.4
3	16 2/3	—1½ : —1	9.2
4	16 2/3	—1 : — ½	15.0
5	16 2/3	— ½ : 0	19.2
6	16 2/3	0 : ½	19.2%
	100.0%	½ : 1	15.0
		1 : 1½	9.2
2 Dice		1½ : 2	4.4
2	2.8%	greater than 2	2.2
3	5.6		100.0%
4	8.3		
5	11.1		
6	13.9		
7	16.6		
8	13.9		
9	11.1		
10	8.3		
11	5.6		
12	2.8		
	100.0%		

Exhibit 8-9 presents the results of a forecast of profits. This was prepared for a lawsuit claiming damages for business interruption. A statistical projection method was employed based on the historical profit and loss accounts of the plaintiff. Damages were claimed in the amount of the projected profit. The plaintiff had projected only the average estimate which showed a profit of several thousand dollars.

The dotted line in Exhibit 8-9 represents the average estimate. The other two lines were added by the defendant and represent 90% confidence limits. That means that according to the statistical projection the chances are 9 out of 10 that profits will be somewhere between the two confidence lines.

This interpretation of confidence limits is important since in this suit the burden of proof was on the plaintiff. As the projection is extended farther into the future, the lower confidence limit falls away from the projection, indicating increasing uncertainty in the projection. A fair settlement should take into account this increasing uncertainty. Eventually the

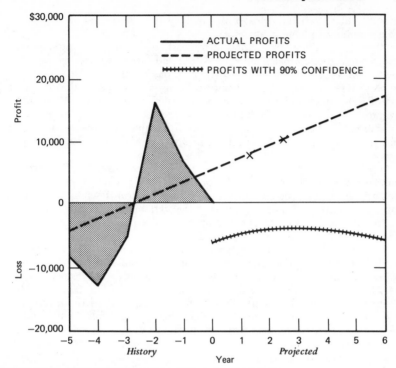

EXHIBIT 8-9 CONFIDENCE LIMIT FOR A PROJECTION

lower confidence line in this exhibit lies so far below the axis, that it is not reasonably certain that the company will be making any money.

It was still correct to say that according to the statistical evidence the plaintiff presented the best estimate. However, the data used for the projection was so skimpy that little confidence could be placed in the "best" estimate. The moral is the same for most business projections used in inventory control. Upside risk is not the same as downside risk. The best estimate should be accompanied by some measure of confidence so that management can assess the risk involved in basing operations on the forecast.

No Escape from Forecasts

Inventory was reviewed at the assembly plant of a manufacturer of business machines (described in another chapter). Much of the interest in the review centers on the work-in-process inventory of parts and subassemblies, many of which are common to a line of products. Company policy is to maintain only a small finished (totally assembled) goods inventory and to satisfy customer demand by the rapid final assembly of subassemblies available in inventory.

When asked about his method of forecast, the manager of production scheduling responds that none is used. The industrial engineering department has tried to develop a forecast which has never been used because its projections are off. The inventory rules used to schedule the production of the subassemblies are order-point/order-quantity rules. When the inventory level falls to a certain point, a work order is issued to prepare a number of subassemblies equal to the order quantity. The work order calls for completion of subassemblies in 2 weeks; this timetable is almost always met.

An item in the subassembly category is a feed arm assembly. The order point for this is 400 and the order quantity, 300. Let us suppose that a forecast has been prepared to project usage of arm assemblies of 400 units per month. Suppose further that the variability in usage has been measured, and in order to satisfy company service policy a safety stock of 300 units for 7 month's time is required.

Since the objective of the work-in-process inventory is to provide needed units during the assembly lead time of 2 weeks, the inventory requirements are about equal to 2 weeks' usage plus safety stock for 2 weeks. This comes out to 200 + 200 = 400 units. (The 300 monthly safety stock adjusts to about 200 units for 2 weeks.) Thus the inventory rule is to prepare a work order when the inventory level falls to 400 units. That is precisely what was being done. In short, the procedure being followed—with no forecast—is equivalent to a forecast of 400 units per month for the feed arm assembly.

This illustrates that "no forecast" is really equivalent to some forecast because some type of forecast is inherently built into the operating strategy. It is not a question of to forecast or not to forecast; the question is, Will a formal quantitative approach yield better results than forecasting by default?

The default forecast in the case of the feed arm assembly is 400 units. Since average monthly usage is only 250, the work-in-process inventory is too high. This is true of many of the items in inventory, with the result that millions of dollars are needlessly tied up in inventory.

BUSINESS PROPERTIES OF FORECASTS

We have seen that inventory control relies heavily on either formal forecasts, using mathematical methods, or default forecasts inherent in the procedures used in purchasing, or production control. The latter are usually based on "intuition" or "feel." Experience has confirmed that controlling inventories through subjective methods is not reliable.

The most common practice with these subjective methods is to use past averages instead of mathematical probabilities. By the very nature of past averages, the data will not be up-to-date. It will not reflect new trends that have crept in.

Suppose that we want to introduce more effective quantitative methods. What is the first step? Since some forecasting technology requires use of mathematics that call for years of graduate study, it would be unreasonable to expect the manager responsible for inventories to become proficient in math. This area must be treated through the black box—with a staff technician assigned to construct the formulas that are contained in the box. The manager responsible for the forecast provides the specialist with the forecasting specifications. The resulting forecast is used by him, not the technician. The manager should be judged on how well the forecast is used; the technician on how well the black box conforms to specifications.

> By way of illustration, let us consider a forecast prepared for an oil drilling company to cover the requirements of such items as tubing, joints, and motors, equipment used in drilling and in maintaining wells. Smaller items are purchased locally and are the responsibility of local personnel. For items forecasted on a corporate basis, the forecast must come up with quantities to be purchased, the delivery points, and schedule for delivery.

Importance of Being Specific

A common error in developing forecasts is to let the specialist prepare a forecast without being given further instructions. Such open-ended instructions are too vague and invite trouble.

> How does the specialist know that an item purchased last year is no longer needed? How does he know that another item is being replaced by a technological improvement next month? How does he know that XB 10173 and XC 10173 are really the same item purchased from different vendors? How does he know that AT 20253 and LG 71112 are different items but interchangeable for the rigs near Tulsa? Does he know that corporate purchasing orders tools for the Midland fields even though the records are maintained at Midland rather than at corporate headquarters? The specialist may not know that Houston's engineering department arranges purchases for the refinery parts even though the paperwork flows through corporate purchasing. These are some of the pitfalls in "letting George do it." To avoid problems, items to be forecast should be listed by those best qualified to provide the answers.

In addition to defining the items to be included in the forecast, the list should also show the units of measure and the stockkeeping units (SKUs).

An SKU is a particular item at a particular location. Three-inch copper tubing used at Midland would be the same item as 3-inch copper tubing used at Hobbs, but they would be different SKUs.

Most items have several different units of measure. Paint, for example, is measured in cans, cases, or gallons. Tubing is measured in number of sections, linear meters, or linear feet. Since purchasing personnel will be working with the forecast, the units used in the forecast should be familiar to the purchasing department. It is the responsibility of purchasing management to specify these units to the forecasting specialist.

Such specifications are used in the output reports. The specialist can select several units of measure, for different purposes, provided that conversion factors are developed. SKU specification is defined by the purchasing department, not by the specialist. For nationally purchased items to be delivered directly to the fields and inventoried there, the vendor must be told the quantity to ship to each location. Such items should be forecast by SKU.

The vendor carries in inventory the more standard items that may be supplied to different oil companies working the same field. Because of competition among the suppliers, vendors often maintain inventories near the field. Items purchased from different vendors are planned according to total need by field regardless of the vendor. The breakdown by source is based on an allocation derived through use of a formula. For these items, the forecast should be prepared by aggregating all the SKUs for like items purchased from different vendors.

Since the requirement for this accumulation is based on purchasing rather than technical considerations, the decision should be made by the purchasing department and given to the specialist as part of the forecast specifications.

After the items and SKUs to be forecast are listed, along with the units of measure, the next step is to analyze in greater depth how the forecast will be used. Forecast timing is an important business consideration and should be included in the forecast specifications.

Timing Considerations

Three aspects of timing must be considered:

1. Units of time: weeks, months, quarters, and so forth.
2. Forecast horizon: 6 months out, 12 months, and so forth.
3. Frequency of forecast update: monthly, quarterly, semi-annually.

The major items handled by corporate purchasing at the oil company are covered by quarterly orders which include a monthly breakdown of requirements which the company is allowed to change during the quarter up to certain limits. Lead times vary considerably from item to item. Some items are ordered 3 or more quarters in advance. In effect, the company is placing orders on a monthly basis but reserving some flexibility to modify the orders for items with long lead times.

If forecasts using either weekly or monthly units of time would satisfy purchasing's requirements, the specifications should indicate either one as being acceptable. The final decision, within the specification constraints, is thus based on systems considerations. If monthly forecasts are to be prepared, purchasing should specify whether calendar months are required or whether a combination of 4, 4 and 5 weeks for each quarter would be used.

The forecast horizon depends on the vendor lead time and varies from one item to another. The specification should, therefore, be prepared in a manner that gives the minimum horizon for each item, and the maximum horizon likely to be needed now or in the future.

A reasonable approach would be to divide the items into product classes and assign a forecast horizon to each class: for example, 6 months for paints, and 18 months for tubing. The specialist can select horizons in preparing the forecast subject to the constraints that the forecast for paints be prepared at least 6 months out, and that the system contain the flexibility to expand that horizon up to the maximum.

Frequency of Forecasting

The third aspect of timing, the frequency of updating the forecast, is primarily a technical problem, although purchasing management can provide helpful suggestions. It would be ideal if all businesses could prepare forecasts only once a year. However, because customers and the economy are unpredictable, this would be hazardous. While some businesses can forecast quarterly and update monthly, probably most businesses should be prepared at the outset to reforecast monthly and update weekly. Once confident of this procedure, the company could forecast and update less frequently. In establishing the specifications for frequency of forecasting and updating, the company must carefully consider a policy that assures reasonable accuracy without "flying blind."

Margin of Error

Another area that warrants careful consideration in establishing forecast specifications is the margin of error. Exhibit 8-10 illustrates upside and downside errors. Error is an unfortunate word to use in describing the difference between the forecast and the actual because of the pejorative connotations. Upside and downside deviation would be better. However, deferring to convention, we use the term "error."

The data in the "Forecast" column of Exhibit 8-10 is the forecasted usage in units. The forecast was prepared using monthly time periods with a 1 year horizon. The forecast was updated monthly from February through June, then left fixed until the following February (note the highly seasonal usage). The forecast shown in Exhibit 8-10 was prepared during April, using data through the end of March.

EXHIBIT 8-10 FORECAST ERRORS

Month	Forecast	Actual	Upside Error	Downside Error
May	270	208	62	
June	184	167	17	
July	96	120		24
Aug.	88	101		13
Sept.	45	36	9	
Oct.	25	19	6	
Nov.	24	40		16
Dec.	60	63		3
Jan.	56	54	2	
Feb.	57	55	2	
Mar.	96	73	23	
Apr.	209	198	11	

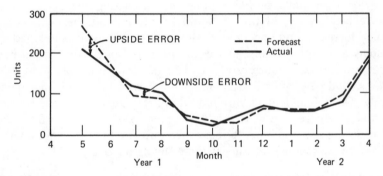

When the forecast is too high, an upside error occurs; when it is too low, a downside error occurs. The error is the difference between the forecast and the actual amount. For example, the usage forecasted for June was 184 units. Since 167 units were actually used, the forecast was too high, resulting in an upside error of 184 − 167 units, or 17 units. In July, however, the forecasted usage of 96 was lower than the actual usage of 120, giving rise to a downside error of 24.

In the case of a downside error, where usage exceeds estimates, the company risks a stockout. This could temporarily halt operations while the needed items are flown in from the vendor or from another location. Such out-of-stock situations could be expensive to the company. An over-estimate, on the other hand, would result in extra inventory in the field. If the item is in continual use, the excess can be adjusted in ensuing months. However, if the item usage is cyclical or if it is subject to obsolescence, the company risks becoming overstocked, with the resulting reduction in return on investment.

In dealing with the margin of error, two alternatives are available:

Method 1

The precision requirement of the forecast is specified in terms of allowable error, say plus or minus 10%. The specification would call for the forecast to be within this range with, say 95% confidence. Since best estimate forecasts tend to have symmetrical upside and downside errors, the specialist can concentrate on developing an estimate with enough of the variation accounted for to satisfy the precision requirement.

In a best estimate forecast there is about a 50% chance that it will be too large and a 50% chance that it will be too small. These risks of having too little or too much inventory are compensated for through use of safety stock allowances. If the downside error is costly and the upside error less so, then a best estimate forecast can be used with ample safety stock carried over and above the estimated usage.

Method 2

The forecast precision requirement could be stated in terms of an asymmetrical requirement. It might state, for example, that in 99 occurrences out of 100, the forecast must be greater than actual less 5%, but not greater than actual plus 15%. It pays off to specify the forecast accuracy before development because it puts the forecast critics on notice that errors must be expected—and that such errors do not mean that the forecast is valueless.

Forecast specifications insure that when the forecast is developed it will fit the needs of the business. Operating personnel should use such a forecast when its specifications meet their needs. Although this point seems self-evident, it is frequently overlooked in practice.

For example, a manufacturer of high quality brushes desires a demand forecast to use in scheduling production. The project is assigned to the data processing department without forecast specifications. The result is a monthly forecast by product group rather than by items. Obviously, the items that make up products need to be scheduled into production. The data processing department favors projections by product group because such forecasts are more accurate. Although this is true, it does not help management's production scheduling needs.

The elements to consider in developing the forecast are summarized in the following checklist:

1. Items to be forecast.
2. Levels of aggregation: SKU location, products, product groups, substitution items, customer groups, sales division groups, and so forth.
3. Units of measure.
4. Unit time of the forecast.
5. Forecast horizon.
6. Frequency of update.
7. Cost basis for items.
8. Flexibility for item additions and deletions.
9. Data editing requirements.
10. Special situation exclusions.
11. Upside and downside error precision desired.
12. Report formating and delivery time requirements.
13. Level, trend, seasonal, and other cyclical component preparation and change detection.
14. Exception reporting requirements.

As mentioned, these should not be left to the specialist, nor should the specifications be developed through the give-and-take of consensus. The requirements of production are specific; accordingly, the specifications should be developed with these requirements in mind.

FORECAST CHARACTERISTICS

Once the specifications of the forecast have been drawn up, the design can get under way. Several characteristics of the forecast bear on how effective it is as a tool for inventory management. A manager who understands these characteristics communicates better with the specialist during the forecast design and in the period following implementation. These characteristics are:

> **The speed with which the forecast adjusts to fundamental changes in the business.** Working with inventories differs in one important respect from working with a natural phenomenon such as radioactive disintegration. The natural phenomenon remains unchanged in time while the business environment is continually changing. In all methods of forecasting the past is studied in order to estimate the future. As long as the business environment remains unchanged, the forecast is likely to be reliable. Fundamental changes such as the Oil Embargo of 1973 can throw off forecasts by a considerable amount.

Some forecasting methods provide warning signals when fundamental changes have occurred. Others can make automatic adjustments when certain changes occur. During implementation, careful testing should be made to determine the answers to questions such as: If demand for the highest volume product were to be reduced 20% tomorrow, how quickly would the forecast react? What if demand tripled?

The stability of the forecast with respect to oscillations. Few conditions are as frustrating to the inventory manager as being continually "whipsawed" by an unstable forecast. "Zigzagged" might be a more appropriate word because the actuals go up when the forecast instructs the opposite.

Exhibit 8-11 demonstrates the whipsaw effect in forecasting. The forecast is applied to estimate the monthly price of Wackenhut Corporation stock 1 month in advance. The forecast method determines first and second trends from recent history and projects this into the future. Note that when the stock price starts up, the forecast takes a while before it follows the same movement. When the forecast does go up, it overshoots and remains high while the stock price falls.

To guard against this, the company should ask the EDP specialist to demonstrate how the forecast will perform in such cases. If the forecast method can't pick the turning points (where the value changes from increasing to decreasing and vice versa), then it should be "damped" so it more nearly holds to an average value. Errors are inevitable but they should be "inside" rather than "outside" errors.

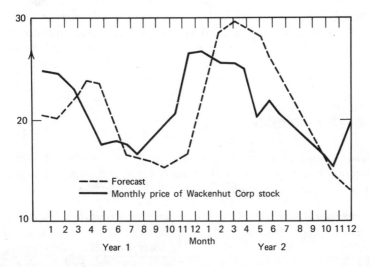

EXHIBIT 8-11   A WHIPSAW FORECAST

That is, there should be a downside error when the actual is high and an upside error when the actual is low.

The ability of the forecast method to provide accurate error measurement. Since the forecast specifications include precision, the specialist must have determined how to measure forecast error. How will actual forecast errors compare to specified margins of error? The specialist should demonstrate the expected pattern of errors when the forecast is used. A number of small errors may not be as much a problem as a few major ones. However, even worse than the random error problem is a forecast biased by unrealistic optimism.

The reasonableness of the forecast in atypical situations. Certain forecasting procedures can exhibit extreme behavior that can hurt the credibility of forecasting. A good example is a forecast based on an exponential function. Such a function may provide an excellent fit to historical data if the data reflects accelerated growth. However, if such growth has leveled off, use of the exponential function will provide results that might show some ridiculous sales forecast such as $5 trillion. Management would question the veracity of persons responsible for such a forecast.

The key is to temper forecasting procedures with a common sense evaluation of the underlying trends. If the accelerating growth of the past, such as petroleum production in the United States, has obviously passed its peak, then the exponential method of forecasting should not be used.

Certain forecasting techniques give undue weight to extreme items at the ends of the range being analyzed. It is possible that only a few of these extreme items, perhaps only 2% of the total items, could produce unacceptably large errors in the forecast. The specialist should be asked to demonstrate the magnitude of these errors when exceptional data patterns are encountered.

FORECASTING TECHNIQUES

The acceptability of the forecast with respect to these characteristics depends to a great degree on the technology employed. Several broad categories of techniques are employed in business forecasting.

Judgmental Methods. As the name implies, these methods are based on the judgment of individuals qualified to render opinions. These estimates are then refined by using committee discussion, averaging methods, or more formal group consensus methods such as the Delphi technique. Judgmental methods play an important role in inventory management, and are widely used. When properly organized and interpreted, they can prove adaptable to fundamental changes.

This type of forecasting, however, does not provide for any error measurement. Studies show that businessmen are poor at estimating how good their forecasts are, perhaps because inventory managers tend to overreact to inventory problems when making forecasts. Assurance of better forecasts, then, is conditioned upon the ability to stem the tendency to overreact.

Formula fitting forecasting methods rely on formulating a relationship between the object to be forecast (e.g., sales) and other variables and/or past values. The formula is fit to historical data and used to project values. Statistical regression and econometric models are of this nature. These methods are very inflexible and unstable with respect to fundamental changes in business conditions. They are rarely of any value in inventory management.

Time series analysis is a branch of mathematical statistics that uses patterns in historical data to project the future. Examples of such methods are exponential smoothing, moving averages, and Box-Jenkins, Wilson, and Shiskin methods. These methods are generally more flexible than other statistical methods and are widely used in connection with inventory management.

The more sophisticated types employing distribution filters adjust to fundamental changes in the business and—barring outright mistakes—all exhibit damping (leveling) behavior. They provide for measurement of error and usually also provide reasonable forecasts even in the presence of data errors. The drawback in using these is that the simpler models are slow to react to fundamental changes and provide good forecasts only in relatively stable environments and over short time horizons.

Simulation Methods. The objective simulation is to formulate a model of the operation and then to run data in one end and observe what comes out the other end. Simulation methods are rarely of value in forecasting inventory usage at the SKU level. They are usually expensive in terms of computer processing and human resource requirements. The desire of a specialist to use simulation techniques should be questioned.

The most effective forecasts employed to manage inventory are integrated forecasts that combine judgmental methods, time series, and, to a lesser degree, curve fitting methods. Volume is important when using econometric or curve fitting methods. To the extent that demand can be related to certain economic variables which serve as leading indicators, economic models can assist in inventory management. Generally, volume must be large for these methods to work.

Since most forecasts used in inventory management are at the SKU level with weekly or monthly time periods and short forecasting horizons, time series forecasting methods are more widely applicable. These methods are intended to produce good forecasts over a time horizon short enough to exclude major shifts in business conditions—typically less than 1 year. They assume that conditions in the near future will be subject to trends but otherwise much the same as in the past. To provide for exceptional factors such as 1) additions and elimination of products and major customers or 2) productive capacity changes, judgmental methods should be integrated with the time series methods.

CHAPTER 9

ASSURING CONFORMANCE
TO INVENTORY POLICY

In Chapter 3, Formulating Inventory Policy, we stress policy objectives. Inadequately defined policy leads to confusion, conflicting objectives, and poor performance.

Policy must be carefully thought out and stated in quantitative denominators such as, 95% of the line item orders will be shipped within 2 days, inventory turns will be 6 times per year, or better—and machine delays due to parts shortages will be less than 2000 hours annually. To the extent that analysis is required to determine the proper course, it is best done as part of setting policy. This approach puts analysis "up front" at the planning stage—before procedures are firmed up and personnel trained. To barge ahead, without considering the "up front" requirements, could require complete revision of procedures, administrative problems in reorganizing and retraining personnel, as well as wasted resources.

Once policy has been formulated, those responsible for planning the inventory procedures have the required knowledge of overall objectives. If the inventory system performs as well as or better than expectations, then the systems plan has fulfilled management's expectations. However, should the reverse occur—bad performance through too much inventory, excessive stockout rates, late deliveries, and so forth—then either the systems planning or operating performance is at fault.

MEASURING PERFORMANCE

The procedures relating to measuring performance are important in inventory system planning and should be distinguished from the operating procedures related directly with procurement, maintenance, and use of inventory. The latter are discussed in Chapter 7 as operating procedures, so-called because they are carried out by operating personnel. The procedures relating to measuring and reporting on the operating performance, by contrast, may involve accounting, financial, and staff personnel.

The starting point for designing performance measurement is the inventory policy. The importance of measuring performance against inventory policy cannot be overstressed. This is illustrated in the case study that follows.

The inventories in question are the manufacturer's finished goods of heavily promoted, high volume, low cost household consumer goods. Obsolescence is a serious problem with such inventories because of packaging and promotional changes—as well as minor product changes. Every year, a "new improved" version is put out, even if new and improved means only that the color is changed and the price increased.

In a company in which production is "king" and the consumers willing, the solution is relatively simple. The sales manager must move all the "old unimproved" product before they can sell the new product. However, when marketing policies reign supreme and heavy outlays are made for advertising campaigns beginning at a predetermined date, then at dawn on the first day of the campaign, the "old unimproved" is effectively obsolete. The production managers must arrange to shut off production of the old product in time. This is not to make a case for either production or marketing predominance in formulating policy relative to obsolescence. Irrespective of which policy "rules," old stocks must be worked down as quickly as possible to minimize obsolescence. This calls for careful planning.

Exhibit 9-1 shows the company's obsolete inventory buildup over a 3-year period. Even though product life cycles for the company's products

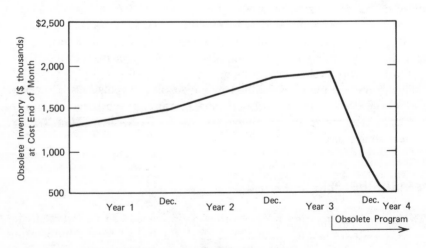

EXHIBIT 9-1 CUMULATION OF OBSOLETE INVENTORY

have been well known, the obsolete inventory has been trending upward rather than downward. The deficiency in this company is that obsolete stock has not been reported effectively. Although the "on-hand" figures for the various items have been available, there has been no attempt to discern trends, as has been done in Exhibit 9-1.

The company depicted in Exhibit 9-1 did not use the available figures effectively. The company procedure was to work down the obsolete items in its stockrooms spasmodically with a flurry of effort when time allowed. This approach was ineffective because the obsolete inventory increased further, during periods when interest wanes. The company finally solved this inventory problem by instituting an obsolete inventory program that was essentially a performance measuring program.

By implementing the obsolete inventory program the company benefited in three ways:

1. Obsolete inventory was prevented from accumulating without notice for months at a time by monitoring performance on a monthly basis.
2. Efficient procedures for selling obsolete items were provided. Monthly reports listed the obsolete inventory by location and provided this information to the sales department for disposition.
3. Standard procedures were substitutes for what had been an undirected and intermittent flurry of activity, thus reducing the management effort required to deal with the problem.

The results obtained from the program can be seen in Exhibit 9-1. The program was inaugurated in July of the year, by which time the obsolete inventory had grown to about $2,000,000 at cost. Within a period of seven months the obsolete inventory had been reduced to a level of about $500,000.

The key to the success of the program was a performance measurement report that, with appropriate modification, could be effective for many companies. The report, shown in Exhibit 9-2, was prepared monthly by computerized procedures and distributed to the field automatically. Note that the report shows the stock status history of the various items making up the obsolete inventory. One can tell at a glance the makeup of the items and whether the problem is growing worse or getting better. The report also provides selling instructions.

Item 12-100-M5, for example, includes a total of 936 cases that have been obsolete for 6 months. Of this total, 6 cases are located in the Boston warehouse, 653 in New York, and 277 in Cleveland. At the extreme right of the report, the selling instructions specify that these items are available at 40% off inventory cost.

This inventory report (for November 1) also shows items 12-100A-30Z and 24-100F-30Z in the 3-month obsolete column. When the salesman receives this report he has in a single report information he could get previously only by making lengthy phone calls and searching through inventory records.

EXHIBIT 9-2 OBSOLETE INVENTORY REPORT (FIGURES IN CASES) NOVEMBER 1, 19XX

ITEM	DATE OBS.	LOCATION	STOCK STATUS MONTHS AFTER OBSOLETE DATE						SELLING INSTRUCTIONS
			1	2	3	4	5	6	
12-100-M5	4/XX	BO	1,459	945	551	6	6	6	Available 40% off cost
		NY	1,343	233	2,594	2,115	962	653	"
		PH	4,649	2,101	160	0	0	0	"
		CL	2,181	2,378	2,121	1,669	1,424	277	"
			9,632	5,657	5,426	3,790	2,392	936	
12-100A-30Z	7/XX	NY	214	204	204				Scrap
24-100F-30Z	7/XX	BO	1,092	492	492				Special price reference sales release no. 132
		NY	2,569	2,569	2				
		PH	4,118	4,068	4,068				
		CL	875	875	575				
		CH	2,893	1	1				
			11,547	8,005	5,138				
. . .	. . .	. . .	. . .	. . .	. . .	. . .	. . .	. . .	. . .

Since the format of the inventory information in Exhibit 9-2 is somewhat unusual, an explanation is in order. An item officially declared obsolete is added to the "Obsolete Inventory Report." The inventory so declared is recorded as 1 month obsolete. At the end of the next month, the remaining part of the one month obsolete inventory becomes 2 months obsolete and is so recorded. At the end of 6 months, every effort is made to dispose of remaining items on hand. This kind of inventory history allows management to judge how fast the obsolete inventory is being worked down. If the particular product classified as "obsolete" is not selling, the selling instructions section can be altered to increase the discount or otherwise make the product more readily disposable.

If the planned disposal discount is expected to work in one location but not in another, the inventory can be transferred to the most saleable location, as was done for 12-100M5 between months 1 and 2 and again between months 2 and 3 in the example. Customers in New York were willing to make purchases at the 40% discount off cost so transfers were made to New York from Philadelphia.

Under the new procedures an item is officially classified as obsolete through an authorization form. The product manager responsible for the new replacement product is one of the signators. At the end of the month, the obsolete inventory for that period becomes his responsibility. He can set the selling terms as he sees fit within certain guidelines. Along with this, the formula for determining his bonus has been revised to encourage him to work down inventories before bringing new products on board. At the end of the 6-month period, the remaining product is automatically scrapped if no markets remain and the loss is reflected in the bonus. This bonus system motivates managers to dispose of obsolete inventory. However, the kind of control measurement available in Exhibit 9-2 is an integral part of the system. Without the report showing the current status of the obsolete items and measuring the impact of sales disposal efforts, the managers would not be able to deal intelligently with the problem.

MONITORING INVENTORIES

Monitoring inventory performance is simplified because only two things can go wrong: too little inventory or too much. The objective of effective monitoring is first to identify where and when either of these situations exists and then to trace back through the procedures to identify the factor or factors contributing to the out-of-balance condition. A limited number of factors cause the inventory imbalance.

First consider an item that is consistently in short supply. The cause is frequently traced to one of the following:

• The product is not available from the source (vendor, work station, etc.).
• Orders are not placed on a timely basis.

- Quantities ordered are too small.
- Deliveries are erratic.

The first factor refers to disruptions such as strikes, fires at supplier plants, and the like. It is questionable whether companies should routinely carry inventories to guard against such contingencies. However, special hedge inventories can be considered to guard against a known probability such as an impending vendor strike or plant move.

The second item—orders are not placed on a timely basis—is indicative of failure to attend to business. This is a common fault with manual systems when it is just impossible for the inventory controller to keep on top of several thousand items. The most widely used monitoring technique for this is the "red line" or "warning line." When inventory on hand plus on order falls below the warning level, the item is listed on a warning report. One company uses two warning lines. If inventory on hand plus on order falls below the first warning line and nothing is done, the level eventually falls below a second warning line. The item is then listed on a separate report. Although the "doubling up" of warnings seems redundant, the company finds it effective. The method triggers two actions. The level 1 warning says: "order immediately" while the level 2 warning says: "check on the inventory controller." The level 1 warning relates to daily operations whereas the level 2 warning relates to procedures.

The third problem—order amounts too small—is the most difficult to monitor. The root cause usually is changing business conditions. Balancing demand and lead times will give the proper order size for an item but last week's order size may not do this week. Further, the change may be difficult to detect. An increase in demand this month may be a permanent increase or it may be a random fluctuation. This is the one point in inventory management where mathematical methods have been most helpful. A good way to monitor order sizes is by using the appropriate statistics and playing the favorable odds.

Another area worth exploring is erratic delivery times. Erratic rather than long delivery times cause inventory problems. If a vendor has long but predictable lead times, a pipeline inventory can be set up so that inventory stocks on hand are relatively low. With erratic deliveries one can never know what action to take. One approach, and probably the most effective, is for the purchasing department to maintain a record of the number of days that orders are open before the vendor makes delivery. If there is a history of erratic delivery patterns, then the vendor should be contacted. If he cannot correct the condition, it may be possible to find another vendor who will follow more orderly patterns in making deliveries.

When companies have problems of too little inventory under the conditions described earlier, some measure of "too little" is required. Some frequently used measures are:

- Stockout rate computed as: units ordered, but not shipped, divided by units ordered.
- Stockout rate computed as: the number of order entry line items ordered but not completely shipped divided by the number of order entry line items ordered.
- Stockout rate computed as: the number of items with zero inventory at month-end divided by the number of items.
- Units backordered divided by units ordered.
- Order entry line items backordered divided by order entry line items ordered.
- Items backordered divided by items in stock.

Variations of the above can be employed. As an example, the denominator in most of the above might substitute shipments for orders.

The stockout rate (or backorder rate) should not be defined and monitored entirely by the inventory supervisors. Top level and mid-level management must assure that the calculations are correct and consistent, and even more important, that proper corrective action is taken when inventories become unbalanced. The proper corrective action cannot be left to inventory controllers. In such matters, profit margins must be considered. When some items are highly profitable and others only marginally profitable, the stockout measure should be weighted; the more profitable the item, the more strict the followup.

A more common error is to select out-of-stock measures on the basis of number of items rather than on the basis of the relative volumes. By doing this, low volume items are kept in excessive supply in order to achieve a low stockout rate while the high volume best-sellers are not given their due weighting according to the volume they represent. Items out-of-stock is a suitable measure when the sales volume of most items is about equivalent in volume.

Exhibit 9-3 illustrates a unit-based stockout measure, which does not require much effort. The clerk who maintains the inventory records fills in preprinted worksheets. The average daily sales figures in units are updated semi-annually. At the end of the month the clerk reviews the inventory records and determines the number of days out-of-stock for each applicable item. These figures are entered in the second column from the right. The days out-of-stock are then extended by the average daily sales to obtain an estimate of lost sales. Finally, the stockout rate is computed

EXHIBIT 9-3 STOCKOUT RATE—JULY

Item No.	Average Daily Sales in Units	Days Out-of-Stock	Lost Sales in Units
5165	1.2		
5170	3.0		
5171	14.6		
5172	8.1		
5200	.2	8	1.6
5205	.7	8	5.6
5230	11.5	2	23.0
5260	2.2		
5265	1.8		
5270	5.1		
.	.	.	.
.	.	.	.
.	.	.	.

Total Lost Sales: 1,672.5
Total Sales: 29,671

$$\text{Stockout Rate:} \frac{1,672.5}{29,671 + 1,672.5} = 5.3\%$$

as the quotient of lost sales divided by the sum of sales and lost sales (5.3% in Exhibit 9-3).

Since the number of items out-of-stock in a given month was rarely more than 15, the entire process required less than 2 hours a month.

The advantages of this type of calculation became obvious. The inventory supervisor soon realized that he would look worse if a high volume item ran out of stock than a low volume item. This encouraged a tendency to pay closer attention to the high sellers. Further, the supervisor realized that a 10-day stockout made him look worse than a 1-day stockout. As a result, he moved quickly to correct out-of-stock situations. This example demonstrates the advantage of changing the stockout measure from a product number item to a unit basis.

As in all reporting, "tricks of the trade" can be introduced so that an inventory controller's performance will not look too bad. As an example, one unit can be shown to be in stock when it is actually out-of-stock. In such a circumstance, cross checks will be available by checking with sales or order entry records. The sales department could be asked to report all items that were not shipped completely during the month and the sales out-of-stock list compared with the warehouse stockout report. Such cross checks, through management involvement, assure proper reporting. Such checks could be applied on either a regular or an exception basis.

It is important to monitor excessive inventories as well as insufficient inventories. This is rarely done, even in companies that prepare backorder reports. Probably one of the reasons is the uncertainty as to what is excessive. Excess inventory means inventory that is not needed to meet the objectives set by policy. Slow-moving stock need not be excessive although many persons would define it so. Some of the inventory in the highest usage items could be excess. In fact, a product could be a star performer with rapidly expanding sales and a healthy profit margin yet part of its inventory could be classified as excessive.

If one of the basic reorder systems described in Chapter 7 is used, excess can be partly defined from the reorder rules. For example, with the order-point/order-quantity (OP-OQ) system, inventory on hand and on order should not exceed the sum of the order point plus the order quantity. Allowing some margin, say 10%, for leveling out quantities provides a basis for the excess. Any inventory above the level of the order point plus order quantity plus 10% is excessive. If, typically, two orders are outstanding at the same time, then excess might more appropriately be defined as any inventory on hand above the level of the order point plus 10%. Similarly for a min-max system, inventory in excess of max plus 10% might be classified as excess. If inventory policy is set by turnover rates, then those rates can be used to define excess inventory. If the required turnover for an item is four times a year, then that translates into a 3-month stock on the average. Allowing a margin for small deviations, we could define excess as any stock above 3½ months' supply.

Excess inventory, as just defined, can arise in several ways. A common method is through overordering. Inventory supervisors frequently order in excess of the rules to provide a cushion against complaints from the sales department in the event of stockouts. It may also reduce the number of times they have to review and/or reorder the items. In the absence of an excess inventory report, who will notice?

In systems where the excess inventory is defined in part by reference to order points, maxes, order levels, and the like, if these quantities are revised inventory may become excessive. If the inventory of an item is at its max when its max is adjusted downward, some of the inventory may be reclassified as excess even though the amount in stock has not changed. This does not mean that the classification is incorrect. It only means that excess inventory can result even when everyone is following the rules.

Obsolete and damaged inventory certainly could be classified as excess. However, if proper reporting exists for these classes of inventory, it is best to leave them out of the excess report. This restricts excess to "good saleable product" and simplifies the design of special procedures to deal with the excess amounts. Another type of inventory that may be included in excess is product soon to be discontinued from stock at a certain location. It may be advantageous to subject such stock to the special attention devoted to excess inventory and to classify all the inventory of the item at the particular location, as excess.

Excess inventory should be monitored by aggregation starting at the SKU level. Excess should be calculated for each SKU and then summarized according to the responsibility for the inventory. If the inventory at a plant is the responsibility of one supervisor, then a plant excess report would be desirable. However, if the responsibility for the plant inventory is divided, say, by product line, then product line excess inventory reports would be indicated.

Exhibit 9-4 illustrates aggregation of excess inventory for the finished product inventories of a division. The report is denominated in dollars since it is part of an executive summary report. The excess portion is good product that previously sold quite well at the location represented by these figures. Now, sales have fallen off so that inventory requirements are less.

Note that the gap between total inventory and non-excess inventory narrows in the latter months. This is a result of a program to transfer some of the slow-moving items to locations where sales of these items are strong. The program was instituted as a consequence of executive review of the report. Without the report, it is unlikely that anything would have been done.

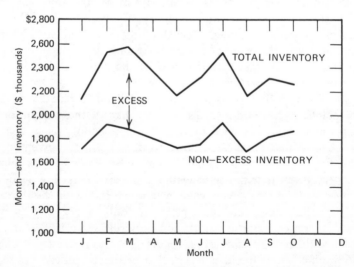

EXHIBIT 9-4   EXCESS INVENTORY REPORT FINISHED PRODUCT INVENTORIES

EMPIRICAL INVENTORY CONTROL

Anyone with an engineering or science background is familiar with control through feedback. Feedback controls are used extensively in process industries, in computer controlled manufacturing processes, and in many other types of production processes. The concept is simple and practical. A good illustration is the thermostat. If the temperature is set for 68 degrees, when room temperature drops the furnace starts automatically. If the system is tied into central air-conditioning, the temperature is controlled on the top side as well.

The following steps in feedback control can be developed from the illustration above:

1. Set a standard in measurable terms.
2. Regularly monitor activity against the standard.
3. If activity is below standard, initiate actions to raise it; if above standard, initiate actions to lower it.

Exhibit 9-5 illustrates the effect of feedback controls on a chemical process. Note that the fluctuations in temperature are not random. As the temperature falls at the beginning of the graph, the feedback control senses the drop and initiates countermeasures. The counteraction at first should be small or moderate. The feedback control continues to monitor the temperature. The countermeasures should gradually bring the slide in temperature to a halt. If it continues to drop, the reverse action may be increased.

As can be seen in Exhibit 9-5, the temperature seems to be steadying at about 120 degrees on the sixth reading. After that, it drops again. Finally, it is stabilized again. When temperatures fall below the desirable range, counteraction is increased in order to raise it.

Inventory level is maintained by feedback controls much like the temperature in the preceding illustration. A standard range is set for the desired level of inventory (as discussed in the chapters on inventory policy and asset management) and the inventory is controlled to that level. The standard range consists of an upper and lower limit. If the level rises above the upper limit, countermeasures bring the inventory down. If the inventory falls below the lower limit, similar measures increase the level.

Fifty years ago, when business was less complex and less competitive, the inventory control manager, upon discovering an unexpected increase in inventory, would try to determine whether the situation was temporary or permanent. If he discovered, for example, that the sudden drop in sales corresponded with a competitor's special promotion, he might consider

**EXHIBIT 9-5   TEMPERATURE READINGS EVERY
THREE MINUTES: CHEMICAL PROCESS**

124.5°	121.9°	106.6°	106.7°
123.4	120.4	107.1	108.3
122.6	117.3	108.1	110.4
120.9	114.2	106.6	112.3
119.8	110.2	106.1	114.5
119.8	108.6	106.4	117.0
119.9	108.1	106.3	119.6
121.4	107.6	105.5	121.8

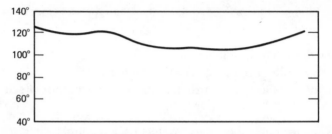

the situation temporary and do nothing to correct it. But a feedback control doesn't think about the nature of the drop, it reacts like an automaton. Although this automatic approach appears to be highly inflexible, it is this inflexibility that makes the system effective.

It is difficult to pin down the cause of increased inventory. Marketing blames sales; sales blames materials management; materials management blames production; production blames purchasing—and so on down the line. Explanations are plentiful. Some sound valid, but a determined effort to assess the impact of each reason given may take several man-weeks.

Feedback controls eliminate the need for analysis. As a result, the job gets done in less time than would be required in probing the reasons why the inventory deviates from the standard range. Even if probing were followed, the causal factors could never be known completely. The result of such uncertain conclusions would lead to a "play it safe" strategy.

Conditions for Empirical Controls

Empirical inventory control is based on automated feedback techniques. It also includes a mechanism for keeping the controls tuned. It may include a time series forecast of demand to adjust the upper and lower inventory level limits (standard). This empirical approach has proved successful in many different industries but it is not applicable to all inventories. Applicability requires:

- Predictability of demand or usage.
- Availability of product.
- Reasonably short lead times for replenishment.
- High volume products with few product modifications.

To summarize, the first requirement assumes the need is known, while the second and third requirements allow the need to be fulfilled. The advantage of high volume is that by the law of averages changes cancel each other out.

Forecasting has had an important impact on the number of products with predictable demand. When the forecasting is restricted to annual budget preparation and thereafter plays only a minor role in operations, the items with predictable demand are the items with stable sales patterns. In a department store, sales of such items as children's underwear, kitchen utensils, buttons, and linens are fairly constant and therefore predictable. Note in Exhibit 9-6 that the upper portion, depicting sale of

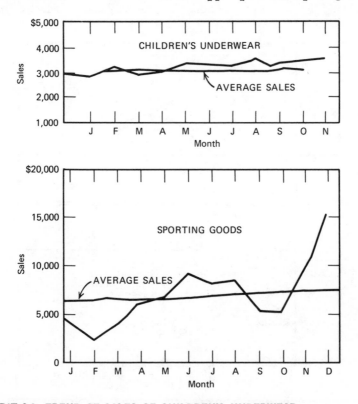

EXHIBIT 9-6   TREND OF SALES OF CHILDREN'S UNDERWEAR

children's underwear, is fairly flat with minor deviations above and below the straight line representing the average. The lower portion shows sales of sporting goods which reflect a seasonal line. Sales of items such as the latter vary markedly from their averages. Basing inventory on the average sales could lead to difficulties in meeting demand.

In Exhibit 9-7, we see the effect of a sporting goods forecast. In the upper portion the forecast is compared with actual data. If the inventory were based on the forecasted level rather than on the average, we would have difficulty only if the actual sales showed marked deviations from the forecast. In the lower portion of Exhibit 9-7, the forecast is taken as the straight line with the actual showing the amount of deviation from the forecast. This illustrates how the forecast in effect changes the seasonal product line into one of relative stability and thus permits the application of empirical control procedures.

An unpredictable item is not suited to empirical control. If a good forecast cannot be obtained, whether or not the demand is cyclical, then control should not be left to an automatic system. Women's fashion items are

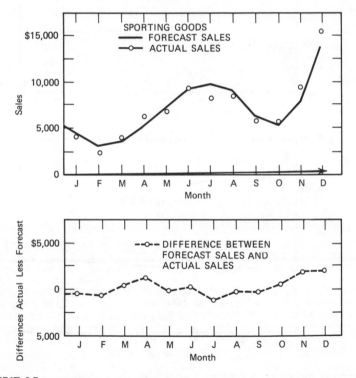

EXHIBIT 9-7

an example. With heavy durable goods such as aircraft and atomic power plants, sales may be large in dollars but they depend on a few decisions made by a relatively few buyers. Demand for such items can be highly unpredictable since the law of averages cannot be drawn upon.

When applied to sales of such items as children's underwear, the feed-back controls are relatively simple to implement. At the end of each month, the store is provided with a sales-by-item report which serves as the basis for the following month's orders. The previous month's sales are compared with orders for the month. The difference is added to or sub-tracted from the forecast for the following month's sales to arrive at the orders for the following month. If orders for an item exceed sales in the previous month, then inventory would be increased by an equivalent amount. Consequently, the orders for the following month could be reduced by that amount. If these rules are used, the inventory at the end of the month equals standard inventory plus or minus the variation be-tween actual and expected sales for the month.

Exhibit 9-8 illustrates the mechanics of this simple feedback mecha-nism. Since most of these items were ordered from a company's central warehouse, delivery was always possible within 2 weeks—provided the

EXHIBIT 9-8 FEEDBACK CONTROLS FOR MEN'S T-SHIRTS

LINE: MEN'S UNDERSHIRTS

			T-Shirts (H) Size	
		34-36	38-40	40-42
July				
	May sales		26	
	May orders		12	
	Differences		14	
	July forecast		12	
	July orders		26	

	May	June	July	August
Beginning inventory	17	3	6	16
Receipts	12	12	26	12
Sales	26	9	16	17
Ending inventory	3	6	16	11

item was available at the central warehouse. Thus, the conditions—short lead times and availability of product—are important to the success of the controls.

An example of slightly more elaborate feedback controls is shown in Exhibit 9-9. The item is a cam made by sintering powdered metal. The production machine operates on a high volume basis but is used to make a number of sizes. The parts are stocked in an in-process stockroom and are used in a variety of products. As in the previous example, the objective of the feedback mechanism is to replenish the in-stock inventory to a pre-determined level.

Two factors complicate the mechanism, however. The requirement for the parts depends on the sales of the finished products containing these parts. Estimates of sales of finished products must first be prepared. Then these estimates are processed through a bill of material explosion to determine the requirements for the cams. The second difficulty encountered is scheduling the machine. Backing out the requirements plan based on standard lead times for assembly of finished goods may lead to requirements in a given week in excess of the machine's capacity. In this case, the requirements are scheduled ahead, taking into account:

- The inventory level of each item produced on the machine.
- Standard production lot sizes.
- A priority for work-in-process items.
- Rules governing the use of overtime and the permissibility of downtime.

EXHIBIT 9-9 FEEDBACK CONTROLS FOR ENGINE PARTS

PART NUMBER: 16-1732C
INVENTORY LIMIT: 600

Week	Beginning Inventory	Deliveries	Usage	Ending Inventory	Requirements	Inventory Short
.	.	.	.	.	.	.
.	.	.	.	.	.	.
12	472	202	212	462		318
13	462	0	185	277	180	553
14	277	206	231	252	230	528
15	252	201	246	207	180	683
16	207	413	290	330	290	
.	.	.	.	.	.	.
.	.	.	.	.	.	.
.	.	.	.	.	.	.

Because of these scheduling rules, the inventory level might not be completely restored at the end of each week. Inventory for a part might rise above standard and still additional production would be scheduled to avoid downtime on the machine. On the other hand, the inventory might be below the standard range without production being scheduled because of requirements for higher priority items. Of course, as the situation worsens, the counterpressures are bound to increase. Thus, when the inventory level of a part greatly exceeds the standard, downtime would be accepted rather than further increases in inventory. As a result, inventories are always pushed back to the standard although the correction could be sluggish at times.

Exhibit 9-9 helps to explain how the controls work. The inventory standard (max) for the item is 600. At the end of week 12, the inventory is 462 units. Since the BOM system projects requirements of 180 units in week 13, the total needed to satisfy this requirement and return inventory to standard is $600 + 180 - 462 = 318$ units. This last number appears in the "Inventory Short" column. Because of the scheduling rules, however, no production is scheduled for week 13. As a result, the end-of-week inventory drops to 277 units and the inventory shortage becomes: $600 + 230 - 277 = 553$. Again, because of scheduling priorities, the full amount of the shortage is not scheduled for week 14. The item continues to qualify for "maintenance" level production until the end of week 15. At this time, the inventory shortage increases above 600. Thus the week-end inventory is not expected to provide the requirements for week 16. Still, because of the high overall requirements for the machine, the full production returning the inventory to standard is not scheduled.

The final element of the feedback control is a semi-annual measure of the standards to test the correctness of the inventory standards for each item made by the machine. The test is run to determine the minimum inventory levels during the period and the incidence of production delays caused by shortages of the items. From the results of these tests the company determines whether to raise or lower the inventory standards for the next 6-month period. In special situations, the standards could be adjusted throughout the 6-month period, but these were rarely required.

CHAPTER 10

INVENTORY MANAGEMENT
AND COST ACCOUNTING
INTERFACE

In recent years the explosive increase in demand for a proliferation of products and product types, coupled with the trend toward larger and more highly specialized manufacturing units, has resulted in a massive increase in the number of different items carried in inventory by many companies. This does not apply to finished goods and raw materials alone. It applies to the multiplicity of components, assemblies, and subassemblies in various stages of completion as well.

A fairly common mass-produced product can have 20,000 items in inventory. An "order of magnitude" analysis by raw material, work-in-process, and finished goods might typically show the following breakdown of the 20,000 items:

Raw material	500
Work-in-process	14,500
Finished goods	5,000
	20,000

When manufacturing units were smaller and the items in inventory fewer, accountability for physical units and dollar value could be accomplished manually. But as the number of items expanded, companies found it more and more difficult to account for them. Production and inventory control records were laboriously posted by hand. Accountants who prepared financial statements found it exceedingly difficult to apply dollar values to movement of inventories through the production processes and through cost of sales. To develop such costs without a computer would require the manual "treeing up" of costs from raw material through the various components and subassemblies to the cost of the finished product.

Such treeing up on a manual basis would require a day to a day-and-a-half, at a minimum, for each finished product. Even if this were a practical approach for 5000 end products, it would be impossible—except at a highly prohibitive cost—to determine the value of inventory. The reason is that even if the costs for the 20,000 items were available, the tracking of physical movement through the process for the various operations would be burdensome. Many manufacturers who have not yet computerized, find it virtually impossible to establish perpetual records of work-in-process manually. When it is necessary to track progress on certain customer orders, this must be done selectively. When it is necessary for the inventory control function to determine inventory quantities so haphazardly, it is difficult to imagine how the accounting function can establish reliable values on such inventories.

With the advent of the modern computer, physical accountability and valuation of the physical quantities can be achieved in a fraction of the time that manual approaches require. Once the system has been computerized, the accounting values placed on inventory can be directly related to and documented by the physical units making up the production and inventory control records.

OVERVIEW OF COMPUTERIZATION

The engineering bill of material is the "blueprint" of how the product is made. It lists the various material items, processes, and processing times for stages of production. Just as a bill of material is important to the physical production process in the manufacture of a product, so the computerized bill is the central point in a computerized inventory control system.

Exhibit 10-1 diagrammatically illustrates the relationship of input and output documents to the computerized bill of material (referred to in this company as the indented bill of material). On the input side, it shows the various types of transaction documents that are run against the bill of material information to produce such output documents as product costs, transaction costing, cost of sales, and variance analyses. Also important parts of the computerized procedures are the ongoing and year-end maintenance programs, the edit lists to assure accurate input of data, and the "where-used" information.

This chapter explains the content of the indented bill of material, where the information comes from, and how the product cost is developed.

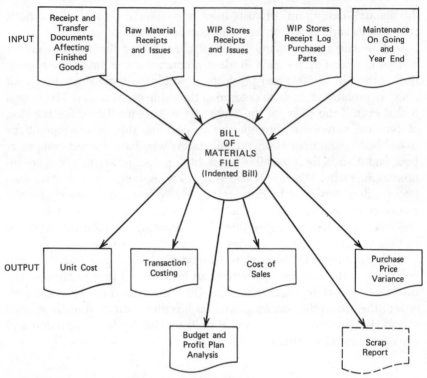

EXHIBIT 10-1   OVERVIEW OF COMPUTERIZATION

It also illustrates transaction lists and describes the procedure for summarizing these and developing the closing journal entries.

INDENTED BILL OF MATERIALS

The end product used to illustrate the indented bill of material is a piece of machined brass rod about 2 inches long and 0.280 inch in diameter. This has a plastic disc affixed at one end. The operations include the mixing of the plastic ingredients, forming the plastic disc, making the brass stem, and then combining the plastic disc and the stem through a molding operation. After some drilling and reaming operations, the item is packed and labeled.

This product, 01 02608 5036, was selected because of its simplicity. The "treeing up" process for this product is illustrated in Exhibit 10-2. Note that five levels are required to diagram the process. More complex

TREEING UP THE PROCESS

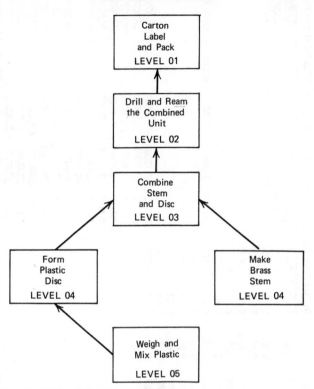

EXHIBIT 10-2 TREEING UP THE PROCESS

products would require numerous sheets of paper to illustrate the treeing up process and could require as many as 14 levels of complex interrelationships of components and subassemblies.

Exhibit 10-3, the indented bill of material, illustrates how the treeing up process is reflected in the computer. The columnar headings in this exhibit are explained below.

> **PRODUCT ID.** As is typical in many companies adopting the computer, this company has had difficulty in trying to use existing product identification numbers. There has been no consistency in the numbering procedures developed over the years. In many instances numerals and alphabetical designations have been combined. In some, additional digits designated special finishes or colors.
>
> To avoid the problems of attempting to use these, a new four-digit "machine code" was added to the regular number. Thus, the old num-

EXHIBIT 10-3 INDENTED BILL OF MATERIAL FOR PRODUCT 01—02608—5036

PRODUCT ID	OPR NO.	BM LEVEL	QUANTITY	START OPN.	COST CNTR.	STND HRS/M	LABOR RATE	VARBLE OVHEAD	FIXED OVHEAD	R/M CODE	R/M GROSS	R/M NET	SCRAP RECOVY R/M	STANDARD R/M COST	U M
01—02608—5036	010	01	1.00000	010	1369	.02	2.497	1.749	3.407	018751				128.6900	2
01—02608—5036	010	01	1.00000	010						011856				8.0500	2
01—02608—5036	020	01	1.00000	020	1369	.05	2.497	1.749	3.407						
.01—02608—0537	010	02	1.00000	010	0267	1.67	2.473	2.093	3.678						
.01—02608—0537	020	02	1.00000	010	0267	1.18	2.473	2.093	3.678						
..01—02608—0005	010	03	1.00000	010	0568	.05	2.752	6.022	4.282						
..01—02608—0005	020	03	1.00000	010	0981	1.16	2.790	1.942	3.237						
...01—02608—0008	010	04	1.00000	010	0447	.15	1.335	4.182	7.121	202800	37.800	17.000	313.75000	638.1700	2
...01—02608—0008	020	04	1.00000	010	0450	.50	1.335	4.182	7.122						
...01—02608—0008	030	04	1.00000	010	0761	.81	3.396	3.326	4.933						
...01—02608—0008	050	04	1.00000	010	0568	.07	2.752	6.022	4.282						
...01—02608—0002	010	04	1.00000	010	1294	.08	2.773	2.978	4.413						
....97—00019—0000	010	05	.00990	010	1291	4.65	2.773	2.978	4.413	059562	350.75000	350.75000		250.0000	2
....97—00019—0000	010	05	.00990	010						055401	17.54000	17.54000		88.0000	2
....97—00019—0000	010	05	.00990	010						051202	3.86000	3.86000		530.0000	2
....97—00019—0000	010	05	.00990	010						058110	4.56000	4.56000		530.0000	2
....97—00019—0000	010	05	.00990	010						057326	7.02000	7.02000		34.5000	2
....97—00019—0000	010	05	.00990	010						054202	35.08000	35.08000		260.0000	2
....97—00019—0000	010	05	.00990	010						057320	87.69000	87.69000		114.2100	2
....97—00019—0000	010	05	.00990	010						055407	86.64000	86.64000		160.0000	2
....97—00019—0000	010	05	.00990	010						057315	3.51000	3.51000		225.0000	2
....97—00019—0000	010	05	.00990	010						059536	70.15000	70.15000		102.5000	2
....97—00019—0000	010	05	.00990	010						059537	224.48000	224.48000		60.0000	2
....97—00019—0000	010	05	.00990	010						051214	21.05000	21.05000		11.7500	2
....97—00019—0000	010	05	.00990	010						054213	87.67000	87.67000		72.5000	2

ber—familiar to the operating people—always prints out with the machine code used in the computer for identification purposes. In the indented bill of material, the existing number used in past years is illustrated by the first seven digits. The machine code follows as the next four digits.

OPR NO. To identify the product further, by stage of completion within each level, an operation number is introduced, shown as 010, 020, 030, 040, 050, and so forth. These are repeated in the different cost centers.

A drilling operation in one cost center may be identified as 010 but in another the same number would mean a coating process. Generally, however, each number within a cost center stands for the same operation on all products. If a product in that center does not require that operation, there is a gap in the operation number sequence.

BM LEVL corresponds with the level of manufacture illustrated in Exhibit 10-2. Note that the indentation of the Product ID is represented by dots preceding the number. The top level—the finished product—is not preceded by a dot. The next lower level is preceded by a single dot, the next level by two, and so forth.

QUANTITY specifies how many of the specific item is required per completed item at that level. This must be viewed in conjunction with the last column, "UM," which stands for unit of measure. In this instance, the code 2 under "UM" means per thousand. The quantity of 1.00000 therefore means that 1000 components, for example, are required per 1000 units that are completed at that level. When 2 units are required per finished unit, then the quantity is shown as 2.00000. In the case of raw materials shown as the 97 series of items at the bottom portion of the indented bill, the quantity is shown as .00990. This means that .00990 pounds of material is required per thousand units of product.

START OPN. The operation number in this column identifies the point in the process at which processing starts on an incoming component. Note in Exhibit 10-3 that the first operation in cost center 1369 relates to raw material (packaging and labels). The first operation for these incoming materials is operation 10 which consists of making up the carton and applying the label. The incoming component (from level 2) is packaged in operation 20. Thus the start operation for the latter is indicated as 020.

COST CNTR. refers to the natural departmental area in which related manufacturing processes take place. The first two digits identify the overall department while the second two identify various work centers within the department. Availability of the four digits facilitates the application of machine hour rates to smaller segments within the department. Although physical inventories are costed at the point at which the latest operation has been completed, the monthly transaction listings do not attempt to follow production from work center to work center within a department. They identify "issues to" and "transfers from" by the two digit departmental designation.

STND HRS/M specifies the number of hours per thousand units that it should take to perform an operation. This figure represents labor hours when a hand operation is required. When a machine-paced operation is involved, these are machine hours. (Machine hours could be synonymous with labor hours when there is a full-time operator for each machine.)

LABOR RATE quantifies the labor cost per hour for performing the particular operation. This rate, multiplied by the hours, provides the standard direct labor cost.

VARBLE OVHEAD is the variable portion of indirect costs. It is based on a flexible budget which identifies separately those costs that are likely to fluctuate with changes in volume of production. Variable overhead would include such costs as supplies, material handling, and equipment servicing.

FIXED OVHEAD is also determined through the flexible budget. This category includes such costs as occupancy, supervision, and depreciation. Segregation of the variable and the fixed overhead facilitates additional analysis beyond that provided in the routine cost system procedures.

R/M CODE identifies the material to which no labor has yet been applied. Included in this coding in the indented bill of materials illustrated by Exhibit 10-3 are the following:

• Cartons and labels used at level 1.
• Brass rod used for making the stem in level 4.
• Ingredients required for making the plastic disc (level 5).

R/M GROSS refers to the starting quantity of material for making the component or assembly. When material is unavoidably lost in the processing of a component, the finished weight is shown under *R/M NET*. An illustration of this is operation 10 of level 4. Here, the brass rod must be drilled out and threaded. The gross weight of the rod is shown as R/M Gross while the finished weight is indicated as R/M Net.

SCRAP RECOVY shows the standard cost per thousand pounds of metal recovered from the process.

STANDARD R/M COST shows the standard cost of the raw material used in the product.

STRUCTURING THE COSTS USED FOR INVENTORY VALUATION

In the structuring process, the computer identifies and accumulates the manufacturing costs by operation and by level. When all the costs incident to completion of a component or subassembly are accumulated, the item is assigned a new part number for the next level. In the next level, it may be further processed or it may be combined with another component or subassembly. When the operations in this new level are completed, a new part number is again assigned as the finished item moves on to the following level.

In many companies, components and subassemblies are moved into controlled stores areas for a period of time before being processed further. It is necessary, therefore, to be able to value these stocked items for balance sheet purposes. The costs at the various levels at which the items are put into stock provide the basis for such valuation.

Many items that are in process but have not reached a completed component stage cannot be valued at a completed level cost. They must be valued at an intermediate value. The structuring illustrated in the indented bill of materials (Exhibit 10-3) provides for costing by operation within each level. When values are needed for production that is in between levels, the accumulated cost at the last operation is used for valuation of the work-in-process "float."

The cost system illustrated in this chapter is based on standards that are revised annually. While such frozen standards are suitable for valuation of inventories, such valuation will not be suitable in cost estimating products for determining cost/selling price relationships. For this reason, many companies maintain a current file of standards which are used for any costing that must reflect current values.

The computer may be used to advantage in maintaining current product costs. A cost implosion program can be developed that permits complete bill of material cost updating based on cost changes entered at any level. For each cost change entered, cost is revised at the entry point and at all subsequent points in the manufacturing process. The cost implosion program must be developed to account for scrap loss and must be flexible enough to adjust to bill of material revisions related to changes in materials and in the production process. A current cost program is most desirable during periods of inflation when rising costs can squeeze profit margins, and quarterly (or monthly) price revisions are in order.

The indented bill of material contains the "formula" for costing the product at the various stages of production. The document providing this basic data must be so organized that there will be a natural flow of information not only on existing products but on new products and on basic changes that are made to present items. The source of this data is discussed next.

SOURCE OF MANUFACTURING DATA

Basic manufacturing data emanates from two sources—the product development group in the engineering organization and the industrial engineering section.

>   **Product Development:** This function is not always identified as such. It may be part of engineering without bearing any special nomenclature. The function is to develop and maintain specifications on the various products made by the company. This covers the specifications of the material to be used, the quantity per unit, and in some instances the vendor source. In addition, this group specifies product performance.

>   **Industrial Engineering:** Sometimes called manufacturing engineering, this group includes a function which specifies the equipment on which the product and its components will be made, the time requirements for processing, and the labor category required to perform the work.

In organizing for computerization of the cost accounting system manufacturing data must be assembled for all active products on a document that acts as a "funnel" to transmit the information. In some companies, the material is summarized on engineering bills of material while the processing data is shown on a route sheet. In the example illustrated here, both material and processing data are included in a single document called the manufacturing process sheet.

An example is shown in Exhibit 10-4 which lists the raw materials used in making up the batch of plastic required in a later operation to form a circular plastic disc.* In addition to the raw materials, this process sheet also shows the time requirements for weighing out and mixing these ingredients. Since only one processing step is required, only one operation

---

* For purposes of confidentiality the ingredients have been changed.

is indicated (operation 010). This is performed in cost center 1291. The weighing out and mixing should take 4.65 hours per thousand pounds and the labor grade to be used is 8.

The manufacturing process sheets must be developed in a manner that fits into the level-by-level progression of the manufacturing operation. This is demonstrated in Exhibit 10-5 for the product shown in the indented bill of material (Exhibit 10-3).

The tie-in of the manufacturing process sheets to the "treeing-up" of the manufacturing process shown in Exhibit 10-5 is also illustrated with the indented bill of materials in Exhibit 10-6, entitled "Data source for indented bill of material." Two manufacturing process sheets are used in this example: the weighing out of the plastic ingredients at level 5 and the fabrication of the stem at level 4.

Exhibit 10-6 identifies on both the indented bill of materials and the process sheets such items as the cost center, operation number, level of manufacture, standard hours per thousand, raw material code, and the weight of the brass used in making the stem.

Since the computerized bill of materials contains all the basic manufacturing information as well as the appropriate direct labor grade, overhead, and material costs, it contains all the elements needed to develop the product cost.

DEVELOPING THE PRODUCT COST

Exhibit 10-7 shows how the material elements are combined to arrive at the total cost of the brass used in making the stem. The starting size of brass rod needed to make a thousand stems weighs 37.8 pounds. In making the finished brass stem, it is necessary to "hollow out" the rod, to tap it, and to thread the outside. The net weight of the finished stem is 17 pounds per thousand—20.8 pounds, or 55%, of the starting weight representing "necessary" scrap. The starting weight is costed by the standard cost of brass which is $638.17 per thousand pounds of rod. The lost brass of 20.8 pounds is costed by the standard cost of scrap brass, which is $313.75 per thousand pounds. When the value of the scrap recovered is subtracted from the starting cost, the resulting cost of brass per thousand finished units is $17.60.

Exhibit 10-8 illustrates the procedure for arriving at the labor cost for product 01-02608-5036. The standard hours per thousand units are added up for all operations in all cost centers. These hours are multiplied by the labor grade applicable to the operations to arrive at a total labor cost by cost center. The addition of the total labor cost by cost center results in

EXHIBIT 10-4 MANUFACTURING PROCESS SHEET

MANUFACTURING PROCESS SHEET

SHEET 1 OF 2

Issue Date	Issue No. 4	Superceded Date	P.C. 97	Basic 00019	Line No. 0000	Mach. Code 0000	Reference	Shop Order No.
Drawing No.			Part Name PLASTIC D785A					Date Issued
			Material Code	Kind	Size			Qty. to Make
			Shape	Spec.	Temper		Hardness	Raw Material Req.
			Unit	Per/M Gross	Per/M Net			Required Completion Date
			Routing MOLDING					LEVEL 05

Oper. No.	Operation Description	Equipment	Dept.	Set-up Hrs.	Lab. Grd.	Prod. Hrs./M	Lab. Grd.	No. Mach.	No. Men	Cost Center
010	Weigh out and mix plastic ingredients (listed below)	Bench w/scale, Mixer	Mold			4.65	8		3	1291

MATERIAL CODE	DESCRIPTION	POUNDS PER "M"
05-9562	Plastic #276	350.75
05-5401	Magnesium LT	17.54

05-1202	Z46	3.86
05-8110	LML	4.56
05-7326	Carbon 6	7.02
05-4202	Alumina 205	35.08
05-7320	Single Ply MM	87.69
05-5407	Black Oxide	86.64
05-7315	Acetone	3.51
05-9536	UPO Black #362	70.15
05-9537	M-34 Black	224.48
05-1214	Gr. Phosphate	21.05
05-4213	Hexo Cl	87.67
Total Pounds of Ingredients		1000.00

Process Engineer

Standard Engineer

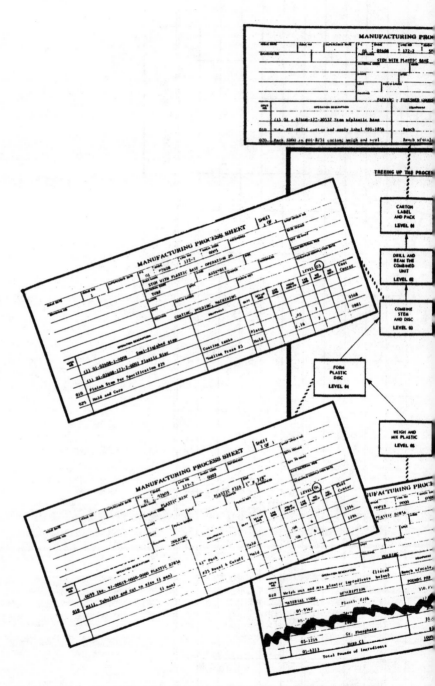

EXHIBIT 10-5   TREEING UP THE MANUFACTURING PROCESS SHEETS

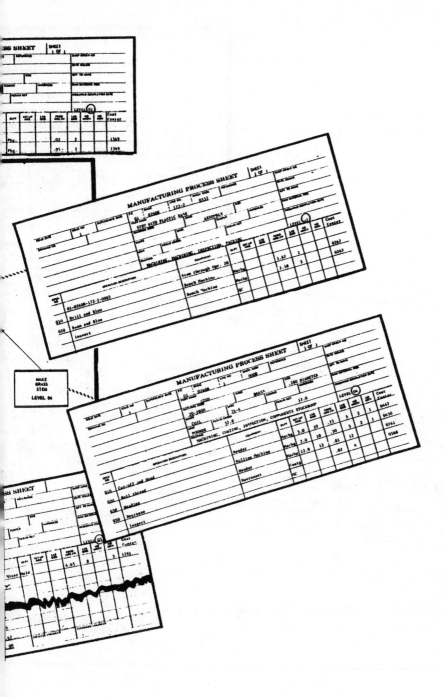

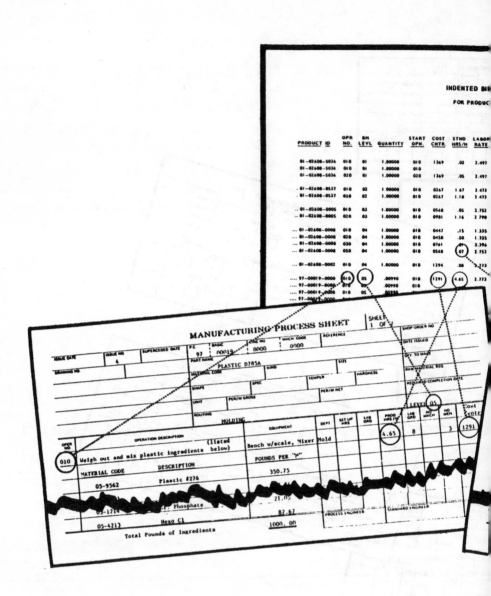

EXHIBIT 10-6 DATA SOURCE FOR INDENTED B/M

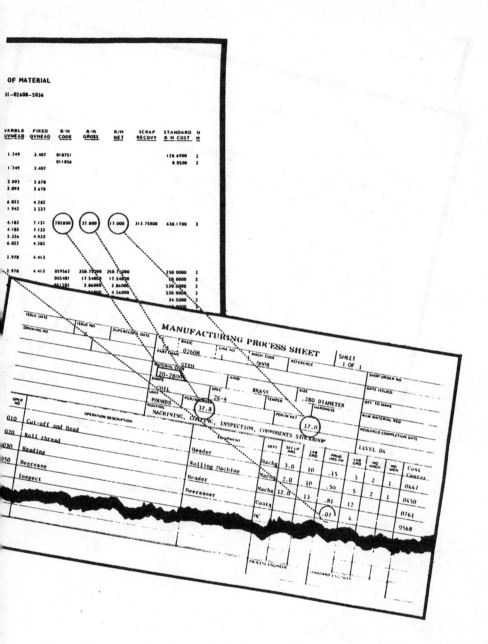

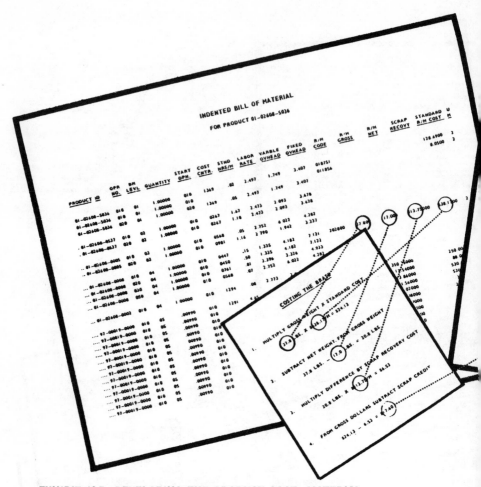

EXHIBIT 10-7 DEVELOPING THE PRODUCT COST—MATERIAL

PRODUCT COST REPORT

PRODUCT AND OPN	ID #	BRASS WEIGHT CRUDE WT.	FINISH WT.	BRASS	SALVAGE	NON BRASS MATERIAL	LABOR	VARIABLE OVERHEAD	CUMULATIVE COST	FIXED OVERHEAD	TOTAL COST
01 0972 R											
010 R		27.80	17.00	17.60		1.53	11.66	12.26			
020 R		37.80	17.00	17.60	6.53	1.53	18.74	18.24	43.05	19.59	42.64
030 R		42.80	18.70	20.34	6.53	2.22	24.00	24.31	56.11	30.11	86.22
S		.56	.27	.75	7.56				72.32	39.92	112.24
W		.73	.66	.70	.10						
					.03						
040 R		42.80	18.70	20.34		14.77	29.17	28.99	95.03	47.39	142.42
S		.98	.51	1.06	7.56						
W		.73	.66	.70	.17						
					.03						
050 R		42.80	18.70	40.34		14.77	34.12	33.17	104.16	54.75	158.91
S		.98	.51	1.06	7.56						
W		.73	.66	.70	.17						
					.03						
060 R		42.80	18.70	20.34		23.66	40.89	38.91	125.56	64.83	190.39
S		.98	.51	1.06	7.56						
W		.73	.66	.70	.17						
					.03						
01 02608 172	5036										
010 R		37.80	17.00	17.60	6.53	1.67	14.63	14.76	48.66	24.00	72.66
020 R		37.80	17.00	17.60	6.53	1.67	14.76	14.85	48.80	24.17	73.05
01 03621 181	5040										
010 R		69.20	26.95	30.09	13.26	23.66	49.62	49.30	154.42	81.32	235.75
S		.98	.51	1.06	.12						
W		.73	.66	.70	.03						

LEGEND FOR PRODUCT ID   R = Rod.   S = Strip.   W = Wire.

183

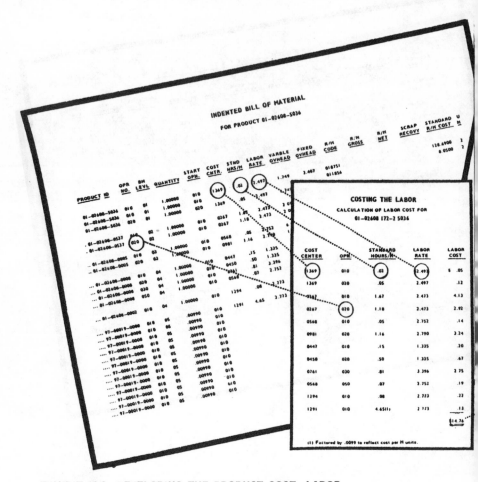

EXHIBIT 10-8 DEVELOPING THE PRODUCT COST—LABOR

PRODUCT COST REPORT

PRODUCT ID AND OPN	#	BRASS WEIGHT CRUDE WT.	FINISH WT.	BRASS	SALVAGE	NON BRASS MATERIAL	LABOR	VARIABLE OVERHEAD	CUMULATIVE COST	FIXED OVERHEAD	TOTAL COST
01 0972 R											
010 R		27.80	17.00								
020 R		37.80	17.00	17.60	6.53	1.53					
030 R		42.80	18.70	17.60	6.53	1.53	11.46	12.26	43.05		
S		.56	.27	20.34	7.56	2.22	18.74	18.24	56.11	19.59	62.64
W		.73	.44	.75	.10		24.00	24.31	72.32	30.11	86.22
040 R		42.80	18.70	.70	.02	14.77	29.17	20.99		39.92	112.24
S		.98	.51	20.34	7.56						
W		.73	.66	1.04	.17				95.03		
050 R		42.80	18.70	.70	.03	14.77	34.12	33.17		47.39	142.42
S		.98	.51	40.34	7.56						
W		.73	.66	1.04	.17				104.16	54.75	158.91
060 R		42.80	18.70	.70	.03	23.66	40.89	38.91			
S		.98	.51	20.34	7.56				125.56	64.83	190.39
W		.73	.66	1.04	.17	1.67	14.63				
01 02608	172	5036		.70	.03	1.67	14.76	48.66	24.00	72.66	
010 R		37.80	17.00			14.76	14.85	48.88	24.17	73.05	
020 R		37.80	17.00	17.60	6.53	23.66	49.62	49.30	154.43	81.32	235.75
01 03621	181	5040	26.95	17.60	6.53						
010 S		69.20	.51	30.09	13.26						
W		.98	.66	1.04	.17						
		.73		.70	.03						

LEGEND FOR PRODUCT ID R = Rod.   S = Strip.   W = Wire

a total labor cost of $14.76 per thousand units of product. The variable and fixed overhead are applied on the basis of the same hours per thousand used to calculate the labor cost. The non-brass material for this product, amounting to $1.67, is the cost of cartons and labels used in the packaging operation in level 1. The total standard product cost, then, is $73.05 per thousand units.

The figures contained in the product cost reports for the various levels are the same figures that are used for costing sales, issues, and transfers.

Before discussing the transaction documents referred to above, let's review two more exhibits, 10-9 and 10-10. Exhibit 10-9 is illustrative of the "where used" file which identifies where the various components are used within the product line. Component #06100746, for example, is used in 749 different end products. In making a change in any of the elements of this component, it is obviously necessary to know which products will be affected by the change. The "where used" file serves this purpose.

Exhibit 10-10 illustrates an edit listing. This relates to the group of transactions identified as #9. The departments involved in the transfers are shown, as well as the quantities involved. The ticket numbers are listed sequentially so that missing numbers can be identified. The edit process for this month (August), would also "kick out" any transactions made to an incorrect department.

EXHIBIT 10-9 "WHERE USED" FILE

COMPONENT #06100746 USED IN 749 END PRODUCTS

02026910209	02026910307	02026910308	02026910309	02052950002
02054310003	02054310004	02054310020	02054310198	02054310209
02054310298	02054320003	02054320004	02054330001	02054330002
02054330129	02054340001	02054340002	02054340197	02054350002
02054350003	02054350020	02054350021	02054350197	02054350209
02054350210	02054360002	02054360003	02054360197	02054360198
02054360200	02054360209	02054360210	02054370003	02054370020
02054380003	02054380020	02055720002	02055720003	02055720019
02055730003	02055730019	02055730020	02055730021	02055730209
90057620099	90057620090	90057620092	90057620096	90057620197
99009900099	99009900100	99052880336	99052890126	99052932401
99053880097	99052453212	99052567820	99061880132	99073201063
99132647761	99133677642	99213674541	99224675132	99567362111

COMPONENT #061001001 USED IN 3 END PRODUCTS

39031001001	39076160419	39078131335

EXHIBIT 10-10   EDIT LISTING

TR	PRODUCT ID	TO	FROM	OP	QUANTITY	TICKET	MO
9	02 07752 0105	73	61	999	1,300	49638	8
9	03 05858 0005	73	61	999	29,000	49639	8
9	21 00423 5305	73	61	999	3,750	49640	8
9	02 07792 0131	73	61	999	4,500	49641	8
9	02 07907 0038	73	61	999	6,600	49642	8
9	02 00150 0715	73	61	999	4,750	49643	8
9	07 00135 0118	73	61	999	4,000	49644	8
9	02 07792 0131	73	61	999	2,400	49645	8
9	21 00416 6299	73	61	999	8,550	49646	8
9	21 50017 9900	73	61	999	180	49647	8
9	21 90001 9901	73	61	999	1,190	49648	8
9	02 07792 0105	73	61	999	1,600	49649	8
9	02 07907 0038	73	61	999	1,100	49650	8
9	21 00413 5299	73	61	999	7,200	49651	8
9	21 00418 0010	73	61	999	1,800	49652	8
9	21 00413 0021	73	61	999	42,500	49653	8
9	34 00316 5217	73	61	999	400	49654	8
9	02 07793 0036	73	61	999	1,300	49655	8
9	06 04374 0013	73	61	999	800	49656	8
9	06 04374 5101	73	61	999	1,000	49657	8
9	01 00015 0009	73	61	999	4,000	49658	8
9	21 00423 5309	73	61	999	9,600	49659	8
9	11 90014 9900	73	61	999	450	49660	8
9	01 00131 0013	73	61	999	8,000	49661	8
9	01 00151 0005	73	61	999	8,000	49662	8
9	21 00413 5090	73	61	999	138,000	49663	8
9	21 03575 5545	73	61	999	15,000	49664	8
9	21 03060 0004	73	61	999	10,000	49665	8
9	01 00131 0013	73	61	999	14,500	49666	8
9	21 00423 5309	73	61	999	3,700	49667	8
9	21 00055 5299	73	61	999	8,000	49668	8
9	21 00418 0010	73	61	999	3,560	49669	8

TRANSACTION LISTINGS

Transaction listings are the most important output documents in a computerized cost system. All material issued to the various production areas, all product movement between departments, transfers into and out of work-in-process stockrooms, and movements into and out of finished goods must be accounted for in terms of both physical units and dollar values on transaction runs. These provide the basis for maintaining inventory status reports as well as providing the documentation to support values carried on the accounting books.

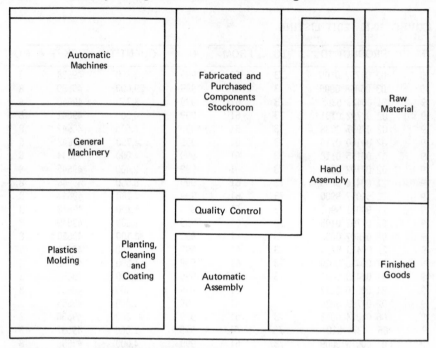

EXHIBIT 10-11   FACTORY FLOOR LAYOUT

Exhibit 10-11 illustrates the floor layout in which the various production departments and stockrooms are shown. These include:

Raw Material Stockroom

Primary Work-in-Process
   Automatic Machines
   General Machinery
   Plastics Molding
   Plating, Cleaning, and Coating

Fabricated and Purchased Components Stockroom

Secondary Work-in-Process
   Hand Assembly (including packaging)
   Automatic Assembly (including packaging)

Finished Goods Stockroom

Raw materials issued out of the stockroom include brass rod to the automatic machines and plastic ingredients to the plastics molding department.

The fabricated brass stems and molded discs are moved to the fabricated and purchased components stockroom until scheduled for assembly. At that time, the two components are moved back into primary work-in-process for combining through a further molding and curing operation. At this point, they usually move into the secondary work-in-process area. Although this move bypasses the fabricated and purchased components stockroom, the paperwork reflects transfers into and out of the stockroom as if the product had moved through a storage area. In the secondary production area, the product will flow either to the automatic assembly department or hand assembly and packaged for shipment, after which it moves into the finished goods stockroom.

Some illustrations of the transaction listings follow:

Raw Material Issues

Exhibit 10-12 shows a listing of raw material that was issued to production. The items have been listed in sequence by part number showing the unit of measure, quantity, and standard unit cost at which carried in inventory. The "Extended Cost" column shows the total standard cost of the various materials issued. Note that item 96-5408 shows a negative quantity and therefore a negative cost, indicating either a return to stock or a correction of a previous issue. The page of the transaction listings

EXHIBIT 10-12 RAW MATERIAL ISSUES

CHEMICALS	DESCRIPTION	U/M	QUANTITY	UNIT COST	EXTENDED COST
96-5408	Powder =6 H	2	30	4750.0000	− 142.50
			30		− 142.50 *
96-5410	Tetrafluoroethylene Resin = 6	2	184	4750.0000	874.00
96-5410	Tetrafluoroethylene Resin = 6	2	138	4750.0000	655.50
96-5410	Tetrafluoroethylene Resin = 6	2	221	4750.0000	1,049.75
96-5410	Tetrafluoroethylene Resin = 6	2	140	4750.0000	665.00
			683		3,244.25 *
965411	Naphtha	2	30	45.0700	1.35
965411	Naphtha	2	60	45.0700	2.70
965411	Naphtha	2	30	45.0700	1.35
			120		5.40 *
			2,062		3,313.98 **
					346,340.81 **

used in this exhibit shows the total value of raw material issued in the period. This amount, $346,340.81, will be shown later in a journal entry relieving the raw material inventory account.

Fabricated Parts Transferred into the Stockroom

Most companies of this type utilize a work-in-process stockroom as a storage and staging area for the primary components and subassemblies. When the finished product is scheduled for production, the required primary components are issued to the secondary departments for further processing.

Exhibit 10-13 is illustrative of a typical transaction listing of components and subassemblies issued out of the work-in-process stockroom. Since no production operations are performed in the stockroom, the operation number used is 999. Note that the columnar format for identifying the costs follows the same breakdown used in the product cost breakdown. Note also that the costs transferred out of the stockroom for this particular group of items is summarized at the lower part of the listing as "TO" departments. The "FROM" totals reflect the costs at which these items were relieved out of inventory; these are exactly the same. This type of summarization is done for all transaction listings.

Cost of Sales

Exhibit 10-14 shows the listing of finished products taken out of the finished goods stockroom for shipment. Product 01 02608 5036 shows a sale of 2255 units. The costs under the various categories reflect the extended standard cost of these 2255 units. The standard cost of Brass, for example, is $17.60 per thousand units. Extending this by 2255 units gives $39.68, the amount shown under the "Brass" column. The same procedure is followed for the other elements of cost.

The percentages across the bottom of this exhibit reflect the percentage breakdown of the various elements of cost for each of the product families sold. This facilitates analysis to determine the material, labor, and overhead content of the various product groupings. Such an analysis frequently helps to highlight changes in mix.

The breakdown of variable and fixed costs is helpful in profit contribution analysis. The cost system provides for full costing of inventories and at the same time shows the fixed cost content of the various components and finished products, so that internal statements can be presented on a direct costing basis.

EXHIBIT 10-13 FABRICATED PARTS TRANSFERRED TO FABRICATED AND PURCHASED PARTS STOCKROOM

PRODUCT ID		OPR NO.	QUANTITY	BRASS	NON-BRASS MATERIAL	LABOR	VARIABLE OVERHEAD	CUMULATIVE OPERATING COST	FIXED OVERHEAD	TOTAL COST
31 05163	0009	999 R	360	3.16	4.54	34.96	43.52	86.18	70.52	156.70
33 00798 D15	0016	999	250		13.13	.00	.00	13.13	.00	13.13
39 01451 198	0019	000 R	1,900	2.36	.00	27.49	3.49	34.87	4.52	39.39
		W		1.53						
39 04414 6	0019	999 R	710	4.36	2.65	18.59	7.40	33.19	9.90	43.09
		S		.19						
39 09155 6	0048	999 R	830	1.75	8.78	51.24	12.54	74.37	21.36	95.73
		W		.06						
41 00931 5	0049	999	300		.17	1.84	1.62	3.63	2.74	6.37
51 01593 4	0029	999	1,000		25.55	9.68	11.15	46.38	13.38	59.76
53 07642 2	0019	999	1,000		2.61	.00	.00	2.61	.00	2.61
53 08385 A3	0109	999	41,620		19.98	155.02	129.55	304.55	223.07	527.62
67 03670 197	0079	999	10		5.85	.00	.00	5.85	.00	5.85
67 08600 16	0119	999	8		.15	.11	.06	.32	.12	.44
67 08600 22	0159	999	7		.24	.57	.63	1.44	1.00	2.44
67 08600 23	0169	999	7		.11	.67	.81	1.59	1.32	2.91
67 08600 45	0269	999	9		.57	.49	.68	1.74	.83	2.57
67 08601 12	0089	999	10		5.20	.00	.00	5.20	.00	5.20
"TO" DEPT. TOTALS		R	48,021	11.63	89.53	300.66	211.45	615.05	348.76	963.81
		S		.19						
		W		1.59						
"FROM" DEPT. TOTALS		R	48,021	11.63	89.53	300.66	211.45	615.05	348.76	963.81
		S		.19						
		W		1.59						

LEGEND: R = Rod; S = Strip; W = Wire

EXHIBIT 10-14 COST OF SALES

PRODUCT ID	OPR NO.	QUANTITY	BRASS	NON-BRASS MATERIAL	LABOR	VARIABLE OVERHEAD	CUMULATIVE OPERATING COST	FIXED OVERHEAD	TOTAL COST
01 00131 AP1	0004 000 R	315,000	4,191.36	17.71	310.16	731.31	5,250.54	837.66	6,088
01 00131 A1782	0013 000 R	57,500	773.78	240.59	481.82	524.23	2,020.42	756.87	2,777
01 00131 17829	0017 000 R	243,800	3,167.79	899.12	2,187.49	2,315.74	8,570.14	3,324.75	11,894
01 00152 17829	0005 000 R	45,500	591.20	248.82	407.35	437.68	1,685.05	631.78	2,316
01 01651 UAH1	0086 000 R	277,500	3,605.67	15.45	287.09	676.08	4,584.29	760.57	5,344
01 02351 7913	5250 000 R	1,200	15.59	11.59	17.31	14.93	59.42	20.94	80
01 02870 7913	5179 000 R	757	12.58	5.29	31.35	20.25	69.47	27.18	96
01 02608	5036 000 R	2,255	39.68	3.77	33.28	33.49	110.22	54.50	164
01 03407 0178	5032 000 R	8,550	137.70	29.88	148.94	186.67	503.19	241.74	744
PRODUCT TOTALS	R	952,062	12,535.35	1,472.22	3,904.79	4,940.38	22,852.74	6,655.99	29,508
PERCENT OF TOTAL COST			42.49	4.99	13.23	16.75	77.46	22.54	100.00

LEGEND: R = Rod

JOURNALIZING THE TRANSACTIONS FOR THE COST SYSTEM

Eleven standard journal entries are used in this company's cost system for purposes of closing the books. These can be broken down into eight categories.

- Purchase price variances on material.
- Issues of raw material.
- Costing production.
- Issues out of work-in-process stores.
- Completed production transferred to finished goods.
- Determining the production variances.
- Costing shipments.
- Closing out the variance accounts.

Purchase Price Variance

Most companies "siphon off" the purchase price variance when the material is purchased. The transaction run from which the amount of variance is determined is shown as Exhibit 10-15. The run lists the actual and standard costs of each item as well as the amount of variance. A minus sign indicates unfavorable variances. The total variance shown in Exhibit 10-15 is $16,191.67. This amount, which is favorable, identifies that portion of the variance that applies to materials booked into the raw material inventory account. Another segment of the listing, not shown here, indicates that $160.87 of variance applicable to purchased components was incurred on materials purchased into the fabricated and purchased parts stockroom. The resulting journal entry to book the purchase of material into inventory at standard cost is:

Journal Entry #1

Material Variance		16,191.67
Raw Material Inventory	16,352.54	
Fabricated and Purchased Stores (WIP)		160.87

The net effect of the above entry is to increase the inventory value by $16,352.54 because the purchase prices at actual cost fell short of standard cost by that amount.

EXHIBIT 10-15   PURCHASE PRICE VARIANCE BY ITEM

P.O. NO.	ITEM CODE	QUANTITY	U/M CODE	U/M	UNIT COST	ACTUAL COST	STANDARD COST	VARIANCE
49999	03 3472	3346	2	LBS	702.700	2,754.43	2,351.23	− 403.20
50344	20 2980	810	2	LBS	620.190	490.21	502.35	12.14
49760	21 3190	1851	2	LBS	625.000	1,110.97	1,156.88	45.91
50134	21 3476	4372	2	LBS	625.000	2,733.37	2,732.50	− .87
50333	21 3476	7378	2	LBS	625.000	4,428.28	4,611.25	182.97
50050	21 3650	344	2	LBS	724.490	206.47	249.22	42.75
50217	21 4450	555	2	LBS	580.000	306.75	321.90	15.15
49799	21 4450	1238	2	LBS	580.000	684.24	718.04	33.80
50591	22 0781	127	2	LBS	1,287.780	109.83	163.55	53.72
50218	22 1562	110	2	LBS	828.000	89.56	91.08	1.52
49215	22 1660	1000	2	LBS	828.000	814.20	828.00	13.80
49216	22 1660	6018	2	LBS	828.000	4,899.86	4,982.90	83.04
49216	22 1660	4383	2	LBS	828.000	3,130.34	3,629.12	498.78
49185	23 0245	6810	2	LBS	625.000	4,087.36	4,256.25	168.89
49186	23 0245	26689	2	LBS	625.000	16,152.18	16,680.63	528.45
49186	23 0245	17314	2	LBS	625.000	10,391.86	10,821.25	429.39
49186	23 0245	20517	2	LBS	625.000	12,416.89	12,823.13	406.24
48958	23 0332	6614	2	LBS	630.000	4,002.79	4,166.82	164.03
48958	23 0332	3726	2	LBS	630.000	2,329.50	2,347.38	17.88
49398	23 0437	7152	2	LBS	585.000	3,988.67	4,183.92	195.25
48971	23 0437	13939	2	LBS	585.000	7,773.78	8,154.32	380.54
49996	23 0438	534	2	LBS	585.000	297.81	312.39	14.58
49670	23 0467	2522	2	LBS	585.000	1,454.44	1,475.37	20.93
50345	23 0531	5066	2	LBS	576.000	2,777.18	2,918.02	140.84
49659	23 0625	1010	2	LBS	549.000	524.90	554.49	29.59
50222	23 0625	1520	2	LBS	549.000	789.94	834.48	44.54
						232,934.06	249,125.73	16,191.67

The transaction listings of purchases should not be limited to the accounting application only. Since material represents an important element of cost, such information should be used for control purposes as well as accounting documentation. Illustrative of three uses to which the purchases listings can be put are the following:

- Purchase Price Variance by Major Item
- Purchased Parts Price History
- Material Receipts compared with Plan

Purchase Price Variance by Major Item. An accounting listing of purchase price variances that shows every item purchased can lose its value to management because of the time required in determining which ones account for most of the money. Exhibit 10-16 illustrates a weekly report that selects only the major purchase price variances that should receive management attention. The guideline for selec-

EXHIBIT 10-16   PURCHASE PRICE VARIANCE BY MAJOR ITEMS

PURCHASE PRICE VARIANCE
BY MAJOR ITEM

P.O. No.	Item Code	Quan- tity	U/M Code	U/M	Cost Unit	Actual Cost	Standard Cost	Variance
49997	03 3472	3?46	2	lbs.	702.?00	2,754.43	2,351.23	403.20
50333	21 3476	7378	2	lbs.	625.000	4,428.28	4,611.25	182.97
50050	21 3650	344	2	lbs.	724.490	206.47	249.22	42.75
50591	22 0781	127	2	lbs.	1,287.780	109.83	163.55	53.72
49216	22 166$	4383	2	lbs.	828.000	3,130.34	3,629.12	498.78
49185	23 0245	6810	2	lbs.	625.000	4,037.36	4,256.25	168.89
49186	23 0245	26689	2	lbs.	625.000	16,152.18	16,680.63	528.45
49186	23 0245	17314	2	libs.	625.000	10,396.86	10,521.25	429.39
49180	23 0245	7859	2	lbs.	625.000	4,716.97	4,911.85	194.91
49186	23 0245	20517	2	lbs.	625.000	12,416.89	12,823.13	406.24
48958	23 0332	6614	2	lbs.	630.000	4,???.79	4,116.82	164.03
49398	23 0437	7152	2	lbs.	585.000	3,988.67	4,183.92	195.25
48971	23 0437	13939	2	lbs.	585.000	7,773.78	8,154.32	380.54
50345	23 0531	5066	2	lbs.	576.020	2,777.18	2,918.02	140.84

tion in this company is a variance of 10% plus any items in which the variance is more than $100 per item purchased. This approach has the advantage in that it monitors purchases more frequently and highlights the variances on an exception basis.

Purchased Parts Price History. Generally, the price information on purchases, in many companies, is maintained in the purchasing department files. To make any meaningful appraisal would require burdensome manual analysis which would be both time-consuming and costly. Introduction of the computer provides an excellent opportunity to develop a price history by individual items over a period of time.

Exhibit 10-17 illustrates an example of two items for which such an analysis is made: part Nos. 01–2868 and 43–9267. The listing shows the vendor (or vendors, when more than one source is used), the invoice number, invoice date, quantity purchased, the unit in which purchased, the total actual cost, and the actual unit cost.

The unit cost is the key to the analysis. This exhibit shows the unit costs for purchases for a year's period. Where the unit cost changes, availability of the quantity provides a clue to whether the unit price change may have been due to purchase of a larger (or smaller) quantity.

EXHIBIT 10-17 PURCHASE PRICE PARTS HISTORY

PURCHASED PARTS PRICE HISTORY

Part No.	Vendor	Invoice No.	P.O.	Invoice Date	Quan- tity	U/M	Total Actual Cost	Actual Unit Cost
01-2868	Ajax Supply Company	42367	02873	2/2	100	ea.	53.80	.538
01-2868	Ajax Supply Company	42367	05091	3/5	400	ea.	215.20	.538
01-2868	Ajax Supply Company	42646	03047	3/6	100	ea.	53.80	.538
01-2868	Ajax Supply Company	43359	06068	5/7	100	ea.	53.80	.538
01-2868	Ajax Supply Company	43363	06949	6/7	900	ea.	522.90	.581
01-2868	Ajax Supply Company	43424	06729	6/8	300	ea.	176.40	.588
01-2868	Ajax Supply Company	43426	07657	7/12	600	ea.	352.80	.588
01-2868	Ajax Supply Company	43468	07657	8/18	600	ea.	352.80	.588
01-2868	Ajax Supply Company	43686	07729	9/12	300	ea.	176.40	.555
01-2568	Ajax Supply Company	4?878	07892	10/13	500	ea.	345.00	.690
01-2868	Ajax Supply Company	46667	07854	10/16	502	ea.	376.50	.750
01-2868	Ajax Supply Company	48882	08861	11/23	501	ea.	375.75	.750
01-2868	Ajax Supply Company	52601	08960	12/14	500	ea.	375.00	.750
					5403		3,430.15	.635
43-9267	Berkshire Products	41031	02802	1/30	25	ea.	408.17	16.327
43-9267	Berkshire Products	42308	0?815	2/5	125	ea.	2,040.85	16.327
43-9267	Berkshire Products	42309	05020	2/18	25	ea.	408.17	16.327
43-9267	Berkshire Products	42656	03023	3/6	50	ea.	816.34	16.327
43-9267	Berkshire Products	42333	05621	4/2	75	ea.	1,224.51	16.327
43-9267	Berkshire Products	43852	068?2	5/9	25	ea.	408.17	16.327
43-9267	Berkshire Products	43962	06731	6/17	25	ea.	416.50	16.660
43-9267	Berkshire Products	43975	01662	7/12	35	ea.	583.10	16.660
43-9267	Berkshire Products	44502	07894	8/14	85	ea.	1,416.10	16.660
43-9267	Berkshire Products	45652	07992	9/16	65	ea.	1,082.90	16.660
43-9267	Berkshire Products	46867	08012	10/18	15	ea.	249.90	16.660
43-9267	Berkshire Products	49001	08862	11/21	56	ea.	932.96	16.660
43-9267	Berkshire Products	51621	09002	12/16	57	ea.	949.62	16.660
					633		10,937.29	16.496

No standard price is shown because the intent of this control is to monitor price trends. This report has helped one company determine where design changes might be useful in eliminating a particular part or substituting another part made with a lower cost material.

Comparing Material Receipts with Plan. Inventory management has a great potential for improvement in many companies. Many executives attempt to reduce inventories after they have become too high. This is, of course, an after-the-fact approach. The better method is to control purchases before they become slow-moving or obsolete inventory.

Exhibit 10-18 illustrates a weekly report which compares the week's purchases with those planned for the week. This is helpful, not only in highlighting deviations from planned targets, but in identifying unauthorized advance shipments made by suppliers.

EXHIBIT 10-18   MATERIAL RECEIPTS COMPARED WITH PLAN

MATERIAL RECEIPTS COMPARED WITH PLAN

Part No.	Purchase Order No.	Description	U/M	Quantity	Standard Unit Cost	Total Standard Cost
01-0126	46236	Casting	ea.	1	22.994	20.994
01-0327	46337	Casting	ea.	10	93.789	937.890
02-0462	40454	Casting	ea.	10	275.000	2,750.000
02-0561	46567	Casting	ea.	10	181.?70	1,810.300
03-0102	46567	Casting	ea.	1	148.870	148.870
04-9362	47668	.067" × 48" Coiled Steel	lb.	20,000	.105	2,100.000
04-98?7	47887	.051" × 36" Coiled Steel	lb.	20,000	.108	2,160.000
05-0002	48882	.020" × 10" Coiled Steel	lb.	5,000	.122	610.000
05-0763	46567	.018" × 9" Coiled Steel	lb.	5,000	.108	540.000
05-0972	46338	.016" × 12" 70/30 Brass	lb.	1,000	.100	600.000
05-27?7	43536	.010" × 16" 70/30 Brass	lb.	2,000	.580	1,160.000
06-9872	43678	Teflon Tetraflouride	lb.	184	4.750	874.000
06-9962	44587	Teflon Tetraflouride	lb.	138	4.750	655.500
07-3212	45867	#110 Switch Plates	ea.	35	.500	17.500
07-3356	43633	#220 Switch Plates	ea.	1,000	1.500	1,500.000
07-5456	42337	Nylon Grommets	ea.	25,000	.028	700.000
07-6768	4124?	Plastic Washers	ea.	100,000	.030	3,000.000
20-3246	46687	#10 Webbing	yd.	1,000	3.070	3,070.000
20-4678	46667	#26 Webbing	yd.	5,000	4.020	20,100.000
20-5762	45452	#32 Plastic Material	yd.	10,000	.500	5,000.000
20-6879	46601	#41 Plastic Material	yd.	5,000	1.100	5,500.000
22-1334	45827	2122 Ferrules	ea.	100	2.100	210.000
22?23?7	45990	3538 Ferrules	ea.	200	3.000	600.000
23-3679	42876	½ HP. Motor	ea.	100	10.000	1,000.000
23-4627	43378	1 HP. Motor	ea.	300	46.500	13,950.000
	Total w/e 10/7					95,968.000
	Planned Purchases					87,690.000

Input into Production

Since in a standard cost system, actual costs and actual performance must be compared with standard, it is necessary to use a "clearing account" to measure the difference. This clearing account, in some companies, is called manufacturing cost control. In others, including this company, it is called variance. In this case study, the variance account is broken down into three accounts:

- Material Variance
- Labor Variance
- Indirect Labor and Overhead Variance

The actual costs are generally charged to these accounts. The standard cost of the finished production is credited to the same accounts. The difference between the two, then, becomes the variance.

Raw Material Issues

Exhibit 10-12 lists the raw material issues for the period. It shows a total of $346,340.81 issued to production. The journal entry to show the charge into production and relief of inventory is:

Journal Entry #2

Material Variance	346,340.81	
Raw Material Inventory		346,340.81

Fabricated Parts Transferred into Stock

The following schedule summarizes the transaction run to show by department the standard cost of primary components and subassemblies transferred to work-in-process stock. The summary shows a category referred to as "uncosted." This means that some items produced did not have costs in the computer file, and it was necessary to cost them separately. Steps being taken to link the order entry system into the scheduling procedure will eliminate this problem because new items will be monitored to assure that costs are available in the file.

From:	Brass	Non-Brass	Direct Labor	Variable Overhead	Fixed Overhead	Total
01 $	13.41	89.53	300.66	211.45	348.76	963.81
02	1.50	38.12	4.08	3.20	4.75	51.65
03	2,085.47	81.80	302.92	678.81	1,029.06	4,178.08
04	4,098.41	11,926.58	2,080.78	2,055.62	2,889.39	23,050.78
05	229,804.96	16,932.22	39,916.46	69,870.01	93,891.07	450,414.72
06	2,913.91	591.33	1,796.39	2,041.96	2,879.65	10,223.24
07	1,408.39	63.53	388.42	433.52	654.23	2,948.09
08	15,413.32	2,473.79	10,881.12	14,917.32	22,872.35	66,557.90
09	541.54	1,204.47	3,340.78	3,096.48	4,880.48	13,063.75
10	97.36	246.72	26.32	28.35	39.43	438.18
11	1,390.27	1,611.96	539.96	628.49	950.28	5,120.96
12		36.72				36.72
Total Costed	257,768.54	35,296.77	59,577.89	93,965.23	130,439.45	577,047.88
Uncosted items	6,666.95	2,003.78	1,495.59	2,368.74	3,444.58	15,979.64
	$ 264,435.49	37,300.55	61,073.48	96,333.97	133,884.03	593,027.52
	(264,435.49)	264,435.49		(96,333.97)	96,333.97	
		301,736.04	61,073.48		230,218.00	593,027.52

The first two columns, which add up to $301,736.04, represent the standard material cost of production. Direct labor represents $61,073.48 while variable plus fixed overhead amounts to $230,218.00. These three figures are the credits to the respective variance accounts while the total of the three becomes a charge to the fabricated and purchased parts inventory account. This is summarized in journal entry #3.

Journal Entry #3

	Dr.	Cr.
Fabricated and Purchased Parts Inventory	593,027.52	
Material Variance		301,736.04
Labor Variance		61,073.48
Indirect Labor and Overhead Variance		230,218.00

To record production of fabricated parts transferred into fabricated and purchased parts stores.

Transfers from Finished Goods to WIP Stockroom

Primary components are sometimes sold as replacement parts. Also, other companies purchase the components and make their own assemblies. Such sales are usually finished goods because the cost of sales entry automatically relieves the finished goods inventory. There are times when excess replacement parts are moved out of finished goods and transferred into the Fabricated and Purchasing Parts Inventory.

This summary transaction run summarizes the current month's transfers. The journal entry is also shown.

	Brass	Non-Brass	Direct Labor	Variable Overhead	Fixed Overhead	Total
Total Costed	$ 47.72	537.22	217.03	188.69	273.50	1,264.16
Uncosted items	31.60	471.41	69.30	47.90	72.19	692.40
	$ 79.32	1,008.63	286.33	236.59	345.69	1,956.56

Journal Entry #4

	Dr.	Cr.
Fabricated and Purchased Parts Inventory	1,956.56	
Finished Goods Inventory		1,956.56
To record transfers of items in finished goods to fabricated and purchased parts stores.		

Transfers from WIP Stockroom

The transaction run summary shown below summarizes by department the primary components, purchased parts, and subassemblies issued to the production floor. Some of the components and purchased parts have been transferred to the primary production area such as Department 01 (Automatic Machinery) and 04 (General Machinery). Department 05 is the Plating, Coating, and Cleaning department. Many of the primary components in the stockroom are sent to this department before being transferred to the secondary departments for assembly.

To:	Brass	Non-Brass	Direct Labor	Variable Overhead	Fixed Overhead	Total
01	$ 48,524.50	21,270.43	18,750.18	23,636.47	32,404.98	144,586.56
02	14,120.43	5,520.33	9,464.68	13,374.62	20,628.73	63,108.79
04	2,454.31	15,257.61	1,861.74	2,285.78	3,029.04	24,888.48
05	152,774.51	6,920.74	14,377.23	24,868.29	34,414.69	233,355.46
06	5,803.94	15,186.86	1,737.66	2,538.59	3,463.66	28,730.71
07	25,787.14	495.34	9,930.40	21,765.50	28,195.78	86,174.16
08	189.76	565.40	41.22	50.95	70.46	917.79
11	1,769.73	373.78	1,077.12	1,791.47	1,738.56	6,750.66
12	14,507.04	59,294.59	5,319.20	7,813.14	10,714.46	97,648.43
13	.34		.07	.11	.17	.69
Total Costed	265,931.70	124,885.08	62,559.50	98,124.92	134,660.53	686,161.73
Uncosted items	4,389.27	1,867.91	1,208.45	1,969.62	2,788.12	12,223.37
	$ 270,320.97	126,752.99	63,767.95	100,094.54	137,448.65	698,385.10

Journal Entry #5

	Dr.	Cr.
Work-in-Process Floor Inventory	698,385.10	
Fabricated and Purchased Parts Inventory		698,385.10

To record issues of fabricated and
purchased parts to production floor.

Customer Returns

Customer returns for which credits have been issued are covered by
Journal Entry #6. Because there were no credits issued in the current
period, this journal entry is not applicable.

Components in Finished Goods Stock Returned to Production

These transactions are similar to those covered by journal entry #4 except
that the items are being returned directly to production for immediate
processing.

To:	Brass	Non-Brass	Direct Labor	Variable Overhead	Fixed Overhead	Total
01	$ 347.41	119.19	243.64	277.24	413.38	1,400.86
02	16.48	96.01	17.43	15.64	25.46	171.02
04	13.08	1.58	28.39	29.87	46.15	119.07
06		61.99	.50	.35	.68	63.52
07	37.87	.12	1.57	3.41	5.69	48.66
08	.05	.21	.50	.37	.57	1.70
11	315.01	850.44	213.87	215.11	333.43	1,927.86
12	1,637.18	1,887.21	1,504.84	1,419.30	2,173.41	8,621.94
32	21.28	77.66	21.30	20.58	31.88	172.70
41	1.42	1.92	2.27	2.20	3.26	11.07
42	.58	.49	.51	.66	.81	3.05
43	1.12	1.06	.62	.60	.93	4.33
47	269.84	63.51	172.31	186.96	289.44	982.06
Total Costed	2,661.32	2,161.39	2,207.75	2,172.29	3,325.09	13,527.84
Uncosted items	547.84	85.95	40.25	47.92	19.42	741.38
	$ 3,209.16	3,247.34	2,248.00	2,220.21	3,344.51	14,269.22

Journal Entry #7

	Dr.	Cr.
Work-in-Process Floor Inventory	14,269.22	
Finished Goods Inventory		14,269.22

To record items in finished goods transferred
to the production floor.

Completed Production transferred to Finished Goods

The transaction summary below shows the costs of finished products that
have been transferred to finished goods inventory. The applicable journal
entry is also shown.

	Brass	Non-Brass	Direct Labor	Variable Overhead	Fixed Overhead	Total
Total Costed	2,661.32	3,161.39	108,217.04	121,741.51	181,154.82	748,832.59
Uncosted items	7,264.81	5,825.78	5,386.64	5,965.95	8,725.37	33,163.55
	$221,975.29	128,834.52	113,600.68	127,707.46	189,880.19	782,001.14

Journal Entry #8

	Dr.	Cr.
Finished Goods Inventory	782,001.14	
Work-in-Process Floor Inventory		782,001.14

To record production transferred to
finished goods.

Floor Work-in-Process

Some cost systems calculate standard cost of inventory input on an operation-by-operation basis. As production is reported at each operation, the number of units completed at that operation is extended by standard cost.

Other cost systems calculate input when the last operation is completed in each department. The product is then moved to the next department.

The problem with recognizing input into floor work-in-process is that the components and assemblies recognized as good production might be scrapped later. While the textbook says to record such spoilage and then remove it from inventory, the real world is different from the book.

Unless dealing with a large and expensive unit, companies generally do not closely enforce discipline for reporting of rejects, because this could be expensive. An automated machine that spews out parts by the hundred or even thousand per hour loses hundreds of components in the course of a shift. These drop down under the machines and cannot be readily recovered and counted. In operations in which parts can be recycled, such as plastics molding or die casting, rejects can be counted as production and then thrown back in for remelting. In many such instances, production can be "doubled up." Monitoring to avoid double counting can be expensive.

What then is the solution? Simply, the solution is not to recognize input into production until the component or subassembly is accepted into the work-in-process or finished goods stockrooms. This leaves only the floor work-in-process to be accounted for. This becomes a two-step process: first, to net out the production transferred into finished goods with the issues of components and subassemblies transferred out of the stockrooms to the production floor; second, to account for the "pipeline" inventory on the floor through a constant floor inventory, a shop-order type accountability if practical, or—if all else fails—a physical inventory of major items on the floor.

The transactions summarized below relate to the first of the above.

	Brass	Non-Brass	Direct Labor	Variable Overhead	Fixed Overhead	Total
Finished Goods Produced:	$221,975.29	128,834.52	113,603.68	127,707.46	189,880.19	782,001.14
From Finished Goods to Production Floor:	3,209.16	3,247.34	2,248.00	2,220.21	3,343.51	14,268.22
From Fabricated Stores to Production Floor:	270,320.97	126,752.99	63,767.95	100,094.54	137,448.65	698,385.10
	(51,554.84)	(1,165.81)	47,587.73	25,392.71	49,088.03	69,347.82

Journal Entry #9

	Dr.	Cr.
Work-in-Process Floor Inventory	69,347.82	
Material Usage Variance (Brass & non-brass)	57,720.65	
Labor variance		47,587.73
Indirect labor and Overhead Variance		74,480.74

> To record standard cost of production between the fabricated parts level and the finished goods level.

The company used as the subject for this case study establishes the "pipeline" value of its floor inventory by establishing a constant value and adjusting this each month by the results of physical counts taken at key points where buildups can occur.

Shipments During the Month

The cost of sales transaction format was shown earlier in this chapter. Like all transactions, the cost breakdown indicates all the elements of cost shown on the product cost sheet. The journal entry is:

Journal Entry #10

Cost of Sales	753,596.69	
Finished Goods Inventory		753,596.69
To record shipments during month.		

Variance Analysis

An earlier section refers to the use of a clearing account for charging actual costs and crediting the standard costs charged into inventory. The net of the three clearing accounts (Material Variance, Labor Variance, and Indirect Labor and Overhead Variance) is the amount of variance. At the end of the period, these three variance accounts must be closed out to cost of sales. This is done in journal entry #11.

Journal Entry #11

Cost of Sales	62,364.67	
Indirect Labor and Overhead Variance	40,740.02	
Material Variance		81,133.75
Labor Variance		21,970.94
To close out variance accounts		

All 11 journal entries are summarized on Exhibit 10-19. Exhibit 10-20 breaks these entries down into "T" accounts. This provides a summary of each of the accounts showing the effect on the various journal entries. From the foregoing journal entries and "T" accounts, the standard cost of sales and total variances provide the basis for preparing the abbreviated income statement shown below:

SALES	$1,260,350
STANDARD COST OF SALES	753,597
STANDARD GROSS PROFIT	506,753
VARIANCES	62,365
ACTUAL GROSS PROFIT	$ 444,388

The breakdown of total variances can be categorized further to show the total material, direct labor, and total indirect labor/overhead. This categorization corresponds with the breakdown of the three variance accounts used for clearing actual costs against standard.

MATERIAL		
PURCHASE PRICE	$(16,192)	
MATERIAL USAGE	97,326	81,134
DIRECT LABOR		
RATE	6,534	
EFFICIENCY	15,437	21,971
OVERHEAD		
SPENDING	12,887	
VOLUME	(53,627)	(40,740)
		$ 62,365

EXHIBIT 10-19 JOURNAL ENTRIES

---

(1)

Material Variance		16,191.67
Raw Material Inventory	16,352.54	
Fabricated and Purchased Stores (WIP)		160.87
To record purchase price variance.		

(2)

Material Variance	346,340.81	
Raw Material Inventory		346,340.81
To record issues of raw material to production floor.		

(3)

Fabricated and Purchased Parts Inventory	593,027.52	
Material Variance		301,736.04
Labor Variance		61,073.48
Indirect Labor and Overhead Variance		230,218.00
To record production of fabricated parts transferred into fabricated and purchased parts stores		

(4)

Fabricated and Purchased Parts Inventory	1,956.56	
Finished Goods Inventory		1,956.56
To record transfers of items in finished goods to fabricated and purchased parts stores.		

(5)

Work-in-Process Floor Inventory	698,385.10	
Fabricated and Purchased Parts Inventory		698,385.10
To record issues of fabricated and purchased parts to production floor.		

(6)

No entry this month.

(7)

Work-in-Process Floor Inventory	14,269.22	
Finished Goods Inventory		14,269.22
To record items in finished goods transferred to the production floor.		

(8)

Finished Goods Inventory	782,001.14	
Work-in-Process Floor Inventory		782,001.14
To record production transferred to finished goods.		

(9)

Work-in-Process Floor Inventory	69,347.82	
Material Usage Variance (brass & non-brass)	52,720.65	
Labor Variance		47,587.73
Indirect Labor and Overhead Variance		74,480.74
To record standard cost of production		

between the fabricated parts level and
finished goods level.

(10)

Cost of Sales	753,596.69	
Finished Goods Inventory		753,596.69
To record shipments during month.		

(11)

Cost of Sales	62,364.67	
Indirect Labor and Overhead Variance	40,740.02	
Material Variance		81,133.75
Labor Variance		21,970.94
To close out Variance Accounts.		

EXHIBIT 10-20 "T" ACCOUNT SUMMARY

Raw Material Inventory

(1)	16,352.54	(2)	346,340.81

Fabricated and Purchased
Parts Inventory

(3)	593,027.52	(1)	160.87
(4)	1,956.56	(5)	698,385.10

Work-in-Process
Floor Inventory

(5)	698,385.10	(8)	782,001.14
(7)	14,269.22		
(9)	69,347.82		

Finished Goods Inventory

(8)	782,001.14	(4)	1,956.56
		(7)	14,269.22
		(10)	753,596.69

Material Variance

(2)	346,340.81	(1)	16,191.67
(9)	52,720.65	(3)	301,736.04
		(11)	81,133.75

Labor Variance

Actual Labor	130,632.15	(3)	61,073.48
		(9)	47,587.73
		(11)	21,970.94

Indirect Labor and
Overhead Variance

Actual Overhead	263,958.72	(3)	230,218.00
(11)	40,740.02	(9)	74,480.74

Cost of Sales

(10)	753,596.69	
(11)	62,364.67	

The further breakdown of variances would identify them by areas of responsibility. Purchase price variances, for example, would be the responsibility of the purchasing department. The transaction listings would identify the price variances by type of material on which the variance was incurred, giving some indication of purchasing effectiveness based on the predetermined standard price. It is possible that because of short lead times given to the buyer, he may not have been able to negotiate out of strength. The purchase price variance, in such instances, should be identified as to the specific reason for their occurrence and given visibility. This would provide information as to the additional cost of orders taken with short lead times.

Material usage, that is, quantity actually used versus quantity that should have been used, can also be identified by type of material. However, it is more important to identify the responsible foreman so that he is prompted to take corrective action.

MATERIAL RELATED VARIANCES

Responsibility of:		
Purchasing	PURCHASE PRICE VARIANCE	
Department	BRASS	$(16,598)
	OTHER METALS	632
	PLASTICS	(342)
	PACKING MATERIAL	116
		$(16,192)
Departments	MATERIAL USAGE	
Using	BRASS	$ 73,499
Material	PLASTICS	22,168
	PACKING MATERIAL	1,659
		$ 97,326

Once the labor rate variances have been isolated (just as the purchase price deviation was), the labor efficiency and other variances can be identified by responsible department heads.

The cost of computerizing a cost system is not small. A company should computerize its materials management system as well. The reverse is also true. Cost accounting and inventory control are inextricably tied together. The physical units reported in the transaction listings and providing the basis for inventory status reports (perpetuals) should be the same units that are valued by the cost department in arriving at general ledger inventory balances.

As competitive pressures intensify more and more, materials management will become even more important to the economic survival of many companies. The steps for computerizing, outlined in this chapter, provide a framework which should support management's needs for effective inventory control.

CHAPTER 11

INVENTORY MANAGEMENT AND AUTOMATED REPORTING INTERFACE

In previous chapters we stress the importance of managing when planning inventory control systems. The aim is to provide systems—informational and operational—that assist management in running the business. For this reason, we tailor the systems planning to implementation of policy and place analysis of inventory problems ahead of design of operating systems. We also emphasize planning systems by personnel who have a good understanding of the realities of operations and operational problems. Naturally, these are not hard and fast rules but they certainly facilitate the development of more meaningful inventory controls.

DECISION-ORIENTED SYSTEMS

One company has touted that its financial information system is probably one of the most sophisticated in the industry—it is completely automated. Each profit center receives complete operating statements, inventory status reports costed up to support the balance sheet inventory figures, production center and service cost center departmental budgets based on the flexible budget concept, detailed scrap reports, sales projections, and product profitability reports.

In spite of the system, however, profits are eroding badly, backorders are high, and scrap losses are double what they should be. The financial information system truly indicates high unfavorable variances but it does not pinpoint the true causes. Volume variances, for example, are shown to be very high. The implication given in the variance reports is that sales volumes are not high enough, but actually sales volume is higher than the factory can produce. Because of unbalanced lines and inefficient operations, inventory has become unbalanced and scrap losses have skyrocketed.

As a result, customer orders cannot be filled. The unfavorable volume variance should actually be a highly unfavorable efficiency variance.

This financial information system is a data collection and processing system built according to "formula." It is not management decision oriented. Inventory status reports show what the inventory actually is but do not provide many clues to the fact that it is greatly out of balance. Turnover figures are available on an overall basis and appear normal. However, the picture is quite different when individual items are taken into account. Some items show as much as a 2-year supply (in one case 10 years), others show no inventory at all even though products using the items are backordered.

The foregoing problems are representative of those encountered with traditional approaches to controls. The emphasis is on data flow and file structure. The skills most frequently applied are data-processing oriented.

Decision-oriented systems focus on the business rather than on data files. The basic methods of managing the function are identified at the outset. The types of problems that can arise are considered and the alternative corrective actions defined. This leads to the decision process. It is, of course, impossible to predetermine all the decisions that management will make and to analyze the specific thought processes that will be followed in making these decisions.

In areas such as inventory the decision process is relatively simple, involving, for example, when to reorder, how much to reorder, and when to transfer. Informational requirements can be readily determined and prepared. To a limited degree, the decision process can even be formulated and given over to the computer. Exception reports are a good example: the computer is programmed to indicate when management should review the inventory status of an item.

To be sure, systems skills are still important, but far more necessary are the business skills relating to the particular function and analytical skills relating to making decisions. Data bases and data files are part of the picture but planning for inventory controls has somewhat different objectives. These are:

- Identify and classify basic problems and corrective actions.
- Define the decision process, including the extent to which it can be formulated.
- Determine the information required and back out the appropriate data collection and processing.
- Formulate the appropriate decision aspects.

Planning along these lines provides management with reports containing timely and selective information that identifies problems and indicates solutions.

Computers can make specific routine decisions previously made by clerks, such as reordering stable inventory items. However, the "human computer" must do most of the planning, revising, negotiating, and establishing standards.

WHAT TO AUTOMATE

Frequently in the preceding chapters, we discussed examples of reports. These include stock status, cost accounting, and listing of obsolete items. Many of these are prepared by computer—others manually. At no time did we designate that the report be manual or automated. The function of the report is not affected by the method of preparation. The key to whether a report should be automated is one of efficiency and economics.

Some reports are automated for the following reasons:

• To obtain a rapid response (e.g., the inventory inquiry part of an on-line order entry system).
• To perform complicated calculations (e.g., projected demand for spare parts aboard a submarine).
• To process an enormous volume of data (e.g., the stock status report for a major steel company).

More often than not, management can get all the reporting it wants—virtually free in terms of incremental costs. Chapter 12 discusses the automation of certain operations relating to inventory management. Applications of the computer to order entry requirements, planning, and statistical determination of reorder quantities are widespread and usually justified by improved operations without regard to management reporting. Once the operating systems are in place, management may already have most of the data base required for reporting on the computer. Where the computer has been applied to such basic functions as ordering, production, and shipping, probably every inventory transaction is being captured on a daily or weekly basis. Since the data is already in the computer, the hard part is done. Experience has shown that a large part of systems implementation is concerned with building and maintaining the data base. Once this has been done for operational purposes, management can obtain automated reports—generated from the same data base—at little additional cost.

Another consideration in determining the feasibility of automating inventory management reports is the timing requirement. To be useful, must the reports be generated daily, weekly, monthly? As we have just discussed, if the related operations are automated, there is probably no obstacle to producing control reports—with whatever frequency that is appropriate. When considering inventory management or management reports on operations that are not automated, timing is important because of the effort required to build the data base.

As an illustration, suppose that management desires a daily comprehensive report on inventory status showing inventory balances, sales, gross profits, discounts—by item, by merchandising responsibility, and the like. This would require that practically every transaction affecting inventory be entered in the computer data file, which in turn may require considerable cross referencing—getting customer numbers, standard costing, and so forth. If the volume and variety of transactions is large, this can be a considerable amount of work. Once the files are set up, further implementation is greatly simplified. The computer application programs that process the data files and produce the reports, at that point, do little more than add up and print the figures. Although data processing managers may try to budget a large time period to program the report, chances are that what has been budgeted in terms of months can be done in weeks.

If the report timing requirements are monthly, the data base problem may be simplified. Much of the desired data may be available by routine processing of accounting data. This brings up another consideration: what kind of data is required for the report? Does the data represent the status as of a point in time or an accumulation over a period of time? Is management interested in backorders at the end of the month or the amount accumulated during the month?

Inventory is managed well when physical units are tied in with dollar values assigned to inventories. In one company, the accounting department has found at year-end that the physical inventory valued at standard cost does not agree with the book inventory, also valued at standard. Management is properly concerned as to whether the shortage is caused by pilferage or is the result of incorrectly applied costs. To solve this problem, accounting personnel have prepared a reconciliation using material as a measure rather than dollars. A discrepancy in the material measurement figures would be highly suggestive of a shortage in units. If the material measurement checks out, then the discrepancy is most likely attributable to erroneous costing.

Exhibit 11-1 illustrates how the inventory reconciliation report is developed. The report covers all items using 1/16″ roll sheet steel. This size constitutes a substantial portion of the inventory, and therefore is a representative sample. Pounds (of steel) is the unit of measure. The beginning inventory figure is taken from the previous year's physical inventory using the engineering standards for conversion of units to pounds. Transfers,

EXHIBIT 11-1   INVENTORY SHORTAGE REPORT: MATERIALS
MEASUREMENT

Month: July
All Items Using: 1/16″ roll steel-glazed
                material number

Number of WIP[a] items: 72
Number of FP[b] items: 35

1. Beginning inventory	22,500 lbs.	
2. Transfer to WIP	14,500 lbs.	
3. Pounds to account for		37,000 lbs.
4. Shipments	18,500 lbs.	
5. Divisional transfer	1,500 lbs.	
6. Scrap	2,500 lbs.	
7. Ending inventory	14,250 lbs.	
8. Total accounted for		36,750 lbs.
9. Total unaccounted for		250 lbs.

[a] WIP = work-in-process
[b] FP = finished product

shipments, and scrap are accumulated from the monthly reports in units
that are also converted to pounds. Ending inventory is determined from
the current physical inventory with units likewise converted to pounds.

Preparation of the report requires only that a program be written to
convert the units to pounds and to summarize the results. The unac-
counted for pounds, amounting to 250, do not appear to be sufficiently
large to account for the large difference between physical and book inventories expressed in dollar values in the accounting records. It is therefore concluded that the difference is caused by incorrect costing rather
than actual disappearance of units of product.

STEPS IN PREPARING MANAGEMENT REPORTS

The operations most commonly included in producing management reports are:

- Arranging
- Selecting
- Calculating
- Summarizing

During the past 20 years, the computer cost of performing these operations has declined dramatically. Today, the low direct cost permits almost unlimited use of the computer in applications that are suited for automation. The limitations of a reporting system are probably more traceable to lack of management resourcefulness and "push" than to cost considerations.

Not too long ago, the executive was reluctant to ask for product returns by customer. He knew that the accounting system accumulated these chronologically with monthly summaries by product returned. To break these out by customer was often an arduous and expensive manual job. Today, returns being accumulated on the computer can be summarized by customer, by product, by nature of the defect, or by any breakdown that serves management's needs—all at little additional cost. Obviously, there is no point in producing a particular breakdown merely because it is possible to do so. The programming should consider breakdowns that are feasible and useful to management.

Arranging was laborious when punched cards were in wide use. The use of cards for returns required sequencing by transaction. The cards would then be re-sorted by customer to provide a breakdown by customer. To obtain a breakdown by defect would require another burdensome re-sorting. Today's computers can sort files hundreds of times faster. The limitation is only the rate at which data can be fed in. Rank ordering—the arraying of items from the largest to the smallest or smallest to the largest—is another operation performed by the modern computer that makes arranging of data far less burdensome.

Selecting has been vastly improved in today's computers. Simple decision rules can be programmed in the computer and the data files passed through to prepare exception lists. Suppose that we want to know what items with inventory on hand are less than 20% of the reorder point. The program would select in the following steps:

• Calculate 20% of the reorder point.
• Compare the result with the on-hand quantity.
• If the on-hand quantity is the smaller of the two, list the item on the exception report.

Such decision rules are easy and quick to program. Once the inventory file has been created, it is easy to produce the exception report.

The *calculating* and *summarizing* operations used for inventory management are also extremely fast on computers. The arithmetic operations include adding, subtracting, mutiplying, and dividing. Square root calculations can also be included.

When the computer is used for optimization, it must be programmed by specialists who are not available in the normal staffing of data processing departments. One company that lacked the particular skills launched a project to determine the optimum forecasting method for inventory management and entrusted the work to persons who did not have the skills. To make up for this, high speed computer groping was substituted for analytical expertise. Another company undertook a project to determine the optimum forecasting method and entrusted the work to a series of individuals, who collectively had only 2 years of graduate training in quantitative methods. During the 2-year project, the project director, whose analytical skills were somewhat limited became deeply involved in using the computer as a substitute for human thinking. Because of this error, the effort was misdirected and the expenditures wasted. A two man-month analysis by competent personnel not awed by the "magic of the computer" could have saved the company a quarter million dollars.

DATA BASE DESIGN

Correct data base design, like any business endeavor, requires foresight and planning. One company whose direct labor costs approximated $600,000 annually established eight digits as the maximum need, assuming with the trend toward factory automation that direct labor would never reach $999,999.99. However, the data processing manager did not know that management was seriously considering consolidating both of its plants at the home location. As a result, upon consolidation some months later, it was necessary to redesign the program—not only for the direct labor, but other areas relating to inventory that might be future trouble spots.

Another type of problem in data base design, can be experienced when a relatively simple change to a report sets off a seemingly unending chain of problems. A company that does much reporting should segregate its reporting programs from the data base.

The objective of data base design is to organize data in the computer files so that many different applications can be made using the same data files. And more importantly, the files should be so organized that the data can be restructured without requiring a wholesale reprogramming. In the illustration of insufficient space to accommodate direct labor, it should have been possible to alter the file to allow expansion of the field.

The application programs that produce reports should be separated from the logical structure of the data files. It should be taken as axiomatic that the data base is always in a state of flux. New data items are added and old ones removed or otherwise modified. Perhaps "dollar sales by product group by salesman" is a data item that will be added next month. Sales zones might be restructured. The logical relationship of data items may change or the physical relationship of data items in the files may change.

One way of separating the reporting programs from the underlying data base is to have the reporting programs work with data items rather than with records. Data items, the smallest element of data recognized by name, are identifiable; they can be found, moved, modified, aggregated, or processed in any of the methods permitted by a computer. Since a data item is the smallest such element, no part of it can be processed.

A record is a collection of data items. As an example, a record in a data base used for a stock status report may bear the name "item" and may be comprised of:

Item number	Units on hand
Description	Units on order
Order point	Vendor number
Order quantity	Vendor address
Stocking location	

If the reporting system is set up so the reporting programs depend on data items rather than records, then the data base software external to the reporting programs is available to recreate different records out of the records currently in the data base. As an example, the exception program to test for excess inventory might utilize a record consisting of the following data items:

Order point	Units on order
Order quantity	Item number
Units on hand	Stocking location

Using these data items, the report could compare the on-hand plus on-order amount to the order point plus order quantity and print out those items showing excesses. If another data item, say standard cost, were inserted between description and order point, no change would be required in the excess inventory program. The data base software would still select the data items desired by the excess inventory reporting program and would organize these data items for the reporting program to use.

The data base must be designed and managed by a specialist skilled in the logic of data organization. This person knows the capabilities of the computer equipment in storing and moving data. If a company adopts a data base approach, someone with these skills will presumably be available to manage the data base. Managers should not have to acquire these special skills in order to plan inventory reports. The report planner can spell out aspects of the logic in the data relationships that might not be apparent to a data base manager. Among the aspects that would be included are:

Data Items: The planner should know which elements of data cannot be further broken down and should give a list of the data items to the data base manager. As an example, the product code may have parts such as 52-103-1713 in which 52 is the code for the producing plant, 103 is the code for the product group, and 1713 is the item identification. The data base manager should be told whether to build three data items (Plant ID, Group ID, and Item ID), or one data item number. If the latter is the case, the 52 could not be used by itself.

Data Aggregate: The planner should determine which data items will be used in combination. If a group of items is to be used as a family, it is usually desirable to establish a nomenclature to describe the group. This is referred to as a data aggregate. Data aggregates may be hierarchical in that one data aggregate may be composed of other data aggregates as well as data items.

Records: A record is a collection of data aggregates or data items that will be addressed in the computer. Additional records can be added to the file by assigning an address. Data aggregates, on the other hand, are parts of records. Another data aggregate can be added only by modifying a record structure. A record is, in a sense, the top level of aggregation just as the data item is the bottom level. The planner should determine the logical content of the records relating to his application.

Relationships: Relationships among records is an important aspect of the logical organization of a data base. Planners use understanding of operations to lay out not only current relationships but possible future relationships. For example, the data base for a stock status inventory report may contain an item master file with a record for each item. Standard cost might be a data item on each item master record. A second type of record might show the inventory on hand but these would be separate records for each SKU for each item location. A program reporting inventory dollars might call a record from the item master and so obtain the standard cost. The program would then proceed to use all the related SKU records containing the inventory of the item at various locations.

The data base manager is responsible for the final organization of the data on computer files but persons familiar with operations and who are planning the inventory reports must provide the logical framework for the data required by the reports. Further, the planners determine the frequency of data collection and reporting, the level of data accuracy required, the units to be used, and the other characteristics of the data. If planners fail to recognize that they are responsible for these tasks, the responsibility is thrown into the laps of systems personnel who are usually unfamiliar with the operations.

CHAPTER 12

INVENTORY MANAGEMENT
AND AUTOMATED OPERATIONS
INTERFACE

The process of automating procedures is more difficult than the process of automating for management information, because personnel who have "run the show" for years resist change. With a computer "taking over," many employees are distrustful. When employees become intimately familiar with and understand the details of the new automated procedures they are more likely to accept them.

TOKEN ACCEPTANCE IS NOT SUCCESSFUL IMPLEMENTATION

Beware of a "gung ho" attitude toward a new automated procedure. It is necessary to see tangible proof that the system is being properly used.

A manufacturing plant in Toronto, Canada, provides a good example of token acceptance of an automated system. The company president has determined that automated inventory management techniques will be installed in his three plants. The budget has been approved for the data processing department to design and implement the required systems.

The data processing function is centralized under the financial vice-president with the computer and personnel located at the company headquarters. There are no data processing personnel at the plants; data entry for existing automated systems (payroll, order entry, sales analysis) are the responsibility of the plant accountants who report to their respective plant managers. To implement the inventory management system, personnel are temporarily assigned from the corporate staff as required. The Toronto plant is selected as the first to be automated.

The kick-off meeting appears to be highly successful. The plant manager has "gotten the word" and seems enthusiastic. He explains (in phrases selected from the president's memo) that he is convinced that his plant needs automated inventory management and is grateful that the corporate staff has finally allocated resources to such a project. The corporate staff is given a tour of the plant and listens to a carefully pre-pared speech on current operating practices and procedures relating to the production scheduling and inventory control.

The lead person of the visiting staff states that the key to success lies in the forecast. The plant manager heartily agrees, adding that if only the system could project what would be sold and then back it out through work-in-process to raw materials through a mathematical formula, he could run the plant more efficiently.

The systems group develops a forecast of sales for the coming 12-month period and explodes it to obtain the material requirements. Then the group compares the requirements with inventory levels to arrive at the scheduling report. This report will be sent to the plant weekly to serve as the basis for scheduling and machine loading.

Throughout the implementation phase the plant manager keeps up a steady stream of praise about what a fine job is being done by the systems personnel and how helpful the forecast will be. He even has the account-ing people in his plant provide the corporate personnel with any analysis of operations that the project requires. Finally, the system is implemented and everyone is pleased—from president on down.

After the new system has been in place for a year, the corporate staff begins to raise questions. Inventory turnover has not improved, customer service is no better than a year ago, and with the improved scheduling overtime is still high. The plant manager states that the system has been a great help but that there are some problems that were not present the preceding year. There was the 3-week strike, for example, and several of the old machines have been "acting up."

The matter is dropped temporarily. A few weeks later, the corporate controller visits the plant manager to explain some recent changes in part numbers. In view of the standardization program that is taking place, a fairly large number of parts have been replaced by interchangeable com-ponents. This means that for some products four different part numbers have been replaced by a single new number. This, of course, simplifies scheduling because fewer parts have to be run and the runs are longer. The controller asks to see the plant manager's copy of the latest schedule so he can point out some of the changes in format. The plant manager pores through the papers on his desk, in the drawers, and then in the file cabinet. Finally, he calls in his outspoken secretary to inquire if she has seen it. Her response is: "It's in the wastebasket. You told me that it didn't contain anything that you didn't already know, remember?"

It is obvious that the plant manager had cooperated fully with the preparation of the automated schedule in order to indoctrinate the sys-tems people with his view of operations. The systems people had been carefully insulated from any direct contact with the plant. They knew only what the plant manager wanted them to know. The plant manager, in turn, believed that he had been successful in training the systems people to his old way of doing things. Because the new system would then reflect business as usual, there was no point in using it. This kind of token acceptance occurs more often than it should.

UNDERSTANDING OPERATIONS

In the preceding example, the plant manager effectively shut the systems planners out of operations. Their only association with the plant is the kick-off tour and their knowledge of operations is so restricted that they cannot see the simple fact: their new system is not being used at all. The controller realizes this. After bringing corporate pressure to bear on the plant manager, he reassigns his systems personnel to get out into the plant operations and to work directly with each department manager who would be affected by the system. Weekly review meetings are held for the entire period of revision until the new "D"-day arrives, at which time the revised system is launched.

The controller then issues a policy with respect to all future implementation, instructing systems personnel to work directly with each department head or designee. They work on the scene—in the stockroom, at the work stations in the factory, in the receiving area, on the shipping dock, and so forth. No longer are they permitted to hole up in a conference room and be directed through an ivory tower approach by managers who want to keep them "out of harm's way."

WHAT TO AUTOMATE

The question as to what should be automated can run the gamut from satisfying the researcher who wants to find new applications for the computer—to the practitioner who has his ear to the ground as to practical application for the most pressing needs of the company.

In reviewing what has been automated by most companies in the manufacturing environment, we find many applications relating to inventory, and most include reporting. Costing, budgeting, and accounting are included as part of the design. These subjects are discussed in other chapters, this section covers the applications that are not included elsewhere. Specifically these can be broken down into:

1. Reordering for uncontrolled demand.
2. Reordering for controlled demand.
3. Order entry processing.

A more detailed discussion of these follows.

Reordering for Uncontrolled Demand

Managing finished goods inventories, as is well known, reduces the problem to that of estimating demand and then providing enough inventory to satisfy that demand in line with customer service policy. In this case, the demand is beyond the control of the firm and the operating procedures deal with how to reorder. The issues involved in determining the appropriate inventory service policy are discussed in Chapters 3 and 5. Various inventory models used to control the reordering are discussed in Chapter 7. When and how should these models be automated?

Reordering for uncontrolled demand is a potential automated application for:

- Retail inventories.
- Wholesale inventories.
- Distribution warehouse inventories.
- Stores inventories.
- Other finished goods inventories.
- Certain raw material and work-in-process inventories.

In short, this covers all inventories where the usage of the inventory is beyond the control of the firm. In some cases the inventories may be within the control of the company but the ability to control is difficult to exercise.

Automation of reorder rules is one of the most common applications of the computer to inventory management. An examination of these rules in the inventory models will indicate the potential for computerizing. These rules all involve some form of calculation to come up with inventory levels (min-max, OP-OQ, etc.) on an item-by-item basis. Such calculations are ideally suited to the computer.

Exhibits 12-1 and 12-2 demonstrate an application of the computer to such calculations.

The company in this example imports wines and spirits from Europe for sale to distributors in the United States. Part of the importer's sales are shipped direct from the foreign port through an import warehouse in the name of the customer. Shipping is arranged by the importer but the merchandise in transit is the property of the customer. The import duty is paid by the customer. The remainder of the importer's sales is distributed through its own warehouses which it operates in a number of states.

As part of its inventory management procedures, the company prepares a monthly forecast of demand for the next 6 months. The method of fore-

EXHIBIT 12-1   COMPUTER APPLICATION TO FORECASTING

MANUAL

WAREHOUSE SALES
WINE & SPIRITS BUDGET YEAR 2

Product Line	Year 1 Sales in Cases	Estimated Year 2 Sales in Cases	Percentage Increase
Scotch A	8,132	8,000	−1%
Scotch B	2,017	2,500	24%
Vodka	23,655	27,500	16%

AUTOMATED

YEAR 2 SALES FORECAST (cases)
NEW YORK WAREHOUSE

Item	May	June	July	Aug.	Sept.	Oct.	Average	Trend
Scotch A 5th	65	60	77	40	53	23	92	−6
Scotch A 5th gift	0	0	0	0	25	213		
Scotch A Quart	52	51	34	19	34	26	58	−12

casting illustrates the use of the computer when a large volume of calculations is required. At the top of Exhibit 12-1 is shown the "first cut" at the forecast prepared by the sales department. It is prepared as part of the annual budgeting process and gives the department's estimate of sales for the year by product line. This part of the forecast is manually prepared.

The budget is deficient for inventory management because 1) it is prepared for a year when a forecast by months is needed; 2) it is prepared by product line when SKU information is required; and 3) it is prepared once a year without updating on a regular basis. Thus, to be useful for inventory management, more detail is required. For example, for 22 warehouses with an average of 8 products per line, the 13 lines result in 2288 SKUs (22 × 8 × 13). If we allow for monthly updating of the forecast, this becomes 2288 × 12, or 27,456 separate forecasts each year. This is quite a few more than the 13 prepared manually by the sales department! Obviously, the computer must be used.

The computer maintains the sales history of each SKU and calculates a moving average of monthly sales. It also provides for seasonal factors. The projection is made by the computer using the average sales adjusted for seasonal fluctuations and then trended upward or downward based on the trend for the product group. The trend calculated by the computer is not used directly in the forecast. It is compared to the trend in the sales department's budget and results in an exception report. The exception report is studied by the sales department and serves as a basis for a manual revision of product group trends.

The lower half of Exhibit 12-1 shows the automated forecast with substantially greater detail than that given in the upper half. Because of the use of past sales history, together with the trend from the sales budget, the detail in the automated forecast ties in closely with the overall picture given in the sales budget. Note that the computer has been programmed to adjust for seasonal trends and part of that is a switchover of product from standard packaging to gift packaging.

The sales department has a feel for the market based in part on nonquantitative considerations. Such a feel cannot be built into the programs. It must remain judgmental. On the other hand, sales personnel do not normally think in terms of SKUs and would be poor judges of inventory behavior at that level of detail. This detail would be built into the computer procedures.

The reorder quantities are determined by comparing the forecasted sales with the inventory on hand and on order. Certain reorder rules are followed. The basic consideration is to have enough inventory on hand and on order to satisfy sales over the import lead time with some safety stock to provide a margin for error. This requires measuring the import lead time and also measuring the sales variability to determine safety stock on an item-by-item basis. Here, again, the volume of calculations is large and computerized operations are necessary. The upper portion of Exhibit 12-2 illustrates part of a page of the computerized requirements report. For each SKU the computer calculates the import lead time (e.g., 1.6 months for the items shown).

Using the forecast shown in Exhibit 12-1, the computer calculates the expected sales over the 1.6 month lead time plus 1 month (requirements). For the first item in Exhibit 12-2, this is 171 cases. Next, the computer determines the safety stock according to certain statistical formulas, and adds this to the requirements to arrive at the max. The next calculation is to determine the available inventory (inventory on hand plus on order less allocated). Finally, the computer compares the available inventory with the max for each SKU. If the available is less than the max, the difference is printed in the "Order" column of the Requirements Report. All this adds up to many calculations, but this is a standard inventory model, sometimes described as the periodic reorder model.

Before automation, a simple form of this model was used to manage inventories. A max was determined, usually without benefit of computations of any kind. Each month the inventory on hand was compared with

EXHIBIT 12-2   COMPUTER APPLICATION TO REORDERING

MONTHLY REQUIREMENTS REPORT
NEW YORK WAREHOUSE

APRIL 30

AUTOMATED

Item	Lead Time (months)	Require-ments	Max	On Hand	On Order	Allo-cated	Avail-able	Order
Scotch A 5th	1.6	171	261	127	100	0	227	34
Scotch A Quart	1.6	123	183	137	50	0	187	

MANUAL

P.O. no. 36751
container: Sea-Land No. 215-667

Item	No. Cases	Weight
.	.	.
.	.	.
.	.	.
Scotch A 5th	100	37 lbs.
Scotch A Quart	50	44 lbs.

this judgmentally derived max. If the inventory on hand was less than the max, the difference was ordered. The more sophisticated method depicted in the upper part of Exhibit 12-2 entails many more calculations and provides much more complete information.

The "Order" column on the Requirements Report shows the orders suggested by the automated procedures. The importer was not willing to rely entirely on this figure for reordering. The report was forwarded to the buyer who used it as a reference or guide in completing the warehouse restocking requisition. The final step, which is illustrated at the bottom of Exhibit 12-2, is manually performed. Over and above the orders estimated by the computer, the buyer needs to consider efficient shipping quantities, boat schedules, possible strikes, and other transporting factors. Enough product has to be ordered to obtain the desired container shipping weights. As a result of these transportation considerations, the computer order quantities are modified when arriving at the final order amounts. The volume of calculations required for this part of the process is not so great as to require use of the computer.

Reordering for controlled Demand

The bill of materials (BOM) explosion represents a different type of inventory management than we have just discussed. The inventories under present consideration are raw materials, work-in-process parts, completed subassemblies, and purchased components.* It is necessary to control inventories at these levels in manufacturing companies using interchangeable parts and components.

Exhibit 12-3 shows four levels of inventory: finished goods, subassemblies, components, and raw materials. The control of usage of the last three items differs from the usage of finished goods. Finished goods usage is determined by customers and is usually outside the control of the company although demand can be influenced to some extent through pricing and advertising. The usage of the other three levels is frequently under the direct control of the company, because the company in these cases is the customer.

Subassemblies can be built on the basis of the company's schedule for finished goods inventory. Since many subassemblies are interchangeable, the company has more flexibility as to the quantities it will keep of each type. The level of component inventories depends on subassemblies that will be built. In fact, any inventory that is input to a process that produces a higher level of inventory has a common characteristic—its usage is under control of the company.

With uncontrolled demand, which is discussed in the preceding section, the inventory control rules are based on a forecast of demand for finished goods. Demand forecasts, by their nature, contain an element of error. Safety stocks are established to adjust to this variability.

With controlled demand, however, the demand forecast may not be necessary. The company can determine demand based on its own actions. For instance, with the four levels of inventory shown in Exhibit 12-3, if the finished goods inventory management procedures are similar to those described in the preceding section, then the company prepares a forecast of finished goods demand over the planning horizon. By following the reorder rules for finished goods, the company determines quantities for assembly. Since these quantities determine the subassembly inventory needs, and the quantities are firm (under control of the company), the company knows precisely what is required. Through this method of backing out demand level by level, the lower level inventories can be determined over the planning horizon. No forecasting or safety stock is required at the lower levels.

---

* Some companies consider purchased components part of raw material inventory.

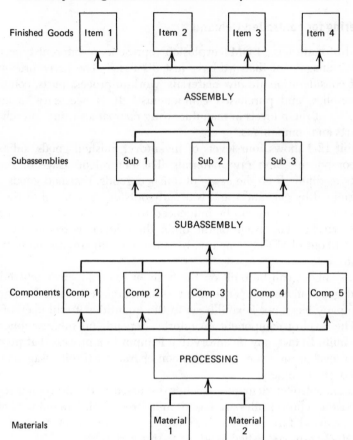

EXHIBIT 12-3 A SCHEMATIC DIAGRAM OF WORK IN PROCESS INVENTORY

The structuring of the bills of materials provides for the interconnection of inventory levels so that finished goods projections can be broken down to requirements for all inventory levels. Exhibit 12-4 illustrates the BOM explosion process for a lock manufacturer. The BOM is maintained on a computer file. The segment of the BOM included in Exhibit 12-4 shows the components of two locks. The bodies of the two are identical. They differ only in length of shackle. One lock uses a 1-inch shackle and the other a 6-inch shackle. As a result, all components of the two locks are identical except for length of shackle. The company manufactures all the components for these two locks except for the springs and pins which are purchased from outside vendors.

Using time series techniques, the computer prepares a weekly forecast

EXHIBIT 12-4   ONE LEVEL BOM EXPLOSION LOCK ASSEMBLY

BOM

LOCK A-1			LOCK A-2		
A	DIAL	1	A	DIAL	1
A-1	SHACKLE	1	A-2	SHACKLE	1
A	DISC	3	A	DISC	3
A	SPACER	2	A	SPACER	2
A	SPRING	1	A	SPRING	1
A	PINS	8	A	PINS	8

SALES FORECAST   Week

	1	2	3	4	5	6	7
LOCK A-1	3,500	4,000	4,500	5,000	5,000	5,000	5,000
LOCK A-2	1,200	1,200	1,100	750	1,200	1,600	1,750

ASSEMBLY SCHEDULE   Week

LOCK A-1	1	2	3	4	5	6	7
Beginning Inventory	18,000	14,500	25,500	21,000	16,000	26,000	21,000
Sales Forecast	3,500	4,000	4,500	5,000	5,000	5,000	5,000
Remaining Inventory	14,500	10,500	21,000	16,000	11,000	21,000	16,000
Scheduled Receipts		15,000			15,000		
Ending Inventory	14,500	25,500	21,000	16,000	26,000	21,000	16,000

Week

LOCK A-2	1	2	3	4	5	6	7
Beginning Inventory	5,300	4,100	2,900	6,800	6,050	4,850	3,250
Sales Forecast	1,200	1,200	1,100	750	1,200	1,600	1,750
Remaining Inventory	4,100	2,900	1,800	6,050	4,850	3,250	1,500
Scheduled Receipts			5,000				5,000
Ending Inventory	4,100	2,900	6,800	6,050	4,850	3,250	6,500

PARTS PRODUCTION SCHEDULE   Week

A Dial	1	2	3	4	5	6	7
Requirements A-1		15,000			15,000		
Requirements A-2			5,000				5,000
Total		15,000	5,000		15,000		5,000
Schedule	7,500	7,500	5,000	7,500	7,500	5,000	

of sales which is shown in units in Exhibit 12-4. Since the delivery schedule for finished goods permits delays of 1 or 2 weeks, the company tries to maintain low stocks of finished goods. An order-point/order-quantity model is used for finished goods management, with the order points set depending on the required assembly time. For locks A-1 and A-2, the order points are about equal to 3 weeks' average sales.

Using the OP-OQ model and the sales forecast, the computer calculates the assembly schedule. This schedule is not final; it shows the desired quantities assembled on a weekly basis in order to maintain the finished goods inventory level. For reasons of production management, the company has decided to assemble in lot sizes about equal to 1 month's usage. This information is stored in the computer. The computer also contains constraints on assembly line capacity for the various products so the computer-produced schedule will be realistic.

In the final scheduling step, the production control section analyzes and revises the computerized production schedule. This is in keeping with the general philosophy of basing the schedule on factors such as a forecast demand, order points, lot sizes, and basic capacity. The final decision, however, should be left to the scheduling personnel. The production control section would modify the schedule based on such additional considerations as vacation shutdowns, holidays, and customer priorities.

Since the company can control the level of inventory requirements for work-in-process and raw material, there is no need to forecast demand as a base for inventory rules, as in the case of finished goods. Inventories are still required as buffers in order to provide control over the operations because it is unreasonable to expect production to flow precisely as planned, however the company should be able to calculate precisely the amount of inventory required.

Order Entry Processing

For firms that maintain stocks of finished goods and plan to satisfy customer demand "off the shelf," the order entry process is interrelated with inventory management. Prior to completing the customer's order, the salesman needs to check whether the product is immediately available. If so, he completes the order as a routine procedure. If not, the salesman may suggest alternative products. If product substitution is not acceptable to the customer, the product is backordered.

In the event of a backorder, the customer usually expects to know the delivery date, which means working out a delivery schedule. This, in turn, raises other questions. Should all the backorders for a customer be accumulated and the total order shipped in one delivery? Should each line item be shipped as it becomes available? Or would the customer prefer some combination? Splitting the order may throw a full truckload order into LTL (less than truckload). Who is going to pick up the cost differential? If product is available but allocated and the customer has an emergency need for it, the salesman has to struggle with the problem of customer priorities. Company rules may prohibit product transfer between warehouses, but if a good customer is applying pressure, it may be necessary to bend the rules.

Add to these problems the considerations of special deals, price discounts, customer profitability, product shelf life, obsolescence, and transportation delays. The salesman's task of effectively matching up product and customer is not easy. Automating order entry expedites the procedures and minimizes some of the problems.

Order entry automation procedures frequently encompass all activities connected with getting the product to the customer, including order taking, stock inquiry, credit check, order confirmation, routing, shipping, customer communications, and at times some aspects of purchasing or production control. While all these activities should be treated as a group when automating order entry, certain of the activities bear little relation to inventory management. Routing is an example and is therefore not discussed in this book. Inventories, however, are an important part of the order entry process.

The objective of the order entry process as it relates to inventories is to provide a quick and efficient way of matching up customer needs with company products. Prior to order entry automation, salesmen were naturally enough reluctant to energetically pursue product substitution. Typically, if the line item ordered was not in stock, it would be a day before the salesman was notified of the shortage. He then had to call the customer back to settle the matter. If the customer was interested in substitution, the entire cycle might be repeated again, and confusing complications could develop.

With an on-line, real-time automated inventory inquiry procedure, the original order is modified immediately while the customer is on the phone. Obviously, this is a great convenience to the customer. The resulting benefits include: increased sales through better customer service, decreased manpower devoted to customer service, and improved inventory turnover through better management of sales.

Exhibits 12-5 and 12-6 illustrate how an on-line, real-time order entry system uses inventory information. The example is taken from a paper products company that manufactures consumer products at four plants located throughout the United States. The products are both custom ordered and stocked. The stocked items account for the bulk of sales.

However, most of the items are custom ordered (also referred to as specials). Since the special orders relate to the designs printed on the products (Coca-Cola, Burger King, and the like), thousands of special order items are manufactured from a relatively small number of basic products. Special order items are made to order as a rule. However, the big name customers frequently exercise their muscle to have their brands stocked. Special orders can be produced at three or four plants.

Stocked items are maintained at each plant and also in a network of warehouses. Each warehouse (and plant) services a specific geographic zone. Salesmen making calls use a standard order form with two subdivisions. A salesman uses the left subdivision to complete the original order and then phones the order entry clerk—if possible, when still with the customer. The order entry clerk takes down the order on the standard form and then interrogates the order entry system by use of a CRT at the order entry location. Such locations are maintained at the plants but not at the warehouses. Thus, each order entry location services several sales zones. If necessary, the original order can be modified immediately while the salesman is still with the customer.

Exhibit 12-5 shows the first display on the CRT screen when the order entry clerk uses the automated system: a list of standard transactions performed by the system. The clerk selects the desired transaction by entering the appropriate code number at the terminal.

For instance, a salesman phones in an order and holds on the line to confirm it. The clerk checks the availability of stock by first entering the code—for example, 01—at the terminal. The computer responds by flashing the top three lines of Exhibit 12-6 on the screen. The second line asks the clerk to enter the area number, which identifies the plant and outlying

EXHIBIT 12-5 ORDER ENTRY APPLICATION TRANSACTION SELECTOR

TRANSACTION SELECTOR
ENTER THE NUMBER OF THE TRANSACTION YOU WANT TO PERFORM

```
01-  STOCK INQUIRY
02-  CUSTOMER CHECK
03-  PRODUCT SUBSTITUTION
04-  NEW ORDER ENTRY
05-  ORDER REVISION
06-  RETURN
07-  OPEN ORDERS BY CUSTOMER
08-  OPEN ORDERS BY PART NUMBER
09-  OPEN ORDERS BY VENDOR
10-  OPEN ORDERS BY DUE DATE
```

---

warehouses associated with that plant. Inventory data is then displayed only for the stocking locations in the area.

On the third line, the clerk is asked to enter the item numbers of the products about which inquiry is being made. Up to three items can be entered and displayed at one time. When the last item has been entered, the clerk also enters "END." The system then displays the last group of items after which control is returned to the transaction selector illustrated in Exhibit 12-5. If "END" is not entered by the clerk, the requested items are displayed and then control is returned to the stock inquiry for more item requests.

The data below the first three lines in Exhibit 12-6 is provided in response to the stock inquiry entered on line 3. This data shows the current inventory status for the three items requested. "Quantity on Hand" and "On Order" are shown. If ordered quantities are still open, the due date order number of the earliest due order is shown. The open order might be a production order at the plant, a transfer order from plant to warehouse, or a purchase order for an outside vendor.

A transfer order from, say, the Newark plant to the Boston warehouse would show as on hand allocated at Newark and on order (available or allocated) at Boston during the interim period between the entering of the transfer order and the receipt of the stock in Boston. If the Boston order is being placed out of new production, the Newark production quantity—shown as available on order—would be reduced by the amount of the transfer and offset by the amount in the Newark allocated on order column. Since scarce product could be all allocated to the outside warehouses under this procedure, the system permits the Newark "warehouse" to order from Newark "production."

Item 53205 in Exhibit 12-6 illustrates how this works. A production order for 700 cases has been entered and the expected completion date is 7/17. Of this 700, 100 cases has been ordered transferred to each of the three outlying warehouses in the area. To insure that Newark gets its fair share, the remaining 400 cases has been assigned to the Newark plant.

Since backorders are shown by the system as net of allocated amounts, the 400 cases assigned to Newark are shown as 377 cases allocated against customer orders and 23 cases available for shipment. Each outlying warehouse has customer orders in excess of available product. Boston, for example, has received customer orders for 102 cases of item number 53205. The 100 cases expected from Newark production is allocated against the 100 cases ordered, with the remaining 2 cases showing in the backorder column. The 12 cases shown as available in New York, in spite of backorders of 65 cases, could represent one of several common occurrences. It might be a data error in the system, an all too frequent

EXHIBIT 12-6   ORDER ENTRY APPLICATION STOCK INQUIRY

STOCK INQUIRY

ENTER AREA NUMBER
ENTER THE ITEM NUMBERS UP TO 3 ITEMS
(END WHEN COMPLETED)

53177	Available Quantity On Hand	Quantity On Order	Allocated On Hand	Allocated On Order	Back-orders	Next Date	Receipt Number
Boston	72						
New York	316						
Newark	1,267						
Camden	60						
53205							
Boston				100	2	7/17	T7331
New York	12			100	65	7/17	T7331
Newark		23		377		7/17	45247
Camden				100	26	7/17	T7331
53215							
Boston	17	40				7/12	T671
New York	252						
Newark	365	400				7/15	45223
Camden	37	100				7/11	T670

---

occurrence, or perhaps 65 cases were backordered by a customer who did not want partial delivery.

· After checking the availability of all the items phoned in on the order, the order entry clerk proceeds with the order processing. Control has been returned to the transaction selector (Exhibit 12-5). If all stock is available, the clerk enters code 04 which displays as shown in Exhibit 12-7. In entering the order, the clerk enters the customer number, salesman's number, warehouse from which the shipment will be made, common carrier if a special one is requested, and the desired shipping date. If the customer number is not known, it is looked up in a customer reference book listing customers in alphabetical sequence.

Next, the address to which the order is to be shipped is entered. If the company is to send the invoice to a different address, as is common with the large chains where deliveries are made to the local warehouses and invoices sent to the national office, the billing address is entered after "BILL TO." Invoices and shipping papers are printed as a byproduct of

EXHIBIT 12-7 ORDER ENTRY APPLICATION NEW ORDER ENTRY

NEW ORDER ENTRY

ENTER CUSTOMER NO.:

ENTER SALESMAN NO.:
ENTER SHIP FROM: TRANSPORTER: DESIRED SHIP DATE:

SHIP TO: _____   BILL TO: _____

            _____   _____

            _____   _____

            _____   _____

ENTER CODE FOR TERMS: _____

ENTER ITEMS ORDERED (AT COMPLETION ENTER END, AT END OF
SCREEN HIT CR)

NUMBER	QUANTITY	UNIT PRICE	EXTENSION	(DISCOUNTS)	SALES	FROM B.O.
53177	13	22.50	292.50	−11.70	280.80	
.	.	.	.	.	.	.
.	.	.	.	.	.	.
.	.	.	.	.	.	.

THIS ORDER IS ASSIGNED ORDER NUMBER 65331, (BACKORDER
NUMBER xxxxx).
HOLD or PROCESS?

---

the same system, with the addresses shown exactly as entered on the screen. If neither the clerk nor the salesman know the addresses, the clerk can interrogate the customer file by entering code 02 from the transaction selector. If the addresses are present in the file, they can be noted by the clerk and entered on the order. The customer file also contains such customer related data as the current credit rating and account aging.

If the clerk starts entering the order and then discovers that additional information is required, he can terminate the order entry procedure. An order number is assigned and the clerk instructs the computer either to hold or to process the order. If the order is put on hold, the clerk performs other tasks and then recalls the order through the order revision transaction (code 05 in Exhibit 12-5). Exhibit 12-8 shows the first screen display of the order revision process.

When the order entry is completed, the clerk orders the system to process the order. At this point, if any backorders are indicated, the

EXHIBIT 12-8 ORDER ENTRY APPLICATION

ORDER REVISION

ENTER ORDER NUMBER:

DO YOU WISH TO EDIT THIS ORDER (Y,N)

START EDITING AT LINE NUMBER:

DO YOU WISH TO ADD ITEMS TO THIS ORDER? (Y,N)

DO YOU WISH TO CANCEL THIS ORDER? (Y,N)

---

system separates out the backordered items and creates a separate back-order. Inventory records are updated immediately so the system reflects the current status supported with the related shipping papers. If two orders for the same item are placed simultaneously, the system might show the stock as available upon inquiry but not available a few minutes later when the order is processed. If this happens, the system should reject the entire order with a message indicating the problem. The clerk can then call the salesman and take whatever alternative action is indicated by the circumstances.

Some companies allow shipments to customers from any warehouse that stocks the product if the nearest warehouse is out of stock and the customer is reluctant to backorder. In such a circumstance several orders are placed with as many of the company's warehouses as needed to fill the order. This is not generally encouraged.

The sections of the order entry system described thus far illustrate the main interface with inventory management and the order entry process. The interface is basically an on-line, real-time inquiry system. The salesman knows, while speaking to the customer, what product is available. He has the opportunity to push for product substitution if there is an out-of-stock situation. The system just described has another advantage with respect to sales planning. As mentioned, the order entry procedure provided for taking down the original order on the left side of the order form. The original order may differ from the order finally placed. Original orders are processed off-line by the system to obtain customer demand figures. Demand figures, rather than order figures, form the basis for sales projections and planning.

Problems with order entry

Attention to detail is required in building an order entry system, particularly for split orders, backorders, and customer freight requests. Order entry applications are generally less complex than applications for material planning or mathematical inventory reordering. However, the impact of errors in the logical formulation of the order entry system can be much more severe because of the complexities of programming on-line, real-time systems.

Much systems work and programming is required to get the CRTs to behave as described. If, after doing all this, some unplanned for transaction or event is discovered, the consequences might be a major and costly redesign and reprogramming task. Careful tests should be performed to assure that the system can handle all transactions likely to occur.

In addition to increased software complexity, the on-line, real-time applications involve increased hardware complexity. Frequently data processing managers who can plan hardware requirements for batch systems cannot plan on-line, real-time requirements. Estimating peak load requirements, for example, usually requires advanced mathematics by specialists. Many new order entry systems continually fail through overload conditions. It sometimes takes months before anyone realizes the nature of the problem, let alone the solution. These problems are discussed further in books on computer science.

MATERIAL REQUIREMENTS PLANNING

Scheduling is the end product of the planning process. The scheduling procedures must be effective to achieve success in MRP. Because of the masses of information that are required to schedule effectively, automation is important. Problems occur in determining which data to automate and which to leave to human judgment. Some factors to consider are:

- Work hours available for the week.
- Assembly work force.
- Productivity rate for the assembly work force.
- Supervisory skills available for the week.
- Current working conditions.
- Capacity of the various working machines.
- Likelihood of machine downtime.
- Maintenance schedule.
- Quality of the material currently being used.
- Expected quality rejection rate.
- Status of long-term production contracts.

- Effect of contract review and facilities inspection.
- Current productivity of subcontractors.
- Quality of subcontract work.
- Planned changes in facilities layout.
- Machine additions or replacement.
- Planned process modifications.
- Long-term availability of materials.
- Possible material substitutions.
- Proposed product changes.
- Availability of packaging materials and supplies.
- Dollar investment in inventory.
- Overtime rates.
- Expected sales.
- Rail strikes, longshoreman strikes, or other shipping disruptions.
- Freight rates.
- Warehousing space.
- Power supply.
- Utility rates.

This represents only a partial list. Which of these factors should be programmed as part of computerized planning and which factors should be left to human judgment?

The lock manufacturer referred to earlier in this chapter leaves certain factors listed above to human judgment because they do not recur regularly or frequently. Government inspections are made twice a year. Rail strikes are infrequent and unpredictable. Other considerations are left to human judgment because it is difficult to determine how the computer should react (the decision process). Working conditions are a good example of such considerations. Finally, certain conditions are left to human judgment because it appears to be more trouble to attempt computerization than to rely on judgment. For instance, production control personnel adjust the production and assembly schedule for vacations, holidays, overtime, and so forth.

The lock manufacturer programs the computer in those instances in which standard rates can be used. All adjustments of the current conditions, other than those that can be standardized, fall in the judgmental class. Personnel availability, vacation, and other similar factors can undoubtedly be computerized because these fall in an area that can be standardized, since they occur with regularity and are predictable. However, management has decided that automation cannot materially improve the application and that the required resources for design and programming are not justified.

The decision to automate (or not to automate) such considerations in the scheduling process differs from company to company. Companies larger than the lock manufacturer may favor automation of the work force and work hour availability because these considerations are much more complicated to handle effectively through manual methods.

Because MRP frequently depends on a BOM explosion, a problem commonly encountered is a data preparation problem. For example, before attempting this application, the lock manufacturer had maintained a BOM used only by the engineering and accounting departments. It was not a source of information for production scheduling. In order to serve the production scheduling needs, it is necessary to rework the BOM files: updating the information in the file and, in some cases, correcting it. (Many obsolete parts are still in the file while some new ones have not been added). Units of measure must be reviewed carefully for application in scheduling. When the necessary changes are corrected, the existing engineering and accounting applications improve.

For the lock manufacturer, the rework requires some restructuring of the BOM as well. Part of the restructuring is definitional. An item inventoried manually has an item number assigned by engineering. However, inventories are not maintained at every discrete stage of the manufacturing process. Lock casings, for example, are molded and then sent to the buffing department to be buffed (finished). The buffed and nonbuffed cases do not have separate item numbers under the manual system.

In order to take advantage of the detailed processing capabilities of the computer, it is necessary to clearly define and name all the work-in-process items. The nomenclature should be such that each discrete step in the manufacturing process is delineated by a named item at the start and a named item at the end. Without this proper identification, the computer cannot calculate the requirements for the manufacturing step.

This step identification should not be carried to extremes. The problem in the buffing operation is that the casting machines and buffers are in different departments. This physical separation creates an in-process inventory of cast but unbuffed cases and thus a need to control that inventory. If the buffer had been physically located by the casting line so that everything coming out of the casting machines would be automatically buffed, then the unbuffed castings would not have to be identified.

An argument can also be made for not identifying product between manufacturing steps if the steps are always included in the same group on a work order. This is a question of judgment that must be dealt with for each intended application. The physical step level as opposed to the work order level of breakdown facilitates future engineering changes.

In preparing the BOM file for inventory management, where does one start? With the lock manufacturer the basic lock is not the finished product. The basic lock might be sold commercially under several different trade names and also used by governmental agencies. For these purposes, the basic lock is considered finished. For some uses, serial numbers or certain finishes are applied to the basic locks. For other uses, the basic locks are packaged in different size boxes or skin packs of a variety of labels.

This one basic lock could result in dozens of different finished product items. This means that the BOM explosion process could be started with requirements for the dozens of finished items or for one basic lock. The computer can handle both possibilities. It is simply a question of how far to extend the scope of the application. In the example, the explosion process is started at the basic lock level. The BOM file is restructured to permit this. As a result, the BOM explosion is simplified and reduced in size. However, the company still requires a manual process to control the final marking and packaging variations.

Further problems in implementing the system are encountered in maintenance of the system. Since it is desirable to use the same BOM file for accounting and engineering applications, as well as production scheduling, procedures have to be set up to permit these departments to have access into the files and to update them for their respective functions. Since these uses of the BOM file do not directly relate to inventory management, these considerations are not described in detail. However, changes in the file by either engineering or accounting could affect the production scheduling process. Production control personnel should be partners in the review of the changes being processed.

CHAPTER 13

INVENTORY CONTROL—
PUTTING IT ALL TOGETHER

Inventories in a manufacturing company represent a major investment. Ignoring receivables, because these are not always considered as part of a manufacturing plant's assets, one will find that fixed assets and inventories are almost equal in size, ranging from 40% inventories in some companies to 60% in others.

CONTROL CHARACTERISTICS OF MAJOR PLANT ASSETS

Of the two major plant assets, inventories and fixed assets, fixed assets are easier to monitor. Control is exercised through appropriation of capital in which each purchase is justified through a return-on-investment calculation and then approved by key executives.

Inventory, on the other hand, is more difficult to control, because it is made up of relatively small unit values spanning numerous product lines. Items in inventory frequently number 3000 to 4000 or even 30,000 to 40,000 or more. In addition to this fragmentation by product lines and components within these products, three general groups of inventories are usually the basis of accounting control:

- Raw materials
- Work-in-process
- Finished goods

The first chapter discusses these inventory groups (classifications) in terms of buffers. Raw materials provide the buffer between the suppliers and production needs. A reasonable level of raw materials assures efficient

241

production scheduling without over dependence on supplier or transportation companies. Accounting control of raw materials is fairly easy to achieve since purchases are recorded on invoices and receiving tickets. Transfers out of inventory can be determined from issue tickets. The key to accuracy is the assurance that tickets are used to support all physical movement of materials out of inventory.

Work-in-process inventories provide the buffer between production stages: a stock of components reduces the long lead time required for multi-stage processes. With such component stocks (including partially assembled subassemblies), finished products can be assembled quickly. Accounting control of work-in-process is not as easily achieved as it is for raw materials and finished goods because it is difficult to follow the many components through the various operations. Accounting for production losses and waste is particularly difficult, as explained in Chapter 2: *Year-end "Physical to Book" Discrepancies—Accountability for Losses and Waste.*

Finished goods inventories represent the buffer between the customer and the production process, assuring better customer service. Accounting control of this inventory group does not present any particular difficulty.

PRESSURES FOR HIGH INVENTORY

Although the purpose of accounting control is to minimize inventories, the underlying pressures within a company favor high inventories.

The sales department, for example, wants a wide assortment of finished products ready to sell. It wants to supply any product ordered by the customer without being concerned with stockouts.

The customer service group, in processing customer orders, also likes all items available so it can order from stock and reduce the level of customer complaints.

The executives in charge of distribution or materials handling activities want high inventories in all warehouses so they can fill all orders immediately, proving to the sales department the value of the distribution function.

The production function wants to have large raw material inventories available so that the production process runs smoothly. Production executives are also willing to pay the price of high component inventories resulting from infrequent setups and long production runs. Production executives argue that sufficient inventories allows leveled, efficient production rather than the expensive ups and downs.

Purchasing likes high inventory levels to be maintained to assure that it need not buy on a crisis basis—with the attendant high costs. This also permits making purchases in larger quantities to assure more favorable prices.

For all of the foregoing disciplines high inventories are beneficial, and rarely are they required to pay the full cost of carrying the inventories. Because of this unrelenting pressure, the inventories of many, probably most, companies are substantially higher than they should be. This is illustrated in Exhibit 1-2, which shows actual figures for a company making a standard consumer product.

Company management felt that a 3-month supply would keep production running smoothly. Of the total inventory of $968,000, 4.8% represents 0 to 3 months' usage, 9.9% indicates 3 to 6 months' usage, while the balance of 85.3% shows greater than 6 months' usage. Thus the company incurs substantial costs because of this excess inventory. Chapter 4 shows that inventory carrying costs can amount to more than 23% of the inventory value per year. In addition to the carrying costs, it is likely that a fair amount of the excess inventory can become obsolete, resulting in 100% loss of such items.

STEPS IN REDUCING INVENTORIES

Inventories can be too high under different operating circumstances:

Planned excess: Hedge against shippers strike or vendor shortages.

Operational excess: Active demand for the item at the inventory point; however, more inventory than required for economic buffer needs.

Locational excess: Inventory at the wrong location. No demand at the inventory point, but demand at physically different locations.

Obsolescence: No demand for the item at any location.

How management reacts to excessive inventories depends on the nature of the excess. For example, a company with locational excess in one warehouse may transfer the inventory to another location. Such transfers could not be justified for obsolete inventory.

What is needed is a continuing review of inventory with the following objectives in mind:

• Measure the amount of each type of excess.
• Identify the weaknesses that contribute to this excess.

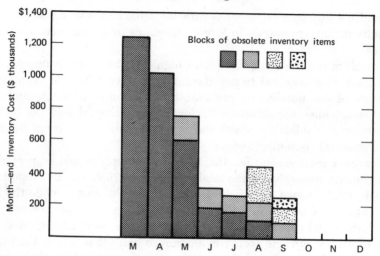

EXHIBIT 13-2   OBSOLETE INVENTORY REPORT: JUNE 30, 19— COST SUMMARY

• Develop procedures to reduce the inventory.
• Strengthen controls.

Such action assures:

• Additional cash flow that can be made available for other uses.
• Less risk of obsolescence.
• Lower inventory carrying costs.

The actual benefits in the control of obsolete inventories in one company are illustrated in Exhibit 13-1. One block of obsolete inventory items is shown as being about $1,200,000 in March. After management took action, this same block of items was reduced to about $1 million in April. In May, the dollar value was reduced to $600,000. By September, this block of inventory was completely eliminated. The same principle applies to the next block of inventory, shown in May and eliminated by September.

An Inventory Review Plan

This plan for developing meaningful controls includes the following steps:

Clarify Customer Service Policy. A service policy is used as a guide for inventory levels. For example, 98% of all catalog items that are ordered are shipped from stock within 3 days. The percentage could apply companywide for all inventory items or it could vary by warehouse. Be sure that the policy is clearly defined and in measurable terms that permit accountability.

Clarify Production Flow Policy. The relation of work-in-process and materials inventory to the production flow should be defined in a measurable way. For example, standards should be set for machine downtime resulting from inventory shortages. This permits accountability of performance against standard.

Measure Excess Inventory. Exhibit 13-2 illustrates how operational excess for work-in-process inventory is measured. Note for the first item that the average experienced monthly usage is 43,873 units of the 212 dial. The maximum allowed inventory for this item (based on an 8.6 week requirement) is 87,071 units. Since the total average inventory amounts to 136,135, there is an operational excess of 49,064 units—56% of the allowed inventory maximum. The 8.6 week requirement had been established by production management as the maximum level of inventory needed to serve as a buffer between parts fabrication and assembly. Thus, management clarified the production flow policy.

The 212 lock is a high volume item, and its component inventory is certainly good stock; however, inventory levels are clearly in excess of production requirements.

Recommend controls for weaknesses. Controls are strengthened to prevent future occurences of excess inventory. Areas where control weaknesses are frequently encountered are:

- Customer service policies.
- Production policies.
- Materials requirements forecasts.
- Production scheduling models (master schedule).
- Work order procedures.
- Expediting procedures.
- Stockroom procedures.
- Inventory reporting.
- Purchasing procedures.

The resulting controls improvements might cover such areas as:

- Development of more reliable sales forecasting.
- Provision for exploding sales forecast and developing master schedule to be used for purchasing and production.

EXHIBIT 13-2 INVENTORY ASSET REVIEW ILLUSTRATED: WORK-IN-PROCESS INVENTORY

RESULTS OF SAMPLE

ITEM NO.	DESCRIPTION	AVERAGE MONTHLY USAGE	WEEKS INVENTORY REQUIRED	INVENTORY MAXIMUM	AVERAGE INVENTORY	AVERAGE EXCESS	EXCESS %
.	.	.	.	.	.	.	.
.	.	.	.	.	.	.	.
212510	212 DIAL	43,873	8.6	87,071	136,135	49,064	56%
212522	212 DISC	131,619	8.6	261,213	820,283	559,070	214%
212531	212 SPACER	87,745	8.6	174,140	299,510	125,370	72%
212556	212 SPRING	48,320	8.6	95,897	431,428	335,531	350%
.	.	.	.	.	.	.	.
.	.	.	.	.	.	.	.

- Establishment of lot sizes and inventory level standards.
- Issuance of work (shop) orders from one central source.

It is clear from this partial list that proper accountability of the inventory asset requires a detailed understanding of operations. The review of control weaknesses might best be accomplished by a team representing both the controller's department and the operating departments.

PUTTING IT ALL TOGETHER

In modern business, inventory can no longer be controlled by measuring the turns per year. Measurements must focus on individual items and relate them to the needs by the product lines on which these items are used.

The controller and operational management groups must develop a partnership to assure effectiveness of controls. With the computer providing the mechanics of control, the operational departments must define requirements in measurable ways so that the financial group can develop controls. In return, the financial group should develop its control with an understanding of the operational requirements for inventory buffers. Coordinating control responsibility and operational needs is putting it all together.

INDEX

Soc
HD
55
D8

DATE DUE

L R FEB 4 1985	MAY 13 1989
R FEB 2 5 1985	AUG 07 1990
M S MAR 1985	SEP 1 4 1990
OT APR 3 0 1986	JUL 2 0 1992
G V DEC 1 1 1986	DEC 8 1995
D U JUL 0 7 1987	
JAN 0 9 1989	
FEB 13 1989	
MAR 1989	
APR 04 1989	
APR 22 1989	